MW01106805

Achieving Sexual Ecstasy

*Using Your Body and Mind
to Experience Total Satisfaction*

AM ROSEN

BARCLAY HOUSE
NEW YORK

A BARCLAY TRADE PAPERBACK
Published by: Barclay House
A division of the Zinn Publishing Group
ZINN COMMUNICATIONS / NEW YORK

Produced in Cooperation with
 Atchity Entertainment International (AEI)

ISBN: 0-935016-31-7

Printed in the United States of America

Library of Congress Cataloging-in-Publication Data

Rosen, Am.
  Achieving sexual ecstasy : using your body and mind to experience
total satisfaction / Am Rosen.
      p.   cm.
  ISBN 0-935016-31-7 (pbk. : alk. paper)
  1. Sex. 2. Sex—Philosophy. 3. Mind and body. 4. Ecstasy.
I. Title.
HQ64.R67   1995
306.7-dc20   95-43159
                                         CIP

This book is dedicated to the
future of our world and the
lovers everywhere who will bring forth a
Planetary Space Age
and launch humanity to its
New Spiritual Destiny
with the intergalactic cosmos.

Contents

Love, my friend,
isn't what you've found
when intelligence goes blind!

Introduction

A soul discorporates. Leaving its life on earth, it passes beyond the corridors of space and time, 'til it comes before the Gates of Heaven.

The admitting Angel comes forth to hear the soul's life story. After listening, the Angel looks at the soul and says, "You mean you lived a whole life on earth, and you didn't make as much love and enjoy yourself as much as possible?"

The soul looks shocked and stammers out, "Make love? Enjoy myself...? I didn't think God wanted me to do that."

The Angel looks back at the poor soul and says; "You didn't think God wanted you to make love and enjoy yourself...? Who could have put those thoughts in your head?"

It's always been a contention of mine that angels get a lot of bad press on this side of the manifestation. If you consider the comparison between devils and angels, you'll find that devils can't really give you any pleasure. They just cause you pain. They can't get it up to energize joyously, they just sort of piss on you. It's the angels who are potent, virile...the best of lovers. But we never quite see it that way.

I'll tell you something peculiar: of all the things I've done, teachings I've studied, disciplines I've mastered, places I've been, people I've met...I've only come across one real devil in this world. Its name begins with a cap-ital "I". "I" for ignorance. **Ignorance is the only devil!**

Now, a fun kind of game you can play with your consciousness is to take the word Ignorance, and substitute it every time you've ever heard or seen the word devil used: The Devil made me do it. Ignorance made me do it. Possessed by the Devil, his body was sick and his soul tormented. Possessed by ignorance, his body was sick and his mind in torment. The Devil held himself up against God and took a fall. Ignorance tried to usurp the divine light of wisdom and crashed into its own shortcomings. The Devil is trying to bring about the destruction of humanity by dragging us into the pit of despair. Ignorance is dragging us down towards the brink of our own destruction and the torments of our own superstitious despair.

Probably the greatest con job that has ever been sold to this world is, *"Ignorance is Bliss."* Now why would anybody not want to understand what's going on? Perhaps, if you don't understand what's going on (down the street, in your home, in a relationship, or with your lover), then maybe you don't have to bare the consequences of your actions. But that's just not true. Whether you understand or not, you still bare the responsibility. Privilege breeds responsibility; that is part of your spiritual maturity.

For example: Let's say you want to try your hand at a serious love relationship. Unfortunately, you don't understand how to communicate your sexual needs and desires. Not only will your ignorance cause you to remain sexually frustrated, but you will also incur the added resentments of your partner who was counting on you to carry your share of that responsibility. Since you're going to bear the consequences for your actions anyway, the more you understand then the better are your chances of fulfilling yourself in any given situation.

The more you understand, the more you can control.

If you put your hand into a fire, you can't say, "I didn't know fire was going to burn me." No matter what you'd like to think, that fire will do its thing. And we're all playing with fire; with various kinds of psychic, mental, emotional, sociosexual fire. This need to understand and take control is with what we're going to be dealing.

So the antidote for Ignorance, and all the devilish problems with which it sticks us, is *Understanding*. Of course, a lot of people think they understand. They have all kinds of opinions about things. Often they're able to out-talk, out-impress, out-con, out-charismatize, outmaneuver...and they may go a long way in terms of their social successes. But that's not understanding.

What is the basis of understanding? Understanding is based upon experience. When you understand how something works, you have control over it. It is clear, simple, direct and works every time; no exceptions. When you don't understand—no matter what you may think, or be able to convince others—you are controlled by the degree of your ignorance. And if you persist in your ignorance, then you suffer distortion in the form of fear, doubt, confusion and anxiety.

For instance: there's this door over here. I've watched as some twenty-odd people have come to try and open it. Out of ignorance, as to the mechanism of how the door works, these people have smashed up their fists and a number of assorted objects— it's one tough door —and still it won't budge. Now I don't understand how to open it either, but after observing I realize that I, too, could break my hands against it and still be unable to get the job done. With concentration and a detached sense of awareness I go forward and examine this door. I get lucky, as in the course of fooling around, I accidentally turn the knob, and the door suddenly swings open. Although I'm not sure what happened, I learn by handling the knob that the door will open. Pleased with my luck, I examine the knob more closely and notice that turning it pulls back a lever which releases the door. From this experience I understand. I have control when it comes to opening this type of door. Never again will I approach it with any sense of confusion, anxiety, fear or doubt. Why? Because I now have a real understanding based upon experience.

One of the most important things I'm going to do, in writing about sexuality and related matters, is to give you an opportunity to differentiate; to give you a sense of exactly how consciousness operates. This sexual act that everyone is so interested in is basic. If it wasn't going on, none of us would be here. What's involved, what determines how enjoyable it can be, has to do with where your mind is at; the quality of consciousness you bring to it (or anything else).

Many people try and conform their life's energies to their preconceived notions about life. For instance: I want to have a really fabulous relationship with somebody; I want it to be like goddess and god; like fusion; like constant multiple orgasms; like walking around in a continual state of love. Or I want to be a free, hip, liberated, uninhibited, open person who lives as a real bon vivant. However, these are just ideas. Obviously, if I had the experience and understanding I wouldn't be immersed in just wanting to, I'd be doing it. So I say to myself, how should a modern, freethinking, sexually liberated person act? Drawing my images from that part of the marketplace which caters to such interests I might think I should dress, smell, act in particular ways and make rounds of the local swing bars, or whatever is currently fashionable. So I make a similar effort as my fellow conspirators who happen to be making the rounds, picking up sex partners, buying gadgets...whatever.

Such conformity is not basing my actions on understanding. If anything, my actions would obscure my understanding. Once I commit my attention heavily to a particular way of being, I stop looking at many other possibilities...as we all too often do. Well, I don't want to look at anything that sours my commitment; I wouldn't feel so good then. Since I've paid my money, and have all this ego and chutzpa invested, I want a good commitment...I want it to be really special for me.

Most of us block out many of the experiences that could give us the answers to our fulfillment. What I'm trying to teach you is how to hone in on your own levels of consciousness, so you can attain exactly what you want out of life. I can provide you with a fail-safe system for gauging your inner involvements. I know there is one— I'm not guessing —I know!

Right now I want you to plant in your mind the idea of creating a geiger-counter out of your feelings. If something really feels good...I mean if you're not just trying to convince yourself, or believe what somebody else is telling you will make you happy...If it feels good, you're doing something right. Move towards it! If something feels bad...If it causes any degree of fear, doubt, confusion and/or anxiety, begin to pull back from it. Now, don't run away from it. Anything in this world can be handled. The only thing you can't handle is what you refuse to look at. You can't shoot at shadows. If you expose them to the light of your understanding, you can deal with them.

A geiger-counter out of your feelings: Say we're making love and the energy is starting to flow between us...maybe it's a highly communicative conversation we're xii ♦ *Achieving Sexual Ecstasy*

having; anyway it feels good—better and better. Suddenly something comes up that as yet we haven't been able to work out. Something unresolved from my past or your past causes the energy and pleasure of the moment to dip. But I was having this good feeling. Should I ignore the negativity crowding my space? I mean I don't want to lose the good feeling. Should I just keep going and ignore the uptightness? No! I stop as soon as I feel anything negative; there's something I'm not understanding. Whether it's coming directly from you, or whether these feelings are just triggering off a pattern in my psyche that I haven't as yet integrated, I stop and examine these feelings 'til I understand and gain control over them.

Later on we will discuss where heartbreak comes from. You'll come to see how you can indulge as freely, deeply and intimately as you want, in any relationship, with anybody, without ever experiencing heartbreak. As a matter of fact, the way you usually have your heart broken is not by involving yourself, but by not allowing yourself to indulge.

Imagine you have two buttons. If you push this first button your relationships with people are absolutely nothing short of fantastic. The communication is excellent, vitality is superlative, sexual responses are terrific, they are an open-ended sort of "I want to work things out in trust, love, mutual satisfaction"...all these things you want. Of course, if you push this second button, you get what you always get—frustration, anxiety, hit or miss moody pleasure-pain vacillation, with lots of competition and gamey one-upmanship. Which button would you push?

Any sane person who hasn't abdicated his or her right to intelligence would push the first button. So why don't we push it? Why haven't you been pushing it? Why haven't we collectively as a species been pushing this button which manifests satisfaction? And you say: "Well, AM, there are no two such buttons. That's just a nice analogy. It doesn't really exist like that."

This first button is *Understanding*. When you understand how something works— whether it's how to turn a door knob, or interpret the workings of your own consciousness along with the neuro-physiology that goes with it —then you understand how you have control. Only then can you come and go as you please.

The second button is *Ignorance*. When you don't understand something, you become controlled by that state. The machinery that should be working for you starts to run your life— you become the slave of the slave. And, if you try to act from such a level you become uptight, anxious and insecure. You're constantly harassed by an inner state of uncertainty; riddled by fear, doubt and confusion.

The question is not really what you do. More importantly, it's a question of where your head is at when you're doing it! Two people get up and look at the day. One says: "My "God, it's a beautiful day." The other says: "Oh shit, what a horrible day." Now, it is the same day. The day has not changed at all. What's the difference? Of course it is each individual's rate of perception. This goes on constantly. Particularly between people having a relationship; sometimes it's kismet, you're melting and everything is delicious. At other times it's not only not there, but you actually find yourself stuck in almost endless antagonism. Why? The act and the people involved are still basically the same.

We all do pretty much the same things: we eat, breathe, walk, talk, defecate (at least I hope we do), whatever; but what's important is where our minds are at while we do them. Are we in a state of understanding and having control? Or are we in a state of ignorance and being controlled?

What is it that controls us when we're in a state of ignorance? It is *the law*. Whether clearly formulated by the intellect, implied by the custom of cultural rituals, or inherent in the natural form and function of any substance-object; law outlines the parameters upon which we consider it acceptable to exchange various energies. In the process of growing up, all of us have been heavily indoctrinated by society. Nevertheless, there are now many of us who are intellectually advanced enough to critically analyze social indoctrination. Intellectually we're saying, "Well, that's a lot of crap. I can see the hang-ups, superstitions, power games; and I'm not going to buy into it." But no matter what we think, this way of socially and culturally responding is a law which governs most of the rhythms of our interactions.

Life may seem much more fun if you ignore, get high or do far out things— many of which weren't even accessible for most people until quite recently. Oftentimes life may be dull and senseless, but if you're caught in the morass of paying your dues, getting your mantra and speaking the party policy, then you are protected— by law. Certainly happiness is not part of the bargain. Rather, you are given permission to be one of the chosen miserable.

To live outside the law of collective society, you must become excruciatingly honest with yourself. Why aren't people honest with themselves? What in the world...(Who could have put those thoughts in your head?) What in the world could possibly keep anybody from wanting to have as much pleasure, joy, satisfaction, and as many good feelings as continually are possible? What? Something must be painful, right? It must be making us very afraid. Yet we haven't consciously identified the source.

Consider: Is there anyone among us who really doesn't want hugs, kisses, closeness, love, warmth and intimacy...as much as you can handle? Look around you: How come we have so much alienation, separation, misery, isolation, mass hysteria...You know, there are a lot of people who would like to see the end of the world; it would justify their apathy. Why are they apathetic? I mean, here are two people looking at life. One sees it's beautiful. The other says life is horrible, it's got to end. Same world, same life; what's the difference? The difference is the rate of perception.

Everything we consider, everything we look at, everything we do is dependent on our level of consciousness. That is the bottom line, not a top line. When you realize that, with all its implications, then you begin to understand that controlling your life requires having choice. Choice doesn't mean you must have so many exceptional things happening because you are compelled to prove something to yourself. You'll succeed only in feeling browbeaten and socially badgered.

Choice means that you have the option to indulge in whatever you want, to move into and enjoy it. It doesn't matter whether you exercise that choice or not, as long as the option to do so is always available to you. Remember, on this level, choice is a consideration of conscious awareness, with all the sensitivity and responsibility inherent at such a rate of perception.

You ask where we have kept our consciousness? For all too long now we've been walking ass backwards into the future through a cesspool of expedient compromises. This is easily discerned and clearly understood when we examine the nature of our consciousness, how it processes energy, and how we participate in the evolutionary process.

Since time began the answer has been right in front of each of us; it is what's most obvious. That's one of my favorite words—obviously. I've known people who say how they really want to have good sex. I observe them and say, "**Obviously** you don't. Despite everything you say, obviously this is what you're into...what you're doing."

Only by understanding the reasons for your actions can you be free. You can't really get out of a trap until you see the trap that's got you. Why don't we want to acknowledge the ways we feel trapped? Did you just rationalize to yourself, "Hey, I'm not making enough love. I'm so afraid if I take a chance and put my heart on the line, nobody will really give a damn, care or want to connect with me"?

Rejection by another isn't so much what gets you. That kind of rejection's kid stuff, not that hard to handle. So you didn't like me today; okay, there will be another day. It's more the idea of being rejected. When were you first rejected? When were any of us first rejected? Who did the rejecting? Who can reject you? Nobody can reject you but yourself! Unfortunately, most of us have internalized self rejection.

Now I'm throwing a lot of stuff out here for your consideration. Together we're going to weave this into an obvious pattern which will give you an understanding of what's been going on and why. Then we'll apply it, since that's what this book is about, to sexual satisfaction...or at the least how to start getting it. And I have a lot of interesting and potentially fun things to share with you.

One of the personal rules I've evolved in my practices is: I don't take something away from you on which you've built a dependency until I have something better with which to replace it. When I was younger, I was extremely adroit at picking apart everybody's fixations and avoidances. It was easy for me to see, because I was delving into these areas so continuously. I'd walk up and psychologically disembowel somebody; I'd say look what you're doing; see where you're hiding. Oh my God, they hated me. And I didn't want them to dislike me; that was never my intention. For me pain wasn't important. To deeply explore the truth of my psyche was all that mattered. Pain felt good in the sense that it indicated I was getting closer to understanding. But that was me.

What I learned to do is make sure that I never expose you to anything that I haven't the skill, insight and necessary techniques to help you change as quickly as you want. That in itself has made significant differences in my own life. I'm now prepared to teach these concepts I have clocked, experienced and understand completely. Had I not experienced these things I would incur only your skepticism and resentment. Since adopting this approach I find a special sense of subliminal receptivity is created between us. You know I'm willing to go as far as necessary to lead you out of your negative space as fast as you want to come.

Much of this will be far more understandable as the book progresses. Another technique I'd like to share with you is how to deal with people. How do you get really close? So many people are full of anger and frustration. God— when inquiring into the nature of their uptightness, I've had people go into spasms, convulsions— literally stop breathing —choking against the darkness of self-denial. How do you get close enough to people and remove that energy without it exploding? For that matter, do you know how to get close even to yourself?

So these are some of the things upon which I'll be expanding. What we're discussing is how we got here, and why we're not enjoying it more. Now personally, I love sex. I always have. I think I've been obsessed with it since

I was a child, but it's taken me a long time to figure out exactly what's been going on between the sexes, and why. Why is hardly anybody really getting what they want? I've seen a lot of people from average walks of life, to corporate heads, models, film stars; and everybody looks their part. Very few people are really living it to their satisfaction. Why? If they could push that first button and have everything they wanted, they'd push it. Why do we keep pushing the other button? That is what this book will more than begin to answer.

Battle Of The Sexes

*F*irst of all, I want to tell you the basis of "war" on our planet.

The basis of war contains a two-fold progression: Initially it stems from the disjointed antagonism in each individual's psyche between the *feeling* and *thinking* levels of consciousness. In turn this split has been characterized through the sociopsychological evolution of every culture as the battle of the sexes.

Most people are at war between what they think and what they feel. They fill in the difference with rationalizations. It's like they take a mental inventory. For example: "It's not that I'm not happy. It's just if this would happen here; and he or she would or wouldn't do this or that, then my happiness would come shining through." Now what I'm doing here is rationalizing about happiness. To whom or what am I rationalizing? My feelings, which for whatever reason, don't feel happy despite all my mental gymnastics. Now if there's nothing happening in my external environment to justify these unhappy feelings, then I'm confronted with inner confusion. If there's no one chasing me with the intention of doing bodily harm, if there's food available, if I'm not being evicted or under any other threat to my well-being, and yet inside I'm beating up on myself, then my actions are not motivated by reality. Rather I'm living in my mind, in a state of self-generated war.

If you spend more time rearranging your life's energies around the fictions in your mind, than you do upon the actualities of your circumstances, you're becoming *neurotic*. And if this kind of expenditure becomes extreme enough to jeopardize your ability to survive physically or socially, then you're becoming *psychotic*. Any of which takes on the particulars of whatever temperaments and circumstances are interacting.

Most people deal neurotically with "ideas about life" rather than real life, thereby confusing who they think they are with whom they really are. Sociologically, the aggressive hostilities ravaging the surface of our planet are a direct reflection of our psyches which serve as battlegrounds for the struggle toward a state of consciousness. These aggressive hostilities, with pseudo-peace marking their cessation as we regroup in preparation for further aggressions, have polarized one aspect of our species development. The other point of polarization— the expansive brilliance of our creative arts, the accessibility of more encompassing superlatives in the evolution of humanity —is the true aspect of peace.

The reasons for this antagonistic split between two of our primary levels of perceptual consciousness, their ramifications, and how they can be transformed are covered in depth in my books on consciousness. In this book I want to discuss how these misunderstandings have socioculturally manifested themselves in the delusory role-playing between the sexes.

Lets look at those characteristics we call male and female. Externally, one of the most easily discernible differences is that the male has a penis which can become erect and ejaculate sperm. The male seems outwardly to be the sexual aggressor. At least it seems that way, probably because he is the one who appears to have something specific to do. Also the male is physically stronger. Now that doesn't make him smarter or better, but ounce for ounce, size for size, pushup for pushup...on the average the male is physically more powerful. Because of his neural-hormonal secretions, he has denser muscle groupings, and can take certain blows that the female can't as easily handle.

The female is softer, more lustrous, usually more flexible, more in tune with the natural earth processes. She's yielding, as in relation to her fertility cycle, and does not aggress as much externally. She's more externally receptive. She is the place to which man's aggression can come; or at least that's how we've been playing it out. All of these traits have been and are modifiable and reversible. But such alternations are a manifestation of consciously applied will. At the moment we're speaking mainly on a biological reflex level in relation to the dictates of natural environmental circumstances.

So the man gets an erection, enters the female vagina, and finally ejaculates placing his sperm within her womb. Now whether it's for two seconds (because the man is that potent and virile), or whether it's for six months (because he's that hung up and inhibited), the man is at that moment empty, void and somewhat lacking in aggressive control. The female, whether or not she takes the sperm and brings it to fruition in terms of a pregnancy, has the genetically programmed psychic imprint to do just that. Internally she's the one who is in control and potentially creative. Recognition of this juxtaposing of male-female control and dominance between the external physicality and internal psyche has been around since the most primitive times. Yet except for brief flowerings of cultural aesthetics during so-called "golden ages" of early civilizations, the reality of these considerations has never really been applied to the moral fiber of society. Instead we've had lopsided oppositional confrontation between the sexes, along with all the dissatisfying destructiveness that it engendered.

Let's take our male and female prototype—the strong guy with the aggressive penis and the soft receptive female—and carry them back to a time before we had our artifacts and implements. Back to that primitive beginning when we were just another animal species struggling to survive. At that level, the measure of survival was *strength*. Whoever could throw a stone hardest and most accurately, run the fastest, climb the quickest, or swing a club most forcefully, was the one who had the best chance of survival. Physical stamina and endurance was the meal ticket, because when it came to the other animals we weren't all that together. Many of them had bigger, sharper teeth and claws than us and were naturally better camouflaged. They could out smell, out hear, and usually out see us.

What we had going for us was the beginnings of an intellectual brain; mostly undeveloped. And manual dexterity, but we didn't know what to do with it. Basically we didn't have much time in which to cultivate intellect, because we were too busy trying to stay clear of the other animals and survive.

Anything that enhanced the survival potential of our species was coveted. And at that stage of survival what enhanced our species was strength. Whoever was stronger got the better share of food, better place to lie down, better choice of mates and subsequent offspring, more maneuverability, more wampum to trade. So strength was coveted.

Whatever took away from that strength, inhibited or debilitated it, was to be destroyed or avoided. Now nothing—and it's rather ironic—nothing takes away from that kind of aggressive physical strength more so than deep complex feelings of tenderness and gentleness. Imagine you are a primitive human lying around absorbed in emotional pangs of contemplating whether or not you're loved while some hostile adversary is sneaking up to crack your head open. What you must have that's so imperative in a survival situation is *reaction time rate*. Your ability to pay attention to everything going on about you determines your ability to survive. And anything that unnecessarily complicates the physical response unit (e.g., sounds, respond; sights, respond; smells, respond; muscles toned and ready) is going to detract from your ability to survive. Feelings of gentleness, tenderness, and openness can diminish that responsiveness. In whom? Especially in the male, leaving him feeling too susceptible to destruction and death. Between male and female, the man is physically stronger. That makes the male superior. Not superior, period—but under pure physical survival conditions, he is in a superior position compared to the female.

So what can the man do with these feelings he's afraid to acknowledge? After all, it is kind of nice after a long hard day of stalking food or worrying about who's going to cave his head in, to kind of relax, cuddle up and let it all go. But he can't really afford to do that. Remember, we haven't got technology yet; we haven't even harnessed fire. We're just huddling and struggling. So what does the male do? He can't get rid of his feelings because he'd have to destroy himself to do that; besides he doesn't even comprehend how the mechanism works. But he did discover that he could *suppress* his feelings. He can repress his feelings by forcing his mind not to acknowledge them.

Such a way of not dealing with his feelings was bound to have some serious repercussions. Although none have been very successful, there are various disciplines we've developed as we became civilized that allowed us to detach from our feelings for short periods and specific purposes. For instance: there's asceticism, stoicism, celibacy, yoga, magic rituals, logical empiricism, and scientific objectivity. None of these systems fully work. Even so, they are complex, intellectual ways of handling feelings based on sophisticated rationalization patterns. Right now we're talking about "el primitivo." This guy not only doesn't have enough intellect to utilize any of these processes, he isn't yet aware enough to even realize he has an intellect. Basically he's just a frightened mass of reactive nerve endings. But not allowing yourself to experience tenderness, while not replacing it with something else basically could drive a primitive nervous system insane.

The male could not exist that way. It's not as if he sat down and reasoned the need to get rid of negative feelings. He just stumbled into his own avoidance patterns. He was very reactive. (As I've said, we've been walking ass backwards into the future—expediently.) Driven by what? **Fear:** "Don't eat me up; don't kill me; what happens when I'm sick; what happens when I die; don't rip me to shreds with your claws." That's heavy; that's fear. That's deep-seated, basic survival, instinctual fear. The male doesn't want to encounter the feelings that contemplation of his helplessness produces. What does he do with his feelings. He can't be cut off indefinitely from tenderness and openness; he'd really go stark raving mad.

What the male winds up doing is repressing his feelings, then *sublimating* and *projecting* them onto the female. After all, the female is the perfect external representation of everything that he feels afraid to be. She's soft, warm, tender, gentle; at least in proportion to him. Although she may be a big hulking cave woman, he's a bigger more hulking cave brute. So she can be that externalization of everything he's afraid to be in terms of his feelings.

Scrutinizing the female; she may not be physically as strong as the male, but that doesn't mean she's not as smart as the male. As a matter of fact, intelligence has nothing to do with sexuality. Rather it is a matter of individual creative potential. Women can just as easily be educated to read books and push buttons as can men.

However he is in this peculiar position. He's the one who is physically stronger. If she disagrees with him: one, he can club her down with this greater bulk and strength; two, he can say: 'Well baby, if you don't like it, go off in the wilderness and survive without me.' She's not equipped to do it; not at that stage of survival. So what's he saying? Not only are you going to become the embodiment of the feelings that I'm afraid to encounter within myself, but in addition you're not going to be allowed to show *power*. Because power belongs to the person who is the strongest. Such became the rationalization at that stage of development.

What is power? What helped us progress from that primitive animalistic circumstance to modern time? Bigger muscle groupings? No, it's our ability to think; to symbolize, cross reference, integrate and transmit sense impressions as thought forms. The basis of power commences from an intellectual level. And even though the female is just as capable of thinking as is the male, at that stage of the game he's saying: "Baby, I'm suppressing my feelings because I can't handle them and at the same time deal with the hostilities of the environment. And I expect you to take up the slack. You know; give me that juice, my fix, when I need it to unwind me." But at the same time he's also saying: "You're not allowed to express your power. You're not allowed to be openly intellectual." He's put her in a life or death situation: "Either you play ball my way, or die!" She acquiesces; she suppresses her right to intellectually structure out loud. That doesn't make it go away, but it does get a bit rusty if you're not allowed to express it. If she doesn't follow his dictates she won't survive. So she is forced to suppress, sublimate her intelligence (her power) in order to obtain his secondhand patronage.

Unfortunately, for the vast majority of people in the world it's still going on today. That's very aggravating (haven't you noticed?). When the female becomes the external embodiment of what the male refuses to consider, she receives through him whatever share of food, clothing, housing and related trinkets he is capable of providing.

Keep in mind this unreasonable, illogical, reactionary pattern of discrimination between the sexes. Let's take this perspective and neurologically advance it through the species...say a few hundred thousand years or so. 'Til we come to a place that has theologically, mythologically, I like to say *neurologically* been called the *Garden Of Eden*. (Whether it's the Bible, rock music, quantum physics, comic books, or whatever; I take my reference points for delineation where I find them.)

In the Garden Of Eden we now find the male and female—respectively Adam and Eve—still living in *a state of innocence in relation to nature*. What does it mean to be living in a state of innocence in relation to nature? It's very simple. It means if you're tired, you find a place to lie down and go to sleep. If you're hungry, you find something to eat and you eat it. It means you let the needs of your body interact with the circumstances of your environment, and your intelligence (whatever part has developed) goes along for the ride. They are there—they have been for hundreds of thousands of years, if you like evolution; or since God put them there, if you like the other story (really the same story)—still in a state of innocence in relation to nature. But, some kind of neurological change has started taking place in them. Although they aren't consciously aware of this change, they've just begun processing through the intellectual based level of perception. They're starting to *symbolize* their relation to everything.

This **naming process** is the *innocent beginning of the loss of innocence*. Adam is no longer content to just let things happen. He no longer just feels the biological urge to erection, finds a way to release through ejaculation, and goes off towards the next thing which catches his attention. He's suddenly moved into the beginnings of a self-conscious stage of conceptual awareness. He's going around putting names on everything: "That's a garden, that's a tree, that's an apple, that's a snake, that's a woman, that's a desire, that's a dilemma..." What is this naming process? It means he's starting to take what he feels, and what he's associated through his senses with his feelings, and reference it through symbols.

Consider: There are three trees over there. What is my relation to them. First of all I've got this need; I'm a physical animal; I get hungry. Right, I'm experiencing this physical sensation of hunger. If I don't satisfy it by eating, then I'll feel terrible. If I do eat something which satisfies me, I feel good. Of course, whenever possible, I go for what makes me feel good. Now this good feeling is a primary feeling; because it's based on a physical survival need, which determines whether or not I will continue to exist. However, after repeated exposures to this process of eating to satisfy my sensation of hunger, I start to develop more complex feelings. After a while I find that if I eat that something here, in this green grassy meadow by this crystal running brook, it feels a lot more pleasing than eating up in the dusty old attic by my lonesome. Well, I keep eating in relation to my hunger, keep changing the qualities of my environment, but I want even more control. This repeated exposure to stimulus is making a particular neurological inroad.

For instance there are those three trees I mentioned. And I find when I eat the fruit from the first tree, I respond with an "uhmmm-hmm". The translation of this guttural utterance would be like: delicious, I want more of that. When I eat the fruit on the second tree my response is "ehhh". Which is like: okay, but nothing to get excited about. When I eat the fruit on the third tree it's "yeccckk". Which is like: disgusting, I could vomit; no more of that. Anyway, after a few hundred million years—if you're an amoeba—or after a few years—if you're a Homo sapiens—the "uhmmm-hum", the "ehhh", and the "yeccckk"...these symbolic associations become vocabulary. They become abstract symbols in your intellect, which refer you back to the feelings that had caused you to associate those symbols. Tn turn, this cues back in the sensations which had originally triggered your feeling responses. So let's say that you've eaten something that has totally satisfied you. But you start thinking intensely about what other kinds of food you might enjoy eating just as much. Even though there is no real food anywhere around you at the moment, if you concentrate enough on these associative symbols, you'll start to emotionally recall the feelings that the actual tastes and smells of the food had stimulated in you. In turn, your feelings may reengage associative physical sensations. Suddenly, without having any real need for food, your mouth has begun salivating, your stomach is rumbling, and your glands are preparing to secrete digestive enzymes. Against your body's needs you begin to crave food. This is compulsion—subconsciously turning the flow of energies from the intellect back against the body. Do we remember this and realize the neurological process taking place? No, we've been walking ass backwards. We've been too busy just surviving, while trying to get away from all of our compromises. But that's what has been going on.

So Adam has become quite preoccupied with naming everything. And Eve comes sauntering through the underbrush, sees Adam and intones: "Let's get it on." She wants to do that sexual thing. Because it's a basic function which can produce pleasure. You see, Eve, the female, not the male, is the sexual aggressor. That's another interesting perspective we've been playing in reverse. Usually it's the male who acts like he's the sexual aggressor. Until quite recently, because it's become chic to reverse role-modeling, the man has always aggressed on the grounds of being the protector and provider.

Anyway, Eve is by nature the sexual aggressor. Why should the female be the one to sexually take the lead? (The implications of which are startling; especially if you want to have good sex.) Unless the male is so tuned into the reproductive process (even then it's doubtful) that his approach is: "Sweetheart, I want you to lie down, spread your legs, I'm going to pump sperm in there, we're going to make a baby. Okay, I'll be back in a few years, have sex and make another baby..." Then any other reason he has for sexually approaching her is an ego trip. That isn't good or bad, but justification of his self image does greatly limit his exchange: "It's because I'm so handsome, so smart, so powerful, so horny, so sexy, so this, so that, I need you, I want you, my mommy said I should have what I want..." ("I...me—me—me...I...me—me—me..." He's got the screaming "me—me's.") It's all a manifestation of his self image; just a way of referencing his own mind. Because most people don't understand how they reference their minds, it does create problems.

Of course the female can be just as egotistical as the male. And often women do motivate their sexual actions from the egocentric compensations of their own perspective. However, superseding all that, she is the *initiatress*—only the female can provide the passage from birth into life. Reproduction is a biological survival mechanism. If we didn't have this ability to reproduce...Well, somebody mutated a million years ago, and that was it, just a one shot deal. Every biological survival mechanism inclines you towards certain psychological traits and psychic abilities. For instance: Sexual pleasure for the possibility of reproduction—Reproduction is survival, but you get the accompanying qualities of pleasure whether or not you reproduce.

When Spring arrives, if you don't let the dog or cat out of the house, the dog will try and hump your leg; while the cat will go around spraying everything with sexual pheromone. Sometimes, in a more peasant oriented society, mention would be made describing a woman *in heat*. Let's zoom in on such a situation: At the rag tag outskirts of a rustic little village, we find the poorest family, just barely subsisting. The couple has a young daughter, who at the age of fourteen is on her way to becoming an old maid. Her parents don't have the customary means to economically secure her through a marriage. It has been a terribly long cold winter, in which they've been most shut inside. Spring has just arrived; the snow bound mountain passes have just begun to clear. And this poor young woman is outside poking at the still half frozen ground she must soon try and cultivate. And she feels so forlorn and desperate as she contemplates the miseries of a loveless life. She looks up to see some man walking down from the mountains. The passes have just cleared, and this young bumpkin has taken a hike to see what's going on in the village below. They see each other. All of her longing, need and desperation well up through her. Suddenly she emits an overpoweringly hypnotic, psycho-sexual magnetism. He is uncontrollably attracted to her. So that before either one realizes what is happening, his pants are down, and he is ejaculating within her, and they're making a baby; as for one brief instance there is ecstasy. (Of course if you can have such exquisite pleasure for even a moment, you can have it indefinitely. But that requires adeptness in higher spiritual techniques.) Then it's over, as the routines of their mundane level of awareness reassert all their subconsciously conditioned inhibitions.

If a healthy male ejaculates, and every sperm fully connects with an ovum, then potentially he could repopulate the country in one good spurt. A female gets one egg per cycle. There will be years when she wasn't yet able to produce an ovum; there will be years when she will no longer be able to produce an ovum. During the period when she is fertile, there are only about two days in any cycle in which she could become fertilized. When a woman becomes pregnant, she doesn't become incapacitated, but she does become somewhat less capacitated. She needs some degree of assistance. A man can—he shouldn't—but physically he can walk away from the reproductive act. A woman cannot walk away. It is her responsibility to bring forth life. With the responsibility of this biological survival mechanism come certain privileges. Her sexual interest, like the male, may be motivated from the vanity of her feminine egocentricity. However, if her actions are motivated by deep egoless attuning with her primal responsibility to bring forth life, then whether she has sex with one man, or a hundred men, or abstains, her actions are free of guilt and shame. If from this psychic orientation she opens up to her erotic pleasure, then sexually aggress on the man before he has time to pump up his justifications, then he can indulge in guiltless pleasure. A subtle point around which a pearl of love may form—such is the basis for why the female is the natural sexual aggressor.

So Eve gets it on with Adam. Now, let's say this isn't the first time they've been sexual. Rather it's the first time they've been sexual since they've started to operated with conscious input from the intellectual level of perception. And they're going rapturously crazy with each other. It's never felt so intense before. Adam starts thinking to himself: "This is the best time we've ever had. We've got to have it at least this good all the time." Adam is becoming premeditated; he's no longer just feeling his way through the sexual act. Changes have begun remapping his nervous system. He has all these new names for things. Instead of simply dealing with his feelings (feel turned on; did it; what else is happening), he wants to compare, make it better, to extend and intensify his pleasure. He doesn't quite know how to do this. He finds if he thinks about what's going on, frames and references his feelings with thoughts, he can emotionally juice the feelings a little more; which in turn seems to enhance his physical sensations. He can also get into psychological trouble this way, but he doesn't understand any of this.

One moment he's feeling: feeling with his skin, his

groin, feeling the electricity of the female entwined with him. The next moment he's thinking: "This is the best it's ever been—can it be any better? Well why hasn't it been better? Wait a moment, is this the best it's ever been? Just how good can it be? They're thinking...thinking, thinking, thinking. They're feeling, feeling, feeling...They're thinking and feeling, bouncing escalating energy back and forth, building, building, erupting...Until they explode in an orgasmic crescendo...! Then they melt back down into little senseless puddles.

As Adam recovers his breath and senses, he turns to Eve and suddenly seems to go bonkers. He freaks out and says: 'You whore, you slut, you cunt, you bitch— I'm screwed up and it's all your fault!' Whoa, where's this coming from? Why does he suddenly turn on this beautiful woman who's given him so much pleasure, and lay that kind of a trip on her?

It sounds somewhat similar to the virgin and whore complex which has so tritely dictated sexual morals through the ages. You know, if the woman is too aggressive, the man becomes apprehensive and pulls back from her. Unless, such an interchange is taking place on a play for pay basis.

But where does this kind of behavior really stem from? The male—prototyped in Adam—a few hundred thousand years ago had big fears about survival. He had super archetypal bogeyman fears about death and destruction; about being starved, or ripped apart by talons and teeth. Not very pleasant considerations. The problem being that he never dealt with those fears, one way or the other. He simply suppressed the feelings that were related to those fears, while also suppressing feelings related to tenderness, which left him feeling too vulnerable to his mortality. By suppressing his feelings he was able to more aggressively concentrate physical strength and puff up his macho power. With this added edge, he was able to beat up and dominate the other animals, thereby becoming the toughest motherfucker in the valley. He'd handled his need for tenderness and the like by sublimating his feelings and projecting them onto the female.

Now for a long time he's been doing rather well this way. He's just been going along, responding to whatever might have stimulated him at the moment. But now he's becoming self-conscious. So that every time he starts to act, he also thinks about his actions. This new consideration of action from an intellectual base is messing up his game plan. He needs her; he needs that fix. Remember, he hasn't been allowing himself to feel...in fact, he has denied his tenderness for so long, that he's no longer even aware that he is not allowing himself to feel these things. But he can no longer just take it for granted. The intellect is opening, and this new level of perception has rules and parameters all its own.

The way he approaches her is directly proportionate to how he approaches himself. Now that his physical sensations are becoming intensified through intense emotions, his approach to sexual release must take on the same characteristics. He can't get to her and get his fix of tenderness unless he opens himself up in an entirely different way. But what happens when he tries to open up to playing with his feelings by way of his intellect? He starts to encounter a lot of pains similar to the ones we all hit when we try to get closer to each other. He is assaulted by the tormented recesses in his mind—the monstrous, the bogeyman, the wide-awake nightmare. So what does he do? Well the male has never been one, at this particular point, to own up to his problems so long as he could club his way out of them. Hence he turns on Eve and lays all the blame on her.

Eve, on the other hand, may not have ultimately figured out about raking talons, death and the assorted as yet incomprehensibles, but she hasn't suppressed her feelings either. Feelings and thoughts are two entirely different processes of consciousness. For the female these conceptual openings in the neurological field add "thinking out loud" as, so to speak, a little dialogue to the pantomime. This is not so difficult for her to adapt to. But what's really bothering her is this: "Look, you son of a..., a few hundred thousand years ago you ripped off my power and relegated me to second class status. You wouldn't allow me to openly express myself out loud as a developing individual. That didn't take away my intelligence. But if you don't get to practice intelligence, it becomes somewhat incapacitated and devious. Now I turn you on sexually; I make you feel wonderful. Don't lie to me; you enjoyed every minute of it. I could tell. I was there, feeling it. You want more of the same right now. But then you turn and bum rap me with all these bad names and feelings. You try to blame me for your fears of inadequacy. Well that tears it! You're an untrustworthy bastard, and I'm going to find a way to get even with you."

In the developing self-consciousness of our species trying to assert itself we first had men of one social faction making war on men of differing social factions. Then you had man, in phobic primitiveness, usurping the power of women; which was the psychological beginning of his making war on women. Now in retaliation to this second great effrontery you have women, deep-seatedly distrustful of the male, polarizing against them in a psychological state of war. One more factional antagonism is left to occur.

What is the male going to do to get his tenderness fix? Without it he'll crystallize and go insane. Unfortunately, he often comes too close to doing just that. We all know modern psychology: You know, you've got to let your feelings surface and express your emotions.

He can't get his fix in the same manner he used to obtain it, because he's thinking too much, and feels too vulnerable to manipulation on the feeling level where through practice the female is far more adroit. He can no longer just push her up against his physical dominance wall and say, give it to me. Or rather he can and will continue to do so as a misguided basic ritual of approaching her; but such physically oriented gestures alone no longer produce the emotional flow-through needed to dissipate his inner tensions. Now that he finds himself intellectually oriented to elongating and referencing his feelings, he also must approach her the same way.

To get to the beauty inherent in the intimacy of the male-female exchange, you have to move through whatever fears and blind inhibitions lurk in your subconscious. Every time the male approaches the female, his fears start to surface, so he pushes her away so he won't have to deal with them. It would be nice if he could say: "Look Eve, I feel confused and upset. You seem to be calm at the moment. Let me run my feelings by you so you can help me sort them out." It would be nice, but you can't help someone who won't admit they have the need to be helped. And he's afraid to get that close to her for fear in opening up she'll get her power back, and he'll have to face up to the fears that he's repressed for so long, that he doesn't even recognize that he has such fears.

So how does Adam formulate his new approach? Well, he had his first great problem a few hundred or so thousand years before this, he'd reached into his little bag of goodies—his developing intellect, rudimentary as it was—and came up with his first set of tools: the artifact extensions of his own physical abilities. As with his new tools of stones, sticks, knives, spears, pits, and traps, he was able to beat up all the other animals. Now he has a new problem, he says: "Let me think about it!" This time he again reaches into his little developing intellect and comes up with a new set of tools. This time he comes up with contracts, promises, commitments, subscriptions and enrollments:

Now he turns to the female and says in essence: "Well sweetheart, now you can safely walk to the water, because there are no wild animals around that will jump you and tear you apart. But I just realized something...No, No...I mean I just had a *divine revelation*: The path you're walking on to get to the water—I own it! The water rights—I own it! The urn you're carrying to draw the water—I own it! The sandals on your feet...In fact I now realize that I own you! And you can no longer get around in our society unless you have some of this barter stuff...we'll call it money. And you can't have any of it directly. You can only have what a man is willing to let you have."

Unfortunately this perspective has not been the exception. Rather it has been the gross general rule that has dominated human development right up to this century. It still does hold sway in much of the world today. And even in our most advanced technological civilizations, equity between the sexes has still not been achieved.

What he's done is to economically power grid society; he's got her feathered in. Why? Because if he's going to open up and make himself more vulnerable, so he can get his fix of tenderness which he doesn't know how to do on his own, then he wants to make sure that she's not in a position to expose his vulnerability. Vulnerability to what? The emotional chaos that would ensue from all the fears he's never wanted to recognize within himself.

His new nest is structured more by the intellect than just by physical necessity. Around the same basic needs he builds these little bird cages and calls them houses. In the back of the bird cages he puts little locked rooms, sometimes called bedrooms. Inside these rooms the rationale is: "Well, you're the potential mother of my children— whether it goes that far or not. Therefore, ninety-five per cent of the time, I expect you to act the way my own mother was forced to act. But five percent of the time, behind this locked door, I want you to be a raging slut-whore-cunt-temptress-bitch, Eve, so I can get my rocks off...and go out and play with the boys again."

For whom is he asking her to be this hot loving lady? For a big strong man who really wants to make the energies flow? No. Usually beneath the personality facade of bravado he expects her to do it for a pent up little boy who won't admit his own neurotic fears of inadequacy. The women who learned to play this game traditionally became known as wives. How this has played itself out in modern marital lifestyles; and how it could play itself out in more fulfilling relationships will be discussed later. For these *wives*, if they did what the man required of them, went along with the patronage arrangement, they still received, by way of barter, survival necessities and social niceties.

The women who wouldn't play this game—either because they couldn't find anybody with whom to play it; or they found it wasn't worth their while to be that structured by the male—became known as *whores and sluts*. Usually, they were able to obtain some of the barter stuff by outrightly trading their sexuality for financial reimbursement.

What was so different in the sexuality of these women compared to the wives? When a man paid for sex as service, he didn't have to care much about what went on beyond the basic act. He was in the position to demand, while at the same time free of the encumbering inhibitions that would require him to sensitize to the woman's feelings. What was he paying for? He was paying for her to be what she already is and assume the natural role of the sexual aggressor: "Now that I've paid you, I don't have to worry about your family, your old age, or even whether you really like me. Why, I don't even have to worry about whether I can get an erection. That's your job. You get him up and make him have a good time." At the least, she was to stimulate the desire which called forth his male sexuality, thereby lifting the immediate pressures of responsibility from his psyche. She represented a level of erotic interplay which brought him precariously close to the brink of surrendering to his own nervous system. It was a nervous system guarded in monstrous drag by the avoidances he'd unreasonably animated. She had learned to keep some of her psycho-erotic circuitry open. Unfortunately, the dark side of their conditioned inhibitions usually slandered the physical benefits of their pleasure.

The male had bowed to the dark gods of his ignorance. He'd sacrificed the wholeness of his pleasure on a libidinally constrained altar of politicized shame. His thinking capacity and physical nature were chasmed by a seemingly unreconcilable array of contradictory feelings. Life had genetically programmed an aspect of human self-actualization to be triggered through sensory stimuli; the results of such interactions both thrilled and frightened the male. From such a perverted point of view, the very path of spiritual evolution by fulfilling his nature, was denied him. Sluts and whores were paid to give him needed erotic contact. He kept such contact from tripping him into neurological confrontation by defaming pleasure as a wicked weakness. Wives were paid (barter is barter) to reinforce the image of his ideals; while inadvertently making him do penance for his spiritual cowardice. Of course, it was a mutual collusion of ignorance between the sexes. To rationalize their impotencies, our primitive ancestors labeled spirit and nature antagonists; thereby taking up the clarion cry of war to distract them from their self-imposed dissatisfaction.

What you wind up with is a four-way cross: men making war on men; men making war on women; women making war on men; and finally women making war on each other. And that is pretty much how it's continued up until the present day. As in this little scenario—with all of its various kinds of social, cultural and psychological ramifications—I challenge anybody to find a relationship they've ever been in, read about, heard of, or seen depicted that does not fall within those confines. I intend to inspire you to reach for new levels within your relationships that go beyond such limitations.

Between men and women exists either a state of polarized opposition, or a state in which each consciously compliments the other. Opposition is survival oriented: there's only so much to go around, and we're always battling for control of the energy flow. In terms of the male and female complimenting each other we're working from the perspective of integrative wholeness. This concept is up and coming; like an orgasm—the coming thing. You're going to be hearing a lot more about it because the level of consciousness to which our species is now approaching is going to require integratively ordering these processes in relation to ever evolving wholeness so we can have all this yummy deliciousness we've been craving and working toward.

This interim shift from subconscious feeling responses to self conscious intellect happens to everybody.

From the womb until about the age of four, you live primarily in the reactive world of feelings. You were not born thinking. In order to think you had to learn to associate symbols in your intellect with sensory objects (e.g. dog, cat, book, house, car, etc.). But you were born feeling. You know pain and pleasure right away (along with acceptance and rejection which are emotional forms of pain and pleasure). If you weren't fed when you were hungry, it made you feel bad. Because the human nervous system has reached such a complex level of processing, all children are born having feelings. Actually your feeling level of response to stimuli started prenatally in the womb. But you didn't develop an intellectual center around which you could consciously relate to yourself, until enough years have passed in which you'd processed sufficient feelings in association with your nervous system, to a point at which you could begin applying symbols to represent your reactions to feelings. That's quite interesting. From conception until about the age of four, children live in a world governed by feelings. It's reactionary; they respond to everything: talking, wandering around, coordinating complex stimulus games that have been presented to them. But they're not intentionally thinking, for instance, that they're going to learn vocabulary in order to communicate better; rather they're being seduced by attention and conditioned by achievement to respond appropriately to their human potential on a neurological level.

By about the age of four, you've repetitively associated enough symbols with actions so that you can start to operate through a symbol that represents yourself. Somebody may come up to you and remark: "What a cute child you are. Who are you?" And you respond: "I'm me..." (I'm so old; I'm a girl or a boy; I'm this name, etc.) As soon as you think, "*I am*," then you are...whatever you've begun identifying yourself to be as a symbol(s) in your mind. By categorizing your mind; you're starting to wheel and deal with yourself. You move from the reactive world of thinking into the premeditated world of thought. You move from being in a state of innocence (in relation to your body and the environment) to a place of power brokering: "Uh-huh, if I smile this way, I get the bigger ice cream cone".

Also, at approximately age four, every male and female child is expected to go through this whole business of psychosexual repression. They're called upon to identify the male as being superior to the female. Now I've tested this a number of ways. In response to the question: "'Do you think that men are superior to women?" Most women will respond with what might be considered dirty looks or well-deserved chuckles. Of course they are right intellectually; sex is not a viable gauge for superiority. But I have yet to meet a woman (I mean I don't care if you were brought up by Jane Fonda or Gloria Steinem) who despite the psychological astuteness of their thoughts really feels that way. Because their intuitive conditioning has been so inextricably rooted in primitive avoidance, that unless they've been *deconditioned*, against their better judgement woman feel that the man is superior to the woman.

Although not a public declaration, by age four you're inadvertently hog tied to this ritual of perception. What happens is, as the child starts to operate functionally from the mental thought plane of consciousness, mother is there to make the child feel that father is the superior sex. Now maybe we've got a well-educated, financially independent champion of feminist rights who intellectually lambasts the idea of male superiority as chauvinistic nonsense. A child with such a mother most probably will grow up speaking and thinking to some degree with her liberated slant. But understand, at this point of barely developed intellectual competency, the child is still mostly operating through its feeling body. The child is primarily relating to the attitude of the mother, not her intellect. Whereas daddy may be a beaten, deballed, shell of a man, who works at a job he hates, gives her the money, never has real sexual enjoyment and dies early of a heart attack just to escape his misery...nevertheless in her feeling mind he is the superior sex; although a lousy example of it. Not because that's right. Let me emphasize that in the feeling body there is no right or wrong, whatsoever. It's strictly a matter of primitive conditioning elaborated upon for thousands upon thousands of years, passing down the same moronic, inadequate, outdated legacy...irregardless of how our intellects try to reference things.

You probably look around and proclaim how you want to be a liberated person: "I want to relate; I want to be open; let's be friends; let's work this out; let's get rid of possessiveness and jealousy; let's love and trust one another, let's really get this show on the road." Those are wonderful ideas...in the intellect. But who is really managing to live that way? Almost every attempt to do so fails. Why? Because the patterns through which the feelings are operating keep pulling you back; because the feelings have never been deconditioned and they're that binding. Although many people feel stuck in an anxiety state of not knowing how to stop their mental chatter, you can't be really thinking all the time. But unless you're unconscious, you're feeling practically all the time.

Power is the self-actualized expression of intellectual potential. Remember, it's not muscle; it's intellect. The female child is expected to sublimate her intellect, and go indirectly to the male for patronage. Whether or not she believes or consciously acknowledges this, it will create a corresponding sadness, an incompleteness and subsequent tension in her body. If you pay attention, as advanced practitioners of body manipulation skills have begun doing as part of therapy, it's not all that hard to spot these body blockages. This planet's psyche is now dangerously imbalanced. The complete liberation of woman's psyche—almost too long overdue—is one of the major components in rectifying the situation.

The boy, too, goes through the same thing. However, he'll give his power to the father and to some extent resent the father. Everybody gives their power to the father (image); who in an amazing supposition represents the embodiment of the Great Daddyo in Heaven. In turn the same resulting fear and hostility continues to be passed on. Later, when the intellect more fully develops, all kinds of ideas will be worked out about being liberated and fulfilled. However, by then, most people are too obstructed to obtain their heart's desire.

So we have war, and the temporary cessation of hostilities which we call peace, going on and on through the ages. And we think we're going to have disarmament? Any highly intelligent persons who are trained to observe, even if they don't know how to manifest it in their own lives, can tell you that everything that's going on in the world right now is directly proportionate to the state of consciousness through which we're operating. If you change that state of consciousness—not just intellectually rearranging ideas (like gee, wouldn't it be nice if...), but actually change it—you can change the external world; which is really the only way that the social reality set does change.

We've polarized against each other throughout history. The reasons for this polarization are directly related to the split between the feeling and thinking levels of consciousness. We've socially extended this by forcing the female to embody and externally personify the feeling level; with the male similarly trying to personify the thinking level. With this in mind we're ready to study some of the ways by which we've tried to socially reconcile our needs to experience sexual energy within the limits we've placed upon them.

Power, Through Legislated Morality

*A*ll considerations in life are polarized between individual desires and the collective needs of our species. The greatest desire, permeating from the core of each individual, is to fulfill one's purpose in life. Regardless of circumstance, that purpose still remains to optimally experience maximum qualities of consciousness through the self-actualization of one's uniquely individual potential. Conversely, the greatest need of our collective species is to safeguard the ever expanding evolution of its genetically latent spiritual potential. Humanity, at large, has grappled to do so by constructing social environments meant to stimulate its individual members to expand further through the dynamic quality of their exchanges. However, from either perspective, the priority consideration is survival.

Just as in the counterbalancing ebb and flow of progress, so does the individual's expectations seem to be in opposition to the collective needs. When you're born you have all this unique potential you desire to actualize: You want to think, act, feel and live in particular ways. But you inherit the collective entropy of society which dictates you should think, act, feel and live according to previously structured patterns. Particularly in the formative years of your growth, these two contending perspectives map out the territory of your consciousness that will later be viewed as your personality.

Survival is the bottom line; to live on regardless of circumstances. Obviously there are certain conditions which make survival impossible. Individuals die; often seemingly before their time. But the collective whole of humanity perseveres—through the horror-filled periods of active mass insanity called war; through plagues, famine and pestilence; through the mass destruction of natural catastrophes, through the atrocities of expedient compromises—and continues to regroup around the startling bursts of insight generated by its more brilliantly inspired individuals.

"For the good of humanity...For the benefit of society...For the greater glory of God..." Such have been the impassioned but hindsighted rationalizations upon which our patchwork social structure has its foundation. For life must go on. The *Life Force* must and will manifest itself as long as possible. Humanity will continue to reproduce itself (if possible). And the basic, primordial drive of this *Life Force* is continuous self-replenishment...continuous self-regeneration of manifestation. *The basis of all manifest movements of the Life Force is sex!*

Embracing, spirit impregnates nature and in union they create life. In the sexual act lies the undeniability of life's urge to manifest. On every level imaginable this urge towards the resolution of differences, along with the productive synthesis of some form which functions more freely and inclusively is the motivating force. Sex is the creative power of life in manifestation.

Do not be so naive as to attempt to reduce the power of this urging of the Life Force to the obviously simplistic thrashing of animal bodies in genitally reproductive heat. Such is as ridiculous as trying to limit the idea of God to some moralistic wish fulfillment embodied to answer the desperate ranting of history at some dire point of social calamity. Sex, at every level, is the urge to fulfillment of the collective through its individual components. It is the urge; it is not the means, the struggle, the accomplishment, nor its results. After whatever nutrients and circumstances necessary to stay alive, sex initiates, at whatever level of conscious development, motion towards fulfillment. Sex is the summit of survival; even as it is the foundation for fulfillment.

Obviously, sex is a power to be reckoned with. As with any form of power, it has no intention of its own. It depends strictly on the functional quality of the intelligence that utilizes it. And from our point of view—from the parameters of that part of the spectrum of consciousness which humanity has so far been privileged to access—how have we attempted to handle this power? Judging by the results, where have we succeeded and failed?

Religion

As already mentioned, power is not muscle. Muscle is just one particular kind of biophysical vehicle for processing a limited range of power. In fact, to process muscle power to its optimum requires coordination, flexibility, timing, restraint, determination and purpose—it requires intellect. All forms of power—physical, feeling, mental or paranormal—must be coordinated through the mental gymnastics of our intellects.

In our primitive beginnings we were out there with all the other animal species competitively struggling to survive. Through deployment of our intellect we found ways of extending our muscle power (e.g., stick and stones) and our safety (e.g., natural rock fortification and difficult accessibility). Although our successes allowed us to enjoy slightly more of the leisure and pleasure we craved, they also produced problems. These were the problems of social organization: Who can do what, to whom, under which circumstances, based on what? The more we progressed in our interactions, the more power there was at our disposal. There developed division of labor, leading to specialization. There was construction that no one person alone could accomplish. There was conquest; along with immediate increases of wealth through the bounty of divided spoils. There was exploration of possibilities to be brought back for the progressive good of all.

Power to make things happen; on what basis are such decisions made? The intellect—relative to its degree of development—decides. Homo sapiens discovered that through the use of intellect they could leverage the forces of nature to their own ends. To control humans, who controlled nature, was to wield power. Budding humanity became a conscripted work force. Those who acquired the responsibility / privilege of decision-making were able to move the times to the beat of their own rationalizations and in so doing, controlled this work force.

It is not all that difficult to reroute the masses. Simply gain access to the psychological jugular vein of their survival necessities. The first necessity, breathing, is too difficult to directly manipulate. However, food, drink, and shelter are much easier to politicize. After all, we have the greatest cravings for those things which directly determines our survival. We all have to eat and park our bodies somewhere. The better the food and surroundings, the more satisfied we feel. We want the pleasure of satisfaction. So create a merit system; dole out degrees of pleasure in proportion to services rendered. Yes, that works; but the process is slow, cumbersome, arbitrary and too easy to argue against.

After the basics of survival come motivating degrees of pleasure. If pleasure, satisfaction and gratification are what people crave, then to manipulate the power inherent in the work force, pleasure must be controlled. That's not so easy; the human species being almost unpredictably varied. For instance, one person may suffer pangs of frustration at being denied a lavish bounty of foods to consume; whereas another may find sublime contentment in simple bread and water. Although controlling the distribution of wealth certainly had persuasive overtones, it was undependable. What was needed to control the power of the work force was a means of controlling pleasure itself. The amount of pleasure experienced was a subjective measurement, relative to individual sensibilities. In order to control the power inherent in human potential, a system had to be established which could dominate and redirect the subjective responses of pleasure in the human mind.

Remember, we're not talking about good or bad, right or wrong, or virtue versus evil. We're dealing with either understanding the energies involved in a particular consideration, thereby gaining creative functional control; or misunderstanding, thereby not only being controlled by your ignorance but suffering the consequences as well. The formulation of a system to manipulate the social masses (from tribal primitives to complex urban technology) was obviously reactionary conformities to basic survival needs, individual desires, and potentials of group interaction—all chased into expedient compromises through the mechanisms of fear.

Fear—reactive patterns to human insecurity. Pleasure—expanding heightened feedback responses from the successful interaction of mind, body and environment. If it were possible—ridiculously farfetched as it may sound—to get people to juxtapose fear and pleasure in the value system of their feelings...to get them to feel intrinsically bad about wanting pleasure, while feeling somehow vindicated by their sufferings and pain...to get them to believe that the only way they could find temporary relief from the perverted torment of such self-defeating frustrations was through the dispensations of some systematized form of authoritarianism...That is, once you can be led into believing that ignorance is bliss, and come to feel that all the things which make you sane, happy, healthy and satisfied somehow will make you wicked, weak and demeaned. And that suffering and pain somehow makes you a better person. Once you begin to feel that way, then you have become extremely malleable to the mechanics of social manipulation.

Actually, if anyone had been intelligent enough to dream up such a way of controlling the populace, they would have also known how to inspire evolutionary fulfillment without damning up society's vital energies. But ignorance, generating fear, politicizing expedience, in a free-for-all of expansion meant gaining power at any cost and by whatever means available. Once power is obtained, use it to maintain the security of your station; then perhaps, to improve things...maybe. However, no system can function any better than the quality of intelligence that wields it. So how did the quality of human intelligence manifest—beyond the basics of survival—the manipulation of power, and towards what proclaimed ends?

There's religion. As a type of system for obtaining and controlling social power, how does it function?

Well, they want to put the fear of the Lord into you. And you're told from such a place you will be able to experience the love of God. Obviously someone wants to conscript you into believing in their way of looking at and responding to life.

I always tell people: If anyone approaches you with fear, doubt, shame, or guilt, then they don't really know what they're talking about. If they did, they'd never try and motivate you by such disorienting methods.

So you find some charismatic puppet, who believes...you know, because it's in their best interest to believe; and he comes and puts the fear of the Lord in you. The fear of the Lord is the Devil. The Devil has been put in you, and you'll do just about anything to get rid of the soul sucker.

Persecuted by this external projection of your internalized ignorance-generated fears, you're pervertedly led to equate suffering and denial with holiness. Restrict your interaction with life, lest it runs away with you and exposes you to aspects of your inner psyche they haven't as yet made provisions to control in you. They con you into damning up your sexual energy.

As emphasized by some of history's more intelligent healers, and more recently by psychologically astute scientists, there is an awareness that most of the aberrations of society have a direct correlation to damned-up sexual energy. You can easily see what such repression does to the body, and to emotional stability in the psyche of most people. Although these thinkers haven't quite understood exactly how this happens, they have come up with some brilliant insights and techniques to help relieve the tension and/or leverage people away from anxiety-provoking stimuli.

So they put this fear in you—why? What good is it? Well, we need a work force out there. Some people tend to become a little more aggressive when promised the *better things* in life. If you can be talked into believing that all the things that make you feel wonderful inside are absolutely wrong for you...if you can be conned into believing that, then you're going to jam up that sexual energy, never be satisfied, feel frustrated and confused, become easy to push around, and work for pennies doing things you don't like or even believe in. It's rather like putting a toll booth on your dream highway to fulfillment. Then, from the profit made on your dreams, those few can afford to have orgies on their yachts, so to speak. Ironically, they can't really be enjoyed to the maximum, because subliminal repression of the toll extracted from others cuts off the sensitivity necessary to sexually open up their nervous systems to full responsiveness—of course they'll have them anyway.

This is a lot of what's been happening for quite some time. By inadvertently screwing around with the psychological motivating factors of the pleasure principle, the basic life urge—sex—has come under systematic control. Sex has been used to manipulate power on this planet. By moralistically legislating sex through religion, we've damned up sexual energy, which has led to all sorts of psychosis.

If you don't damn up sexual energy, if you don't cut off the psyche from its need to release, to know, to touch, if you manage to move to some degree into that current of pleasure where: "Oh God, yes, I love it...it's delicious. I want more!" At such moments you don't want to kill anybody, be hateful, or listen to a lot of bullshit. More than likely, you probably want more. You want deeper communication; something feels satisfied; something beautiful is spreading through you. At such moments you're inclined to follow your own lead and begin to question things that take you away from feeling satisfied. You become hard to control.

Well, if we all experience such moments, to whatever degree of intensity or whatever duration of time, then why don't we use them like a Geiger-counter and follow our feelings into more of the same? On one hand we simply don't understand how to do so. On the other, we've created a psychological con game out of our religious view of the world. It's one that's so binding that we can't go directly to pleasure; and when we do experience pleasure, it's so tied into emotional pain that we want to let go of it as soon as we've released the tension we could no longer deny.

I call it the **spiritual con game**. Not only has it been played beautifully by religions, as well as with ingenious psycho-diplomacy by Madison Avenue, but most incredibly we've so internalized the process that we run it on ourselves continuously.

The first of three steps in playing the spiritual con game is to tell you something you want to hear: "You're a wonderful human being. You have such potential. Your soul is divine. You can be great." So now you are tripping over all your possibilities...like: "Gee, do you think so? Gosh, it's so great to be loved and appreciated. Golly, you really care for me."

Then comes the world's greatest excuse in two words..."**Yes, but...!**" Watch out for the *but*, it gets you every time. "Yes, but you've got a few problems." And you, the bewildered pigeon, envisioning all your most secret hang-ups and self-tormenting inadequacies asks, "But what happened? I was feeling so fine. Now it's lost and I'm fucked up. I've got to get back to feeling beautiful. I'll do anything you say, just get me back to feeling good about myself."

Finally comes the con's third line—"**However...**" That's the great hook, the one that gets you, the poor sucker, to dig deep and shell out. "However if you pay your money, and speak our party's line, you have our permission to be miserable. Now we never give you permission to be happy. If you were happy you wouldn't need (to follow) us." But the victim gets to be one of the chosen, elected miserable ones. You get to be among some kind of elite. And you keep suffering...and suffering...

This is the spiritual con game: "**Yes,** you could be sexy ...! **But,** your teeth aren't white enough. **However,** if you keep using our toothpaste..." Or: "**Yes,** God loves you and will forgive your sins. **But,** unless you follow our rules, it will go against the spirit and send you to eternal damnation. **However,** by following our path of suffering, you will become redeemed by God to everlasting joy." Or: "**Yes,** I am a sexy person. **But,** if I really expressed the way I feel, I'd make other people uptight. **However,** at least I have a few friends who like me."—*The spiritual con game!*

Law

Whatever the system that takes control of organizing the human work force, it must deal with all aspects of socialization. Directing the flow of goods and services is accomplished by influencing the belief systems of the populace. These belief systems must also take on the sublime domain of speculation as to the nature of the unknown (i.e., God, after death, other dimensions, etc.), along with any considerations such contemplations might raise. Religion and its organizing capabilities served to pull our species up from the brutal muck of its primitive origins.

Religions form around those individuals whose personal explorations into their consciousness open up more encompassing vistas of spiritual potential. They become prototypes, exemplars of the as yet undeveloped qualities inherent in collective humanity. To potentiate themselves, they had to answer the needs created by the demands of the time. By doing so they came to represent an approach to living that others of similar disposition could emulate. Unfortunately, those who follow are usually less adroit. They often substitute ritual, techniques, and attitudes to compensate. As for those who follow the followers of the original source of inspiration, insight dilutes into ritual, which compounds into complex social customs as bureaucracy.

Religion is a particular form of approaching Life (living, itself, being the only true religion). Religious institutions hold in trust a path by which honest followers may gain access to the neurological rate of perception that was originally encoded in the actualized experience of a specific human prototype. For many, some of the earliest paths still offer a viable means by which they may further unfold their own level of development. However, the re-creative urge of the Life Force cannot be denied. Continuously new levels of social response to expanding neurological integration require proportionately evolving social systems for the control of the human work force's potential.

Living takes energy. Power is consciously directed energy. The basic power urging life is sex. This sexual power is the fuel through which creation fulfills itself, from manifestation to manifestation. It is an energy which can, with conscious determination, provide the power for self-actualization.

Religion found crude ways to control sexual energy by

emotionally manipulating the psyche. It organized a collective damning up of sexual energy, which it redirected into the work ethic, along with a few peek-a-boos into more fulfilling (or more often, less self-tormenting) states of consciousness. For a long time, in its various approaches, religion offered its participants far more gain than loss. There has been the promise inherent in religion that you will receive far more in the Light of the Spirit, than you ever could in the shadow of compromise, which is material manifestation.

As the conceptualizing aspect of mind gradually developed, it progressively brought more of the unknown of the unconscious into the knowable conscious territory of self-choice. Religion still held sway over the feeling patterns that had been set, but gradually lost control over basic social commerce. A new system began to emerge. Social organization had provided accumulation of wealth (power to control symbolically represented by money) beyond the basis of survival. People wanted to use their energies to experience what they thought would provide them greater satisfaction.

This new system of social organization became known as **Law**. It superseded the religious edicts of conduct which had been constructed to socially justify a theological point of view. Rather, rules of conduct were to be enacted on supposedly reasonable evaluations of earned privilege. Still, life, liberty and the pursuit of happiness which people were seeking had to be counterbalanced against maintaining a conscripted work force. Intellect asserting itself over feelings, made it necessary to form rules insuring the distribution of power. Upon what were these rules based?

At first these rules were but mere rationalized extensions of the social momentum established by religion. However, as power continued to decentralize—to become increasingly represented through money—the rules of law readjusted to whatever benefitted the marketplace. There was room for rapid growth and expansion; there was room to sweep unfair inconsistencies under the rug of expedient compromises. What seemed imperative to the collective good of all was to keep expanding the flow of power through an ever expanding marketplace. Being able to legislate the public psyche into buying what you wanted them to buy, became the controlling key to power.

That which was most profitable for the public to buy—in the shadow of short-sighted expedience—was whatever could most quickly give the seller (power-broker) the fastest and greatest returns with the least effort. A debatable philosophy at best. But even more important, by keeping the public sufficiently dissatisfied, they would continue to produce and consume distractions.

With the increasing development of self-styled individualism, a lot of people began looking once again for satisfaction. Peer group pressure of religiously dictated social ostracism was simply not enough. No, the presumptuous populace had to be kept dissatisfied (supposedly for their own good). Many of the rules concocted for social conduct continued to revolve around criminalizing fulfillment through sexual pleasure. Not that this stopped people from seeking it; but the relaxed sensitivity required for achieving such an experience became swept into costly risk-taking undercurrents of social persecution.

Because the antisocial criminal element multiplied in direct proportion to the laws established by the power structure, society had to be policed. Psychological aberrations and disease kept pace with the guilt and shame of being bullied into denying sexual fulfillment. As the populace became more intelligent, greater quantums of energy could be conducted through individual nervous systems, and the libidinal drives of sexual energy pressed more powerfully against the conscious mind for fulfillment.

Illicit Trafficking

Saints and sinners...cops and robbers...psychologists and cons...they're all the same ball game; it's just that some like to pitch and some like to catch. The dividing line is most often circumstantial. Quite frequently the roles juxtapose themselves within the same person.

It's a buyer's market and a seller's paradise out there. Repressed physical needs and perverted feelings don't disappear. They just keep resurfacing in ever increasing complexities of social interplay. The more they complex, the more impossible becomes their resolution. Actually, attempts to desensitize or rationalize your dissatisfaction only makes it worse and you become a consumer of anything that will distract you from the pain generated by your self-denial. Religious promises of after-life reconciliation may make you self-righteously holy about your suffering. Social prestige and position may seem an ample reward for tolerating your discontent. And plenty of products are produced around these systems of reward and punishment.

What the legal system peddles is conventionality. Those who conform to whatever power structure happens to be in control shall receive its benefits and tolerate its mandatory inhibitions...or else... Or else be unconventional! Explore those possibilities within and around you that you were conned into believing you had no right to experience. Get your red hot, ice cold unconventionality! Step right out of your patterns of social conformity and prove you have a mind of your own...become a certifiable closet individualist.

It's easy. All you have to do is what you've always

wanted to do, but were brought up to think wasn't proper—satisfy yourself / feel pleasure.

It's easy that way. That's why a good psychiatrist may need therapy from a knowing prostitute. It's easy, but it doesn't work. But ooohh, do those financial bells peel forth in the marketplace with glee. Although the marketplace is neither particularly spiritual nor humane, it is the epitome of barometric fairness. If your product can get into a position to produce a cash flow, the machinery will transform the illicitness of your product into a bona fide necessity for public correctness. As all the holy and revered throughout history were slandered as sinful wicked defilers of the public good (status quo of the marketplace) when they first introduced their own slant on things.

A house divided against itself cannot stand. A mind chasing after its own understandings only catches sight of its efforts. Consciousness, lacking a centralized resonance with the wholeness of its being, cannot operate from within a feedback of satisfaction. But it can be tripped, led, or maneuvered to at least temporarily passing through such so-called peak experiences. And you will pay handsomely to be led through rituals of pleasure, pioneered by self-styled social outlaws. You will pay for what can never satisfy, only justify your frustrations.

Power is the ultimate commodity. Manipulating the psyche by controlling the basic manifest energies of the Life Force, by psychologically perverted programming of the pleasure principle has been the way to control the marketplace throughout most of history. It creates endless variations on the same basic need which can only be intensified by such an approach and generates the production of endless commodities to barter. Whether to pitch or catch, lawful or illicit, these are the social basics of manipulating power through legislated morality.

Abstention

"Whoa there ego, you're galloping away with me, and I'm getting old just trying to control you. Like stop the world...! How do I get out of this...! I mean, if that's the way you're going to treat me, then I just won't buy into your silly game anymore. It's not worth the price. I'd rather do without than have to put up with all that. If it's not going to give me what I really want, then why should I even care about it?"

Some people need a rest from the social struggles of pursuing the chase. Sometimes, it seems the only way to catch up with yourself is to stop chasing yourself. Or you may view abstention as a combination of protesting the social order while validating the integrity of what you believe: That is: "I may not know how to stop the madness, but I won't contribute any of my personal energy toward furthering it."

So instead of trying to sexually satisfy yourself, you deny it as unfeasible. You take a rest and feel a little lighter to be out of the struggle. Yes, you have to pay a heavy price; but look at the power you gain over your feelings, and potentially over others.

Abstention is interesting. I've tried it for variation; I wouldn't try it for long. It's healing if you've been emotionally scathed, or suffered the loss of someone to whom you were attached. It's appropriate when you're worn down, need to regenerate your system and regroup your perspectives. There's a naturalness to abstaining.

But many times it's used to induce false suffering, which is but an unwitting justification of the perverted sense of holiness slyly conditioned into the primitive feeling responses. It can also be most effectively used to produce disproportionate energy blocks in the body, leading to altered attributes of consciousness. Quite often monks, yogis and various ascetics use such techniques to gain amazing insights. But by denying one part of the psyche to experience another, such insights usually can be maintained only in relation to the techniques, which at best only illustrate other possibilities for the human psyche. It cannot be brought into perspective in a socio-sexual context to really better mainstream conditions.

It becomes a way of denying life, in order to exalt life. It doesn't really work except within the circumstance of mind-generated particulars. Too often it can lead to other aberrations. Yet it is undoubtedly a way of manipulating power; an individualistic approach through self-negation.

Esoteric

There have been other forms of approach to individualistic control of power which have been oriented to a more inclusive affirmation of self. By way of inherited genetic potential, transcendent experience, and/or direct training there are those who have accelerated their nervous system to a point where they are less swamped by the conditioning factors of conventional social indoctrination. Having experienced the pleasure of *self actualization*, they seek to further increase the process through special techniques and lifestyles. They pursue unconventionality not in rebellion or denial, but as a carefully chosen path of exploration and experimentation to experience what the average nervous system is afraid to acknowledge. Such clear-sighted awareness permits them to translate the perspectives of their insights into considerations which can heal society's confusion.

Throughout history there have been those who molded their thoughts and actions around more esoteric considerations. Esoteric thought takes you beyond the normal, the average, and the conventional. Being esoteric is fun, as long as you keep the fearful masses, who justify their sacrifice of pleasure as a sanctimonious duty, at a respectful distance. To do this, you need to take on an acceptable front of social commerce. Religion, of course, is the most obvious and widely accepted arena for pursuing the ramifications of things beyond the mundane. But, as we know, it is very conformist and limited as to what you may see, and how you are supposed to proceed.

Well, if you're not going to follow the crowd, you need a perspective on which to orient your activities. You need a philosophy to guide your quest for knowledge; to direct the utilization of what you discover. The sexual act being basic, you must search for a philosophy that enables you to explore the more esoteric realms of sexuality.

If you're making love to get a little pleasure, to release tension, and/or to make babies, that's normal and mundane. But, if you're making love because you want to move incredible currents through your body and change your whole consciousness, that's esoteric because your actions are no longer dictated by the needs of circumstance. Rather, you set a course based on your desire to transcend the mundane—the average. And there are some very interesting ways of playing with sexual energy.

Socrates, one of my favorite philosophers, had an expansive appetite for understanding life. His pursuits led him to examine the nature of thought (i.e., the thinking process). Although he couldn't always arrive at exact formulations, he was wonderfully adroit at clearing away the cosmetic debris of other people's faulty thinking. A vital man, he was one of the few philosophers who based his conjectures on actual experience. In order to gain a better understanding of sexuality he went directly to a woman for instruction.

Unfortunately, too many philosophers have been armchair quarterbacks. However, they do create potential pathways of mental orientation that may be better utilized by individuals who don't need to deny so much outside themselves in order to examine what's going on within. Philosophy is a means of disciplining yourself to step outside the bounds of normal, structured thought processes by which you were programmed to respond. When you learn to step beyond those boundaries—even if you don't know exactly what you're doing, or feel comfortable inside—you begin avoiding a lot of the guilt and shame which usually inhibits the range of individual responses. You may experiment, and come up with a better rationalization than another person who's been trying to program you. Something like: "I may not feel comfortable in what I'm doing, but I can out think you. So at least I have as much right to feel uncomfortable doing what I want, as I have to feel uncomfortable doing what you expect of me; because I can out think you."

Philosophy, when integrated in your psyche, can provide a leverage for organizing and processing the information you're continuously receiving. The ways in which that information is processed depends on an interaction between the quality of the environment, sociocultural particulars of circumstance, level of perception, and the vitality of your body's psychophysical equipment. There are honeymoon periods in the marriage of perception and circumstance, during the emergence of a new organizing system, which manifest themselves as sociocultural golden ages. As for a short time—before politics and religion catch on and incorporate the newness, again reclaiming the right to mediate the distribution of wealth and power—there is a surplus of resources which allows for social experimentation. These cultural flowerings are well illustrated by the ancient civilizations of China, Greece and India.

There was in ancient China a philosophical system

called *Taoism*. The basics of how Taoism incorporated sexuality into an alchemical art are mapped out with functional simplicity in quite a number of books. However, the main source of confusion most people have with the practices described in these books is that unless you understand the meaning of Taoism then the mere practice of these techniques will not lead to the exact level of fulfillment which could be available to you. Understanding Taoism will not come from simply reading the dictionary either. It's a living system continuously recycling your nature with the greater Nature of which you are a part. Taoism uses a wide variety of psycho-connective images: mountains are broad-based, solid, reach toward the sky and interact with the elements in a particular fashion; water continuously flows, fills up places, molds to circumstance, wears down obstacles. Taoists observed the interaction of elements with topography. They noticed how people have similar elements interacting within their own personal topography. They then attempted to correlate attitudes which would allow for harmonizing the greatest symbiotic benefit between humanity and Nature. They wanted to harmonize the alternating polarity of all forces in Nature—the Yin and the Yang.

In terms of sexuality, Taoistic practices are oriented to optimize potentials of the body, in order to bring consciousness into ever expanding fulfillment. This meant to partake of both Nature and Spirit in their entirety. Later we'll expand this into a modern context which is appropriate for the current trajectory toward which we're evolving.

In Taoism, as with most esoteric sexual practices, the female is recognized as the initiatress, the priestess, the teacher...the more sexually competent. It's the female who instructs the male. Remember sex for her can always be an egoless trip. She takes a man on the ride by opening him up through the processes of leveraging her own pleasure circuits, which enables them to glide and soar through the neural apparatus. It becomes a mutual recycling process of cross currenting energies through the nervous system, releasing correspondent hormonal and enzymatic secretions for the optimal maintenance of body potency and clarity of the mind. In order to experience these different states of consciousness, man must learn to retain his sperm, in reasonable proportion to his age and stage of development. In other words, by his holding back, and her letting go, they are both sexually transported into a rapturous gestalt, an energy field in which the whole they represent can resonate with the greater spectrum of the whole of which they are a part.

Men have a particularly nightmarish fear of sex draining their vitality. When sex is done intelligently, not only is it fulfilling and releasing, but also can be rejuvenating and a prime factor to increasing longevity. However, to practice sex in such a manner requires *cooperation between equals* based on a clear understanding of what's involved and what you intend to achieve. As the population's expanding work force brought with it social imbalances, the brief period of psychosexual equality between the sexes was deprived by social power manipulation—chauvinistic sexual demarcations.

Each of these philosophical systems developed according to the sociocultural specifics of its time. Because these systems were geared to a different head level, and people were living at another ratio of stimulus-response to environment and nature, they don't work completely in today's society.

In ancient India, many philosophic techniques evolved around reaching the qualities inherent in transcendent

(transconceptual) states of consciousness. Esoteric sexual practices oriented toward transcendent ends were referred to as *Tantra*. In Tantra, individuals try to manipulate
the recycling of neural resonance frequencies, by aligning themselves with archetypal images which characterize
spiritual entities (e.g., gods and goddesses). For instance,
the male and female in ecstatic sexual embrace is an
archetypal image. In whatever way an individual perceives
God, God would be the one to ultimately actualize the full
power of sexual fulfillment inherent in that image. At that
level, God is the creator of and power source behind all
archetypes, which have been structured to convey a particular aspect of Divinity through manifestation.

As such, I might want to conceive of that aspect of God
which represents the greatest lover in the world. What I
would do is try to align with the resonance frequency
connected with God when manifesting as a great lover.
How can I use this to modify the resonance frequencies
I'm capable of operating through? How can I connect the
transcendent and the personal, so I can partake of that
quality of sexuality? What techniques will allow me to do
so?

Tantra, as compared to Tao, deals with imagery that
expresses the superlatives of an individual's needs. Rather
than harmonizing the flow of nature within you with
Nature at large, you're looking at the possibilities of controlling nature to achieve transcendence, fulfillment, and
ecstasy. By doing that you give personification to certain
forces. Noticing how they process, you can attempt to
harness these forces through visual images within you own
psyche. You look for techniques associated with the manifestation of these forces, and try to approximate them.
Accordingly, you shape the nature of your sexual activities to facilitate these inner goals.

While oriental culture created social systems based on manipulating their relationship with nature, and the cultivated minds of India founded their social structures to transcend the limitations of nature, western civilization developed more along the lines of obtaining power (mundane and esoteric) to stabilize the rationalizations of the intellect. The occidental mentality demanded social systems that bent nature to the will of its collective destiny. The philosophical basis of western systems was rationalized eclecticism: Take whatever you want from any source; subjugate it to your purpose; and make it work to glorify one's power to dominate circumstance. Oriented by such psycho-socio structures, the esoterically-inclined occidentals developed systems of magic.

Magic is a means by which you control the forces of nature through ritualized attitudes of the mind. As with any such esoteric system, you attempt to find techniques for rewiring your nervous system to paranormally take control over phenomenal manifestation. Magically you neither transcend the intellect, nor sublimate it to the normal processes of nature. Since magic is conducted through the intellect, the practitioner must find ways of expanding and rearranging the information to be processed. As such, you must look for rituals which create different levels of attitudinal feedback in your consciousness. By breaking the normal stimulus-response rate of perceiving the environment, you can rechannel whatever available energies are present toward those ends you desire.

Esoterically, the sexual act is a powerful archetype for harnessing energies. It represents a functional act which is tied directly into the experiences of your own nervous system. At the same time, it can be used to access all the basic polarizations in creation, right up to the dynamic interplay between the forces of Spirit and Nature. How much this potential can be actualized has a lot to do with your need, your purpose and the developed integrative qualities of your nervous system. Sexual magic was set up along just such lines of thought. Many of its rituals were meant to gear the rational mind into more powerfully inclusive rates of vibration through various psychological combinations of consciously damning up and sequentially releasing energy.

Any of these practices conscript energy. When you're charged with an abundance of energy, you feel good; you've got vitality. So there are problems to be handled? No matter what, if you've got the energy to do it you feel terrific. But if you have no energy...even if there's caviar, champagne and a beautiful lover beside you, but you can hardly keep your head up...nothing feels very good. So how do we get more of this energy? Well, magic essentially uses different ritualized forms and symbols to commandeer your own consciousness to resonate with things in nature and gain control over the power indigenous to them. And one of the greatest forces in nature is sexuality.

There are many ways of evaluating human worth. Scientists noted that the human body when reduced to its chemical constituents, is probably worth less than a dollar...of course, with inflation the market keeps fluctuating. Also, on the average, incredible amounts of bioelectrical energy are constantly being channelled through our bodies. Over the course of a lifetime, any one of us probably puts out enough wattage to keep a large metropolitan city functioning for quite some time. Consider the utility costs in a city for even one day, and you start to see a small fragment of almost inestimable potential value of our bodies. Our bio-machine is capable of so much. It's a receiver, a transmitter, and has a feedback system that we call consciousness.

What is important to keep in mind when studying any of the past systems of social organization (and they are fun to uncover, decode, and play with) is that their structures depended on the sociocultural particulars of the time in which they were formulated. We're no longer living in a tribal society or an agrarian-based pastoral society. We're living in a totally different kind of society now. Most of these ancient systems dealt with sublimating the intellect, then ritualizing your feelings into certain attitudes, to achieve experiences beyond the normal states of consciousness. For a long time there wasn't that much intellect to sublimate; intellect being only one level of processing intelligence—not intelligence itself. Because we've advanced to such an incredible level of technology, applying the ancient treasures of a more inclusive state of consciousness can be accomplished only with complete intellectual awareness of our goals.

Space Age Technology / Stone Age Emotions

$\mathcal{W}$elcome. So glad you could join us as we transit into the future. It's just around the bend, you know. Whatever their orientation, anyone who pauses to think knows we're on the eve of the profoundest changes humanity has experienced since our prehistoric ancestors first facilitated language. We're in that limboesque state of transition. Increasingly, most of the emotional-based mental formulas which served our collective development for hundreds of thousands of years no longer seem to work. Sensing impending doom we've tried to amend and patch these directives in accordance with our recent discoveries. Yet escalating mass social unrest continues to crack the seams of civilized proprieties.

Every exit is an entrance; every ending is but a beginning of something else. A lot of people believe they are living in the "last days." Some want to believe they're pioneers of the future. While others have already begun attenuating their nervous systems to a few of the possibilities implied by more encompassing levels of perception, most people simply continue to practice modernized variations of centuries old patterns of social conduct and individual inhibitions. Afraid to acknowledge their insecurity, the majority straddle the fence of desperate curiosity.

What is the future? How does one clearly demarcate it from the past?

Life—as our consciousness has so far been capable of perceiving it—matriculates itself in cycles. If you want confirmation of this just listen to time-wise Frank Sinatra songs; or delve into quantum physics with its biological implications; or hang ten with the profoundly clear philosophically poetic prose of Dane Rudhyar; or open your mind and *pay attention*. There are cycles within cycles. They are precisely structured, and thereby limited, units of energy, manifesting according to their nature, with a definite beginning, middle and end. Psychologically they've been referred to as gestalts. They encompass the entire range of considerations potentially possible in anything being considered. There are a variety of legitimate techniques which can enable you to center your awareness at the point where all energies within your consciousness integrate and emanate from. As from this balance point you become capable of simultaneously perceiving all the possibilities which can manifest in the entirety of your being.

For instance, an atom is a unit of energy by which the qualities inherent in the nature of its substance displays certain physical characteristics and patterns of behavior. An element (e.g., uranium) can be altered into different functional states (i.e., isomers and isotopes), yet still retain the basic integrity of its character. But if the energy particle configurations are altered too much, they become transformed; gestalted into a new substance, which in turn represents a whole other range of structural potentialities. The wholeness that an atom represents can combine with the wholeness which a different atom represents, and form a molecule. This molecule becomes a still more encompassing whole with yet different properties.

And so it goes. Wholes actualizing within greater wholes: from subatomic particle / wave configurations, through the psychophysical complexities of human nature, to the barely comprehensible vastness of the universe...all held together through one common medium—the mind of God.

Lets look at the wholeness represented in human nature. It connotes, at the very least:

1. every physical sensation and biological process of which you're capable;
2. every gradient of complex, compounded, approach-avoidance responses you're capable of feeling;
3. any and every symbol-thought-idea of which you can conceive;
4. every level of experience into which you've somehow found a means of extending your awareness;
5. the vast complex of subtle telepathic energies that impinge on your unconscious potentials from other wholes, in the greater whole in which we exist as a part;
6. your ability to consciously hook up with the resonant frequencies of other wholes, and channel their energies into your own territory of creation;
7. the ability to identify with the part of the image-making process which is generating the territory of space contained within any system of wholeness.

Obviously, the combinations and degrees to which any of these levels of perception interact through your nervous system depends on your level of development, the circumstances in which you're operating, and the intrinsic need motivating you at any given time.

A whole exists in a comprehensive polarity based on the interplay of energies between its center and perimeter. Between these two considerations, the energies inherent in the whole go through polarity-defined cycles of manifestation. As they run their course, these cycles proportionately refine the expenditure of energy. In turn, the changing of their energy redefines the emphasis on tension, tone and flow in the quality of the cycles. The most basic example is living breath of which we all partake; a continuous inhale-exhale cycle essential to the metabolic processes of the body. Breathing can—with conscious intention—augment the quality of your perception. It is one of those cycles in the wholeness of your being which enables you to interact with everything else. Perhaps, from nervous anxiety or some physical ailment, your breathing has become constricted. This in turn could result in further physical and mental impairments and possibly a negative attitude to the living process. There are countless variations on this basic cycle; any and all of which contribute to the way energies play themselves out in the polarity of your wholeness.

Within the collective whole represented by our species, myriads of cycles have already exhausted their realm of possibilities, and gone on to transform their energies into other cycles. There exists countless combinations of these interactive cycles that we can already identify. While looming on the horizon, awaiting verification through our experience of them, are the soon to be manifested newer cycles. These spirit specters of our evolving consciousness are already pressing their way into our consideration. They are functional cycles of collective humanity's future range of experiencing itself. This grand procession of unceasing change goes on whether or not we acknowledge it. However, If your awareness has evolved beyond the hypnotic redundancy of the mundane, you may be able to discern, and thereby move into a co-creative relation with the wholeness operating through your consciousness, which is coaxing us to release the energies we've invested in outmoded systems so they can be reprocessed through more expansive structures.

The wholeness of humanity came into existence with self-consciousness (i.e., the ability to retain, symbolize and cross-reference experience through thought forms). At that time, the potential of all which we are capable of manifesting was initiated in this quadrant of space, on this still greater planetary whole. At first, the cycles through which human awareness manifested were dominated by the level of perception which biologically coordinated us with physical nature. Through the aeons, numerous interactive cycles contained within the whole of our potential have continued to transmute our consciousness, sophisticating the ways in which we exchange energy. Currently, in terms of the collective whole that is humanity, we have reached the mid-point of that cycle.

Our past is everything we've experienced leading to this point. We have come from being relatively unconscious and totally at the mercy of environmental nature within and about us, to our present self-conscious ability to alter and direct the flow of nature. The more we are consciously aware of this, the more we exist in the present. What then is the future?

The past was dominated by *survival* of our species; by whatever means, no matter what the cost. While we were struggling through the psychic swamp of our own avoidances, we held a promise of hope within our hearts. It was a promise that someday a *quality of life* would become accessible to humanity...a quality which would redeem, heal, rectify, and somehow justify the sacrifice and suffering through which we'd labored. It became a juggling act, trying to find balance between the collective psyche of humanity and the boundaries by which its potential was contained. From slavish, blind, instinctual conformity towards open minded, free thinking, enlightened individualism, we've slugged our way through the social ramifications of evolution. The balance point we've been half believingly trying to hawk in the market place of "carrot before the horse" idealism is that consciously recycling, mutually beneficial, tantrically symbiotic, synergistically synchronistic, functional state of social commerce— *Unity through Diversity*.

Of course we suspected as much all along. Occasionally, under the auspices of various cycles of energy, we've experimentally tried to make it a reality. In the process of our social experimentation we kept accumulating information which brought us ever closer to that goal. At last we have the ability to actualize humanity's every dream into daily commerce.

The past is that which we've already processed.

The present is our unavoidable need to make a choice: What is the most effective way to utilize the energies available to us, in order to socially actualize the optimal functionality of our human potential.

The future will begin when the quality of life that we've been so earnestly chasing after, ceases to exist as a goal to be attained. When such is the way we live; when our greatest and dearest longings are the mere stepping stones of our everyday way of life, then the second half (the future) of the wholeness implied in being human will begin.

Even now we are hurtling through a transitional corridor toward our future. The birthing contractions of this passage are intensifying; flowing into one another, with practically no discernable space in which to pause and reflect. Every operating social system for manipulating power seems poised between long-promised fulfillment and total annihilation.

Welcome. So glad you could join us as we transit into the future.

What—you might very well want to ask—has all this to do with a book on sexual satisfaction?

The absence of pain is not pleasure! Though, if you've been in pain, and manage to get away from it, it may seem like pleasure. We're talking about pleasure as a positive feedback system, which allows you to gauge the quality of your relation to continued, ever expanding, well-being.

The sexual act is basic: It can be draining or invigorating; demeaning or uplifting; satisfying or frustrating. It can facilitate greater ranges of communication, or induce feelings of ostracized isolation. It can be transcending, enabling you to experience more encompassing spiritual levels of your own consciousness. Or it can lock you into an obsessive blind fascination with your own physical sensations. It is—as with everything else within the range of experience—a matter of your state of mind when experiencing it.

In discussing the pleasures of sexuality as they relate to the level of consciousness now overtaking us collectively, we will proceed with the premise that good sex—intense physical sensations of enjoyment and heightened emotional sympatico—is not what we're looking for. That good friends, good food, good loving, nice environments,

fun times are not what people should be trying to obtain—
they are the least that any intelligent person should accept! We're going to expand our considerations of sexuality.
The self-actualizing potentials of eroticism can augment
your abilities. Heightened sexuality can be used in self
healing to boost intelligence, extend longevity, and psychically expand consciousness. From such a state of mind
you can engineer the appropriate coordinates for fulfilling, open-ended relationships; which, in turn, will help
facilitate more appropriate social applications of power on
this planet.

Before we can successfully deal with experimental
abstracts, we must first master the basics of classical form.
This chapter represents a transition (directly proportionate
to the changes now establishing themselves throughout
humanity) between what human sexuality has been based
upon, and what will enable the erotic arts to become more
advantageous in the future. The rest of this book will deal
with mastering the basics of human sexuality, and transforming these energy-patterned forms into more satisfyingly expansive functions.

In the past, sexuality was inadvertently used to manipulate power (by conscripting a work force) through morally institutionalized inhibitions aimed at controlling your
response to pleasure. In turn we responded to this compromised state of perception by accepting the power party's
dictates. Or by rebelling into opposite extremes, avoiding
sex and / or trying to transcend our limitations with cautious esoteric disciplines. Although the conditions which
fostered such reactions to sex are no longer dominant, the
emotional patterns utilized to deal with such conditions
still control too much of our love life.

Future shock: The future is arriving—what makes it so
shocking to us?

The first rule of humanity is survival; all considerations such as pleasure, salvation, enlightenment and self-actualization take second place to that primal necessity. While our nature has been evolving towards more spiritualistic concerns, maintenance of the integrity of our biophysical vehicles has been paramount. Maintenance and continuance—at least keep the thing alive and operational 'til it can reproduce itself. How well we were able to fulfill these basic survival requirements formed the most primary feelings in our nervous systems. That is, pleasure-pain / approach-avoidance. Although our feeling responses progressively sophisticated in complexity, they were still dominated by our biological survival-reproduction necessities.

Representational symbolism developed as a self-conscious part of our intellectual rate of perception in relation to neurologically encoding our sensations and feelings. Through emotions, conceptualizing became a self-reflective way to manipulate our feelings; thereby affecting our physiology. While I cover this subject much more fully in my books on consciousness, I do want to mention here how this process was used to develop emotional patterns in our psyche.

Feelings are pure, experiential, and within the moment of their happening. They are qualitatively distinguishable by the duration of their intensity, and how much of your consciousness is involved in their experience. If I stroke your arm, you may either find it pleasurable, not worthy of notice, or offensive depending on the circumstance and your orientation. Whatever the response, that is your feeling about what you're experiencing. Now, you may either not want to let go of the feelings, if pleasurable; or be afraid to reencounter. Either way, you identify and remember them by conceptualized thought symbols in your mind;

so that at your own leisure you can try to experience them at will, or at least have them available for future introspective analysis. When you produce feelings from intellectually associated thought symbols (concepts), while nothing in your circumstance actually generates these feelings in you, you are creating *emotions*. These earliest emotions are generated as a semi-conscious reflex of trying to satisfy your physical survival needs of maintenance and reproduction.

Initially the symbolizing capacity of your self-conscious, self-reflective intellect is emotionally commandeered to enhance the focusing capacity of the still dominant, mostly subconscious, feeling level of perception. You want to arrange your relation to circumstance so you experience more pleasure; or organize to avoid more painful feelings. Emotions bridge the shift between feelings and the conceptual process. Emotions are a way of organizing thoughts, to orient your actions and achieve certain levels of feeling. Organization gives you a greater control over your circumstance. You can see how In tribal primitivism, the emotional patterns of the strongest became the collective pattern of its society; all of whom were dominated by biophysical considerations of survival.

Our earliest feeling-based patterns for organizing our thoughts to direct our actions were instituted as reactive patterns (expedient compromises) to the challenges of environmental circumstance. Between the sexes, the male usurped the power over the female and established his social dominance so that the natural biological distinctions between the sexes were crystallized into modes of behavior and conduct.

After survival and reproduction the next consideration was *power*. In whatever form, power was the social means to advance these basic emotional patterns. As humanity grew, diversified and specialized, it mentally tried to re-direct itself into qualities of social commerce that would take it beyond the grip of biophysical limitations. Pleasure was not the commodity, but rather the means of manip-ulation. These reactionary emotional patterns—established in the all but forgotten recesses of our collective antiqui-ty—formed the character for how we would develop so-cial commerce and traffic in power. The results were the *work ethic*.

I've worked with people from all walks of life and strata of society, assisting them, as much as they were ready, to commune more comfortably with their own unfolding individuality. Whether I was dealing with an international celebrity, media sex symbol, corporate executive, house-wife or student, I've always been struck by the emotion-al-based dichotomy of their performance level. In relation to their job they usually perform with a reliable degree of competency. But when it comes to the quality of their personal lives, that level of competency too often is re-duced to anxiety-related inadequacy. The movie star may be the epitome of sexual confidence on screen, but be unable to have either a meaningful or fulfilling sexual relationship in her personal life. The executive might handle hundreds of details and efficiently direct the movements of dozens of people which includes keeping an active interest in their personal well-being, but at home his family life may be chaos. Why? Because the same emotional patterns which formed our primitive reactive psyches are still very much in control. One of these is the work ethic: Individual power sublimated; held in manip-ulative control by the most aggressive; supposedly for the greater collective good. Personal power to make yourself happy, to get more pleasure and satisfaction, sacri-ficed...harnessed into the socially organized collective work force. You may give your all for the marketplace, but not when it come to achieving personal satisfaction.

These biophysical survival patterns have continued relatively unabated for hundreds of thousands of years. They were organized into social power structures in their earliest stages as religion. All religions up until the advent of science were basically matriarchal. Regardless of who seemed to be running the show, within the consideration of developing neurological rates of perception, religions were formulated as a response to the feeling level of consciousness. Religions serve to socially organize power, and provide rationales and distractions to comfort the powerless. Power derives more and more from the increasing utilization of the developing intellect. Religion uses emotional patterns of ritual, attitude, imagery to engender states of consciousness. These collective states of consciousness are necessary to placate the inadequacies of lesser-developed individuals. Less developed, not so much because of a lack of capability, rather, you will mostly find a lack of intellectual-based discipline; with the power they would have needed to face the challenge of life given over to a representational system which doles out rationalizations as to why they should covet the dissatisfaction of their powerlessness. Religions are matriarchal in that they're set up to comfort the feeling body.

It wasn't until the development of humanity's first patriarchal religion—*science*—that the means were formulated to augment and redirect these patterns. Like religion, science is a socially applied system for organizing power. However, it is not based on the bio-survival necessities of the body as structured around reactive feelings. Instead it is based on relatively objectifiable, proportionately measurable, physically demonstrable qualities of the conceptual intellect.

When discussing religion, I use *matriarchal* to exemplify those qualities of mothering (nurturing, caring for, etc.) to illustrate how society distributed the power to conduct social commerce to its masses. With science, I use *patriarchal* to refer to those highest of attributes of the conceptual level of thought, usually propagandized as the domain of the father, as a basis around which social commerce (i.e., logic, reason, proportion, analysis) is directed. Art is a different sort of organizing system, which can be used neurologically to connect the feelings and / or conceptual intellect with transconceptual states of experience.

The gradual social takeover by science was attributable to an individualized coming of age of humanity at large. Too often, crude, inefficient and wasteful as they've been, the emotionally structured patterns of religious societies provided the means for various factions of individuals to actualize beyond their collective contemporaries. Gradually the discoveries of these experimenters created a climate in which the benefits of reason could be organized into a more logically oriented social structure for directing power.

It's not a question of which is better. Just as feelings and thoughts have their places, so too does science and religion. Neither is really complete without the other. No whole is complete without integrated functional access to all of its parts. Once a degree of competency is reached in assimilating the mechanics of any learning process, your attention is liberated to more creative considerations, while having full access to whatever skills you've already acquired. Gradually you transit from social commerce dominated by feelings, to one controlled by intellectual constructs. Now feelings no longer respond merely to the bio-physical survival requirements of the environment. Just as your body had needed the complexities of compounded feelings and emotions as an incentive toward furthering its refinement and expansive qualities. So too, feelings needed the more encompassing structures of thought to motivate their expansion.

It's taken hundreds of years for science to provide the intellectually based objective tools enabling individuals to function independently from the collective patterns. It has had to sludge through the inertia of past religious systems, much of whose content is still valid and desirable today. And while the ground rules for science (the *scientific method*) are relatively reliable within the bounds they were meant to operate, the quality of the mentalities using this method too often have been just as compromised in their social structuring as were their religious predecessors.

Yet ready or not, here we go. Suddenly, in less than a hundred years, we find ourselves with the means to actualize our full potential and rectify our past. In less than a century we've come from transportation dependent on human or animal muscle, wind and water currents, and beginning of fossilized fuel burning railway engines to...We've come from word of mouth, to printing, to coded bleeps along a telegraph line to...We've come from handwritten recordings, and the relatively recent development of the printed word to...We've come from ignorance and superstition as to the functional workings of the human body to...We've come from moralistically punitive restrictions against hedonistic pleasure and relaxation to...We've come from the narrow confines of local territorial politics to...We've come from the social structures and implements motivated by Stone Age emotional patterns for survival to the frontiers of—*Space Age Technology*.

Technology of the Space Age: Humanity on the verge

of extension beyond its planetary womb (gestalting its consciousness into realizing the cyclic formations of more encompassing wholeness). Why? What's the motivation? From the emotionally patterned mental configurations of our past the answer is simple; the answer is more. More raw materials to finance our wants, along with *more* territory into which we can expand. And in answer to what currently wreaks of desperation on Earth: More opportunity to outdistance the toxifying implications of our compounded compromises.

When pondered from the newly emerging level of consciousness beginning to inspire human interaction, the answer is still forming. This new level is one in which the operative ranges of physiology, feelings, intellect and environment are structurally understood. The energy fields these rates of perception generate, and the experiences to be had by interacting with those energies yet remain to be consciously chosen. Each individual has available an almost infinite number of possible combinations in accordance with what will further expand the interactive potential of their own nervous system. *As above, so below.* There are corresponding parallels between past escapades and our future potentialities: Our technological ability to expand into outer space is directly proportionate with the neurologically controlled accessibility into the inner space of our perceptual processes of consciousness.

Remember, humanity is in transition between which of these dominant rates of perception will orient our future thought processes. We've already invented—in less than a hundred years—the basic equipment necessary to begin our new Space Age level of activities. Telephones, cars, planes, televisions and computers are all new. In less than a century we've arrived at a means of living out that which was dreamed about, speculated on, and worshipped as divine for hundreds upon thousands of years. At the rate these changes are complexing themselves, acceleration has barely begun. But why are we having such a tough time with these changes? Why are they shocking us? Isn't this what we wanted and worked to achieve? Isn't this the "someday soon" that we've sloganized, as we relentlessly kept marching into battle to justify our aggressiveness? Isn't this the ancient, long awaited promise, the means to satisfying our most deep-seated emotional longings? Well, it seems to be; except...Except they don't satisfy. They do everything but satisfy!

Let's say you're about to undertake a journey. You have plenty of reasons why this journey is necessary and hopefully beneficial. From what knowledge and resources are available, you make your plans. Prepared as best you can, you set off on your adventure. Sometime down the road, you find that circumstances are not exactly what you expected. You have to adapt. You become inventive with what provisions you've brought, and start to combine them with things you find available locally. You discover new ways of interacting, which in turn generate new insights about yourself. Eventually—after many successive readaptations—you arrive at the place for which you set out. But the person you've become is no longer bound or driven by the things you originally set out to find. Your motivations are as different as your thought processes have changed about yourself. What you will do with the fruits of your journey is far different than you would have thought at its beginning.

We set out in the bleakness of our primitive ignorance to resolve our basic survival necessities; hoping that by so doing, our situation would someday improve. Most of the pain we experienced along the way resulted from our internal avoidances and corresponding social compromises. Now we've reached the end of that journey and are about to begin still another. Yet we seem stuck with the accumulated social paraphernalia of our Stone Age trek. No matter what material form that paraphernalia takes, the basis of it is our *ego*. That *self image* was molded around feeling-charged, subconsciously structured, emotional reactive patterns. These patterns were in keeping with the level of perception which dominated our range of social possibilities for hundreds of thousands of years. However, they're as out of tune with the times through which we're transiting, as humanity is with its current potential.

It's not that humanity is right or wrong; it just misunderstands itself and is therefore out of focus. Actions—individually and collectively—must be based on something. Up 'til now actions have been based on disjointed, defensively speculative factionalism. To be successful our decisions must be founded on the most encompassing and integrative view possible. To exist in an optimal self-actualizing continuum of ever-expanding and recyclable fulfillment we must consciously make choices based on *a functional understanding* of the wholeness through which our parts inter-relate.

Privilege breeds responsibility. The privilege of activating greater levels of perception breeds a responsibility to invent the technology which frees us to live in accordance with our individual inclinations; to insure our creativity is utilized to further extend the benefits of our relationship with the collective whole.

Unity through diversity is not a competitive encounter. When unity occurs, not just as an idea, but through the core of our motivations...when technology and consciousness deliberately recycle each other...when life, liberty and the pursuit of happiness is no longer a goal to be striven after, but a reality for germinating human fulfillment, then—and only then—will the appropriate forms of social exchange be launched into existence. And the changes of consciousness at which we're arriving say, that time is now!

Though barely dry from the womb, design technology is providing the means for decision-making power of such immediate actualization, that we can no longer afford to close our minds and play pin-the-coverup (excuse-avoidance-compromise) on the social standard. *High tech* must be balanced by *high touch* social modalities. Both must be encompassed in appropriate social systems.

How does all this relate to sexual changes taking place in the nature of the male-female relationship? Whereas physical strength was once the measure of survival-success, and the necessity around which patterns of social conduct were grafted, it is no longer so today. Intelligence is now the prevailing criteria. Although the approach to intelligence by the male and female has been oriented differently by social role-playing and reinforced by neural-hormonal physiological functions, in our present age both sexes are equally able to traffic in this commodity. Men and women are mutually capable of pushing buttons, reading information, articulating thought through modern means of communication, and for that matter, spending money.

Money, you should always remember, is nothing more than a representational symbol for bartering power. You bought some food; you bartered for that which would power your body. You bought this book; you bartered for thoughts that would empower your mind with greater understanding, stability and pleasure. In striving for our individual freedoms we established a marketplace to re-circulate the distribution of power as represented through money. Inadvertently we allowed ourselves to be conscripted into a work force because it seemed the best way. We fueled the productivity of the marketplace, creating an emotional treadmill called the work ethic. This work ethic manipulated pleasure by perverting the energies of sexuality. And to some degree it worked; it got us where we always thought we wanted to be.

But robotics and design technology is making that stone aged generated process unnecessary and obsolete. More and more machines will take over the rudimentary drudgery of mundane chores which do little more than prematurely exhaust our vitality. Money, which if you understand anything about economics, really doesn't exist; it's a phantom joke for which people will numb their sensibilities and toe the line. It's being phased out by computer-tracked distribution of accessible goods and services. Humanity is living longer; and if health was approached more as an art, longevity could expand far beyond current expectations. We have worldwide mobility; or at least the means to facilitate it. And we have the potential for total dissemination of any available information among the entire citizenship on this planet; that is, a link up of individual nervous systems around the globe. If you consider even a little of what this implies, you will start seeing the last one hundred years as being distinctly transitional compared to the hundreds of thousands of years which preceded them.

Of course, there is concern that all this could mean the ultimate homogenization of individuality into a collective mush. That instead of fostering the elemental freedom of creative decision-making, which is our inherent human birthright, they could squelch individuality out of existence. And if we consider these changes with the Stone Age emotional patterns that have structured our thinking processes, unfortunately, that kind of apprehension seems all too justifiable. Of course, that's exactly the kind of thinking which has made the marketplace function...that has made war and its temporary cessation a viable industry...that has made the wheels of social commerce go 'round...and around...and around. No wonder we're dizzy; we're punch-drunk chasing ourselves.

Yet through the products of its own inventiveness, the marketplace is being transported to a whole new level for consideration. As machinery advances, and is intelligently employed, the need to conscript a labor-oriented work force is diminishing. Work will be seen as a privilege in the future; the privilege to manifest your intelligence will hold the highest personal value. The motivation for sexually manipulating power in order to control the work force is subsiding. Yes, we now have the means to actualize almost any kind of society that we choose. Through social application of design technology, we could eradicate the fear of need, which has harassed us through the desire for security, which has made us slaves to our own mental imagery, rather than its masters. It kind of makes you stop and think when you consider the implications implied in one statement by the dedicated brilliance of the late R. Buckminster Fuller: "There are over a billion billionaires living on this planet in poverty."

Now that we can see what's happening, where does that leave us? What do you do with all the possibilities implied by what our more disciplined intellects have provided? What do you do with nervous systems directed by the compounded complexity of reactive patterns, reinforced for hundreds of thousands of years into expediently compromised social behavior structures, generated by life and death survivalism? How do you release and socially reintegrate the barely tapped sexual energies which are no longer needed to conscript the work force? What levels of social interaction are in keeping with these new possibilities and can replace our old modes of conduct?

These questions will reach into and transform every area of life. I can tell you that if you don't enjoy yourself in discovering and implementing their resolution, you're missing the point. If you're not enjoying yourself, you're not doing yourself or anybody else much good. I mean, if you have good food, good friends, good loving, good environments and fun times, what else have you got to do besides see how well you can make things work!

For instance—good sex—where and how does it fit in? Obviously, I have some interesting (highly enjoyable, delightfully expanding) things to share with you on that subject. But if we're going to talk about our present transition into future possibilities, let us first reach a more substantial understanding of the major system now dispensing power—*science.*

Science evolved around a technique from a need to objectively validate the relation of perception to apparent existence. Patterns connecting patterns—science began by accumulating a reliable reference index of verifiable conditions which gave rhyme and reason to the activities of nature. Once confirmed, science could communicate and trade its findings with others.

Science is a discipline of the intellect; not the feelings. It is concerned with objectively measuring and cataloguing the energy patterns involved in the activities of any phenomena. These measurements provide a more accurate understanding upon which we base our individual and collective decisions. In offering its services in such a manner, science advises that the main factor in any consideration should be only that which has been experimentally tested and measurably validated. At the same time it implies, too often with dogmatic intimidation, that what has not yet been so experimentally validated should be given little credence either way...that it is wiser to base decisions on what you can prove positively, rather than on the unproven; no matter how persuasive or logical it may seem when considered through a different discipline of thought. Anything can be politicized, made into an art form, a philosophy; everything has economic, sexual and/ or spiritual implications. Yet science, politics, art, philosophy, economics, sexuality, and spirituality are all separately evolved disciplines of thought; all equally valid within their own considerations.

Still, science has become one of the main vehicles on our journey into the future. As such, it has not only provided the means, but usurped the highest authority of deciding our social structure. Although I applaud and respect science as one of the most prized tools of the intellectual mind, it is only a part of the whole—and by itself is not adequate to set the social course on which we're now transiting. I'd like to help free science to more succinctly accelerate its activities. I would like to see the burden of ultimate decision-making lifted from the shoulders of the scientist. I would like to see—obviously in keeping with the needs of the time—a new functional gestalt of perspective for decision-making made accessible to every capable person. This would be an integrative discipline in which art, science and philosophy are mutually recyclable. Now, most certainly, the means for such is available. But this book is not where I intend to discuss the full implications of such a level of consciousness. However, I do think it important to understand the shortcomings as well as the inestimable values of science as it lends itself to the decision-making process of socially structuring our activities.

The basic concerns of science center around investigation into the nature of phenomena. Everything that we are aware of as existing—whether through our senses, or some sophisticated mechanical extension of our senses— are phenomena. We want to understand how things work; their cause. We want to know the range of possible interactions by which phenomena can manifest their effect. *Cause and effect* are the polarities in the wholeness of the mental discipline and application through which science generate the cycles of its activities. Those cycles may involve simply the gross classification of a particular species by detailed cataloguing of the functions of its observable structures. Or it may be the quantum implications of particle-wave activity as they aggregate into structural energy patterns.

For instance: Perhaps you want to investigate the visual impact of erotic stimulation on the men and women of a particular age group. Your hypothesis could be anything. Let's say you hypothesize that the men viewing said stimulus will verbally express different emotional reactions than women viewing the same stimulus. You run this experiment keeping such factors as age, cultural background, education, etc., constant among the participants. From the results you draw a conclusion as to whether or not your hypothesis was valid; and then determine whatever other experiments are necessary to corroborate and/ or extend your findings.

Now two factors are important to keep in perspective. The first is that the type of questions you ask has a lot to do with what you're going to discover. Using the scientific method you cannot ask questions about things you have no way of validating (e.g., as yet we can't measure scientifically the spiritual magnitude of the Godhead). Those questions you do ask must be propounded from what has been objectively determined already. Secondly, as Heisenberg so aptly pointed out, 'The amount of energy used in observing phenomena, changes the nature of that which you're observing.' What this adds is the "X" factor, or rather, the *human factor*, in all scientific observations. It is an illusive variable which can never be totally pinned down.

When it measures phenomena objectively, science seems infallible. For example: The precise and always duplicative reactions of specific chemicals, under constant conditions in a test tube allow random variables involved to be controlled exactly. But when those same chemicals are placed inside the human metabolism, non-specific and unexpected effects quite often occur. The results may vary from application to application. This variance is not only detectable from person to person, but also from moment to moment in the same individual. Because the way in which our nervous system (particularly self-conscious reflective thought) interacts with our metabolism cannot be pinned down precisely by scientific measurement. Why? Because every objective form of measurement needs a more inclusive subjective rate of perception from whence to apply the measurement. No instrument can ultimately measure itself; it can only compare the isolated measurements of parts of its performance capacity to other parts; or measure phenomena less inclusive than its own capabilities.

The unknown factor "X" in scientific calibrations is our level of perception or, the interactive rate at which we think. Consciousness is of itself the reason for its existence. It is as illusive as trying to find a way to expand our awareness to a level of perception from which we can objectify what had seemed previously to be a subjective consideration. Simultaneously, a newer and still more encompassing objective state starts to intrigue us.

I'm not negating anything. Rather, I want you to be aware that *relativity* and *relevance* are poetic ways of scientifically describing recyclable states of subjective-objective consciousness. As in relation to the pattern of discovery-integration-creativity (thesis-antithesis-synthesis), science gradually has assumed control of social conduct. In that sense, too often, science has become a frustration unto itself.

There are times we get the feeling that in order to glorify its own authority, science, (much like religion) sacrifices the dynamics of the individual to the so-called collective good. Of course, such has been the peril of any social system conducting power once it reaches the self-justifying state of bureaucracy. Every distinctly bureaucratic system is necessarily divided within itself. All measurements are relative to the state of the perceiver. In science, this in-house fighting has revolved around the considerations of *Nature versus Nurture*.

Ever since science began to distinguish itself, the question it has generated is on what—and consequently how—to base the social application of its findings. First it observes a reliable pattern of functionality in nature. With fresh insights, science produces a new framework on which to base activity. In turn, this information processes new social forms to nurture the interactive levels of society. Suchly, newer discoveries (nature) keep leapfrogging over existing patterns of social interaction (nurture).

For instance, Sigmund Freud's discoveries into the nature of the human psyche replaced former patterns of social conduct. Darwin did the same with his flood of information pertaining to the scale of human development. Along with Einstein's findings on the constituent nature of energy, the means were created for entirely new ranges of social interactions which have continued to erupt through the twentieth century. *Psychology of social behavior* has become the nurturing factor of our time. Regarding the nature of the sexes, psychology has tried to outline a proper perspective for appropriate modern conduct. This has been but another attempt to create order out of objective views of nature; hopefully to end the conflict within ourselves and between each other. This unavoidable incompleteness upon which social science bases its approach, coupled with the incredible insights of newer research, even now is banging down the doors of our current value judgments.

With new means of probing and manipulating the body-mind complex just starting to trickle in, it is obvious that more radically encompassing social patterns must make their appearance. We're finding that the brain and neural endocrinology is physiologically distinct between the male and female. Was this the original design? Or has it been modified and reinforced by hundreds of thousands of years of socially dominated patterns of nature and nurture? And what perspectives can be created from this information so we don't continue to recycle these same limited social patterns into newer, more technologically amplified versions of life in the Space Age?

That we've reached a point of transition is obvious. We simply can't go on repeating these delinquent patterns of social maladjustment. The balance between sanity and insanity is inescapably precarious. The stakes for which our planet is gambling are at the maximum: at the very least, either a new order which transcends, encompasses and fulfills the functional coefficients for *unity through diversity*; or total annihilation of the human species.

Of course, you're probably saying to yourself: "I know all of this already. No sweat, baby; it's just so easy to pierce the dark shrouds of past aeons of superstition and corrupt survivalist bullying, dude." Okay, so now you are free to live your life the way you really want to, except...you aren't quite sure what it is you want, are you? Actually, you've only spiritually conned yourself into believing you already know. As yet, you haven't attained enough inner freedom to want much beyond a means to break free of your old restraints.

Sexual Barter

*E*verybody is saying:
"Love me, touch me, notice me, care for me."

Everybody else is saying: *"Fuck you; love me, touch me, notice me, care for me. And then maybe..."*

The question seems to be who is going to win; who is going to get their way? The problem is that when one person does manage to psycho-emotionally dominate the other, what they take dominion over never satisfies them anyway.

The situation changes: When you're inwardly centered and integrated to where you can love, touch, pay attention to and care for the other person, they're so thrilled that they want to give back to you. Or, at the least, they want to give back whatever will keep you interested enough to stay there and keep feeding them some positive attention.

However, you can't do more (give more to) for another than you can for yourself. No matter what you say, think, or do, the real quality of what you convey is directly proportionate to how much you've opened your own nervous system.

And never forget—no matter what the intentions—whatever someone can do to themselves, if you let them, they can most certainly do to you. Consider the source. If they can live in self-deceit, frustration and self-denial, they can certainly subject you to the same.

What this amounts to is: "I'll love you the way you want/need, if you do just one thing. What's that? Love me the way I want/need."

Armed camps—one upmanship always involves at least two down in some hole of aggravated self-denial. Power struggles to survive in this day and age are like trying to climb a mountain when you're already on top.

Let's examine the situation: Despite easy access to the collected works of the world's greatest minds (on spirituality, philosophy, science, psychology, art, history, etc.) combined with all the computer wonders of instant communication, most people still operate through a haze of emotional compulsion. It's not that they don't think progressive and enlightened thoughts. They quite often do; as in their own way, most people would truly like to see the world as a peaceful place. When they stop to think about it, they don't really want to be unfair, prejudiced, unjust, or any of the other states of power dominance we all too often display. Yet despite their best intentions, most people continue to conduct their lives along the age-old patterns of emotional fixation we've mistakenly come to accept as human nature.

No one is an island. We're born naked, ignorant and totally dependent. We inherit the human legacy of hopes and fears of all the compromises in the cultural milieu which were acted out before our arrival. From the moment of birth we start struggling for independence. We seek it out in whatever understanding that will leverage us into more control over our circumstances. A goal never totally achievable, yet, it is always relatively within our grasp. For *to be*, from the human perspective, is to be related. Independence, for those who achieve it, is the means to function mentally and/or socially beyond the indoctrinations of upbringing, to which most people will conscript the rest of their lives. It is the ability to consciously function in relation to the whole of human potential.

When the infant self-consciously starts to identify itself by association to thought symbols—*I am me*—it moves from the reactive world of feeling responses into the mental world of social barter. In response to memories of pleasure and pain it calculates, anticipates and structures its future potential. As to whatever degree of capability, each person must start to assume responsibility for their own success and satisfaction.

Increasingly, each developing individual must potentiate their means to access power. We must learn to obtain power for our body-mind metabolism to perform (e.g., nutrition), to enable us to mold environmental circumstances (e.g., tools, knowledge), to command social position (e.g., customs of culture), to name but a few. The child must learn to obtain whatever will satisfy those undeniable needs which motivate its psyche. Gradually the child learns about the equipment with which it's been endowed. Appearances, intelligence, dexterity, personality projection, muscle coordination, etc.; to each of our developing attributes we assign a value. Later we cultivate and transpose these attributes into the skills we can use to barter our way through society's marketplace (i.e., art, craft, labor, technical know-how, social aplomb, high procreative promise, etc.).

Regardless of what you're inclined to pursue, or how

you go about bartering for the necessary power, it is (as with everything else) a matter of from what level(s) of perception your efforts are structured. Mentally, we've come a long way down the civilized highway. Emotionally, we have not. We've devised modes of social conduct based on the highest qualities of our reasoning abilities. Then we harnessed science and technology to bring them into functional reality. We've got manners, legality, customs, morals...you name it. But when it comes to our interpersonal dealings with one another...When it comes to the important things we've collectively sweated out the aeons to achieve...When it comes to the personal satisfaction we hoped to be able to someday fulfill with one another...When it comes to love, affection, warmth of shared feelings, closeness, tenderness, intimacy, communion... When it comes to simple, straight-forward, open, honest exchanges, despite all our achievements, we're still going about trying to emotionally power-trip one another.

One upmanship; who can best manipulate; who can maintain control. If it were a question of basing our relationships on the highest qualities of the intellect, then logic, reason and truth would prevail. Obviously, this has not been the case. We shout our civilized, intellectual slogans from the coverup institutions of pomp and circumstance. We go through all the motions, paying homage in lip service. Our literature and art sentimentalize the nobility of our yearnings, or make heroic our moral frailties, as if failure was its own justification. Now we can watch it being enacted with endless variances of savoir-faire on public cinema screens and home televisions...all the too human foibles of betrayal, unethical dealings, bullying...all of them paraded before our eyes. The suffering of the ages, personal and collective, are dramatized in an endlessly entertaining stream of repeat performances. And they will continue until the emotional reactive patterns of our consciousness have been deconditioned and more appropriately self-reprogrammed (open-ended and flexible). Or, until the stage is dismantled.

What are these emotional patterns we keep manifesting? What are they based upon? Obviously, the need to manipulate power to your own desired ends. What do you desire? It depends on which level of consciousness is structuring your priorities. On a survival level it's the needs of our physicality. When you detach and simply contemplate, it's the highest disciplines of thought which characterize human idealism. For those who manage to peak beyond the conceptual limitations of their self-imaging, it is the balanced state of mind which allows them to feel connected to the more encompassing supra normal forces of life. Indeed, most everybody at some time and to some degree manages to experience the qualities of these different rates of perception available to the human organism. But for the most part, people are motivated by the reactive response patterns subliminally conditioned into their nervous systems at the feeling level of perception.

Feelings have no right or wrong; there's no good or bad to them. With feelings it is simple: You get what you (were patterned, conditioned, and programmed to) want. If you get it—whatever it may be—it produces pleasure, you approach it and your feelings become validated by satisfaction. Or you don't get what you feel you want; which produces pain, you avoid it, and feel guiltily anxious. What you've been made to feel you should want may be degrading to your health and demeaning to your spirit. For instance: You may have been conditioned to feel that you're a miserable, screwed up sinner, and you should spend your life suffering and repenting. When logically examined, such an orientation is psychological crapola. But once you've been subconsciously made to feel this way, the only time you feel good is when you're miserable suffering and repenting. While if for the most logical and scientifical- ly validated reasons your intellect sets a course counter to your conditioning, you will feel wrong and fight your- self. All the other values we hold up as civilized measuring rods have their place; but they are values of the intellect, not of the feelings. In other words, when the feeling body takes over, there is nothing which cannot be justified as a means to the programmed ends.

Most extremely, this can be seen in the case of a vio- lent criminal. I don't mean the fancy dan con man who strategically sets about outmaneuvering the already socially sanctioned merchant. Rather, look at the brutish psycho- path who sexually assaults, destroys property, and too often takes other lives. In such a case, the ethical safeguards of society were unable to take priority jurisdiction in the intellectual level of consciousness. Instead, the person lives in their feelings, bending their thoughts into emotional fixations. In such a person, even the survival needs of their physicality have lost perspective. Every aspect of their consciousness becomes sucked into a whirlpool of their feelings. The same age-old feelings we all have, but without the structuring of other qualities of consciousness to give them stability. Aggressive, assertive, dominating, destruc- tive patterns of feelings reactively established in the sub- conscious of the human psyche to motivate primitive Homo sapiens to materialize power to defeat its enemy. But this ultimate enemy was always the dark deep-seat- ed fear of its own misunderstood psyche. The evil enemy within that we've characterized and battled in so many forms throughout the ages. Getting away from the pain of this enemy becomes the main motivating criteria. For so imbalanced a psyche there is no pleasure; only the pseudo-imitation of pleasure in temporary respites from pain. This is the only rightness to such a person. The only wrong is in tolerating anything that cues in the pain-charges in its negative feelings. When feelings are the dominant evaluator, there is nothing which can't be justified.

This is one of the main reasons that rehabilitation of the criminal psychopath has been tenuous at best. You remove them from the source of their anxieties; then structure in them intellectual patterns of activity that are re-inforced by the mandatory nature of their surroundings. The cuing factors of feeling-based aberrations recede. The responsibility for decision-making is no longer one that taxes their self-image. But unless the original feeling blocks can be deconditioned and the person taught to self-consciously reprogram, then as soon as they are thrust on their own, the same feeling patterns will reassert themselves.

But we don't have to go so far to see this in operation. For instance, before women recently began to assert their individual rights, men had found many quaint ways of cataloguing the feminine nature. From the lopsided male perspective women were said to be fickle, and quite often, deceitful liars. Men thought of their sex as logical, reliable and forthright. Now what had been going on between the sexes was the result of the primitive male usurping power (intellectual rights of self-expression) from the female. The female, until quite recently, was forced to work mainly from the feeling level of consciousness. On top of which the male economically corralled her to spending her life's energy within the confines of what he'd talked himself into believing was proper. That is, she was supposed to partner (sexually mate / economically marry). Reinforced by attitude and ritual, this was one of the main directives of the social programs that were instilled in her from birth. Remember, the only real criteria of feelings is that you get what you were programmed to want, or you don't get what you want. Men tried to overlay what they had denied in their own feelings with patterns of logic. They established measurable norms which they called truth and dependability. Men measured the correctness of their social interactions by how dependably honest and predictively coherent was the quality of information exchanged between individuals. Very logical, but it's all a product of the intellect. Women were working from their feeling level. For them, the only measurement was satisfying whatever the program was to which they'd been conditioned. If the program was to obtain and keep a marriage partner for the purposes of accepted social procreation of the species, then anything they did to satisfy that purpose was right, true, and justifiable on the feeling level. If they changed their minds twenty times in the course of a few minutes, if they contradicted what seemed to be the apparent truth of the circumstances repeatedly, if they were clearly inconsistent but even when caught at it refused to concede they'd done anything improper, it was because they were being honest from the basis of their feelings. From that level, their only honesty was to fulfill the program. Of course, with most men having cut themselves off from adroitly perceiving through their feelings and trying to stampede their consciousness through the disciplines of their logic, women did indeed seem to be fickle and liars. But they weren't; women were being honest and true to their own priorities of criteria. *There are no paradoxes—only the same point of consideration being viewed from two different levels of perception.*

Unfortunately, this feeling-based level of self-justification all too often plays itself out through the emotional power games of social one-upmanship. Real security is

based on *understanding*. Those people who apply themselves to working through the particulars of any function,
'til they've mastered it and can utilize its properties at will,
are very secure within their own knowledge and abilities.
They've earned the right to power. After achieving such
control of their own potential, the only thing which can
further enhance them is to extend their range by working
with others of like mind. Knowing the struggle involved
in self-actualizing, they can afford to cheer others on and
help instruct. But many people get into positions of power
through social grace, inheritance, or skulduggery. Because
they really don't understand the formulation of energies
over which they've managed to gain decision-making
power, inwardly they always feel insecure about their
position of authority. Without such understandings they
don't know how to progress on their own and are therefore always afraid of falling down the ladder to the less
prestigious rungs which they never successfully climbed
in the first place. Such people attempt to maintain their
position of authority not by excelling in creative merit, but
rather by trying to keep the other person below themselves.
This too, goes back to primitive emotional dominance,
when might was equated with right. When coupled with
the psychological perversion of the pleasure principal,
where you're taught that good people should be unasser-
tive, humble and meek...When you combine all that, too
often people with the brains, and sensitivity to create,
wind up having the least say in the application of their
inventiveness. For those reasons people who work from
the feeling-based patterns of their emotions are prepared
to dominate—as long as you let them.

Perhaps you're locked in a confrontation with such a
person. You're trying to use logic, reason, truth, etc. to
show them the correctness of your perspective. You're

being reasonable. They, on the other hand, are operating from their feelings where the only real criteria is whether or not they can get their way. For you there is honor and correctness. For them there is only power control. The more honest, open and sincere you are, the more you play into their hands. Their measurement of success is in their ability to emotionally manipulate you. So what if you have brains, talent, looks, whatever; that's fine, they can manipulate you into placing it at their service. What this means, from the pettiest of nitpicking levels on up, is that as long as I can emotionally push your buttons I'm in the driver's seat. That no matter what you may know, if I can get you to respond and get emotionally bent out of shape, then you're not so together after all.

It was the realization of all this as I reached the end of my youth which inclined me to vow to myself that: **I will never allow anyone to steal from me what they could have for the asking!**

Remember, the intellect developed after the feelings were already operable. And until rather recently, we've used mainly our intellects to formulate and justify the emotional patterns we created from the reactions of our feelings. After populations became too large to simply live off the land, we motivated codes and customs to organize our expanding social exchanges. As discussed in the first chapter, one of the earliest forms of socially encoded barter was sexual barter. At first it was reinforced through superior male muscle power. Women indirectly received material necessities by male patronage. Later, as our nervous systems complexed into more organized forms of social exchange, the male economically power-gridded society. Economics became the media through which the sexes escalated their bartering with each other.

Whatever the media of exchange, the quality achieved

always depends on the level of consciousness from which your social structures are formulated. The intellect and feelings should work together in a flow through coordinating the greatest benefit for each individual; instead they too often exist in a sly state of unannounced war. The male and female could consciously work together for the greater fulfillment of human potential; instead they continuously aggress against the weaknesses of one another in a recycling battle that is as sexually boring as its modus operandi is primitively inane.

Social barter between the sexes—with thick coatings of various nuances, innuendos, and affectations—is patterned exactly the way it has been since humans first became self-consciously socialized. There are a number of differences between the sexes around which we could have intelligently based our social structures. But we didn't establish our criteria from a logically analytical point of view. We established our social structuring upon the reactionary survival criteria of the obvious differences of muscle power and the social functions each might serve.

Thus was the *double standard* established. In a survival state, the superior muscle power of the male gave him dominance over the female. Across the board he used that perspective to justify his superiority over the female, and has tried ever since to usurp a number of exclusive rights and privileges for his sex alone. Actually, it was an unadmitted mutual conspiracy between the sexes. The female learning to manipulate the male who manipulated nature. While despite all the outraged squawkings that have rattled through the ages, there was a kind of unhealthy fairness in past sexual barter, which today's modern hindsight should acknowledge.

Because our intellects are more encompassing in the rates of perception they can invoke than are mere feelings (for the moment not including those transconceptual states of spiritual implications), it has been too easy for us to mentally envision harmonious states of human relations which we really don't know how to actualize in everyday life. It is easy to picture a society where there is an abundance of food for everybody. But to develop the tools which can make this a reality is another thing. Its not just the science and art of proper cultivation, and the means of distribution, but also the cultural sophistication which allows for this to become a political and economic feasibility. We are on the verge; but because of the confusion of past compromises, despite the already perfected technology, this is not obtainable even now. Children die of starvation every day, while we dump perfectly good grain down the tubes of power dominance toilets. Why? Because, no matter what we think, the emotionally-based economic distinctions by which we allocate power are not set up to allow for such distribution. They are survival-oriented at almost any cost. Now we know this isn't the way to be most productive. And it's easy to postulate a system which could be erected to handle human needs more equitably. But no matter how much sense seems to be made, we are drawn back to updating a patchwork survival of the fittest.

The answer, of course, is a system based on a far more holistic rate of perception— one which doesn't counter the already existing human tendencies, but rather views all aspects for what they are and how they've played themselves out so far on the world stage. A system is needed which can order those established, and often imperative, social functions, while not activating the residue of their compromises. Such a system cannot be thought up first in reference to some social need; that is how we've been doing it up 'til now. Many people are being opened to these more encompassing rates of perception; and as more and more people learn to operate from these vistas, they will begin to experience new forms of social exchanges in keeping with their escalating nervous systems. It is from such an overview that we will draw the understanding around which the already existing social systems will be transformed into a coherent workable answer to humanity's Space Age needs.

Even now the social ramifications of the outmoded double standard are heading towards extinction. New formulations based on individuality will soon replace sexist mandates. From more encompassing vistas of understanding we'll project our will through whatever machinery is available to us (including the sexuality of our bodies); according to what will optimize our potential at any given moment. In fact (as we'll discuss more fully in the next chapter), based on experiential understanding, this greater range of potential responses, balanced on an inner security which reaches far beyond states of consciousness that any amount of sexuality can produce, will enable us to explore and develop our sexual differences to their fullest.

If we're going to master and have these functional human proclivities at our disposal (instead of being continually disposed by them), it is necessary that we first understand how they've played themselves out, up 'til now, in our development.

Out of ignorance and force of habit, our feelings are generally conditioned during infancy by our parents or whoever represents that level of connection and authority. They may be very idealistic, with all sorts of progressive ideas. At that stage of development you are most likely to imprint on the patterns of their feelings, most of which they are themselves unaware. These imprints include all the qualities of social interaction up through the responsibilities of raising a family and earning a living. Usually, you will not be aware of how your consciousness has been conscripted. But as you approach each level of personal maturation and social exchange, these imprints erupt like psychological time bombs, exploding reactive feelings through your consciousness, quite often usurping the logical proportions of your reasoning faculties.

We have been collectively successful—at various periods of time—in erecting modes of social conduct which repress, reroute and / or contain the irrational excesses of our feelings. However well this has been managed or mismanaged, when confronted by the nature of relations between the sexes, we throw up our hands in whimsied mystical helplessness—"All is fair in love and war." And the way we've responded to our feelings, often it is hard to distinguish between the two. When you understand how the development of your consciousness is structured, it becomes remarkably easy to see exactly how we've conditioned our range of choices in responding to each other.

You're either in love, or searching to be. That search may be a deranged, backward withdrawal into the cesspool-ridden compromises of your self-avoidance. But ultimately, that's what you're seeking. We will put off expounding on what love is 'til the next chapter. Instead let's look at the predictably mechanical way in which we conduct ourselves in the pursuit thereof.

As a legacy of the Judeo-Christian mindset, most people have been subliminally conditioned to *feel* that men are superior to women; that basically women should exist to serve men; that to have a mind of your own and assert yourself in the pursuit of pleasure is somehow wrong; that being erotic is demeaning in a man and sluttish in a woman; and that somehow suffering makes you spiritually a better person. Also most people rationalize some internal daydream scenario in which they postulate the kind of uplifting situation which would make it alright for them to unleash the full potency of their passionate nature.

Let's say you finally meet the person of your dreams. There is attraction on all levels. You speak your hearts and minds to each other, with candid honesty, holding nothing back. You decide to form a marital union where you will continue to be open, honest and work everything out. You both have a desire to be faithful to one another. You set a date for the wedding; you design the ceremony to fully express the deepest feelings you want to acknowledge publicly. You find a spiritual person whose dedication and insight you respect to perform the ceremony. You invite your families and dearest friends to give testimony to the commitment of love you're making to each other. Now you are married and committed in every possible positive way. You want to make a go of it. Under such conditions is it good / right to be erotic with your beloved spouse?

Unless your feelings have been deconditioned from the quagmire of past social programs—no matter what you may think—the answer is no! Under no circumstances does this still too pervasive legacy of primitive control mechanisms allow you to feel good about being erotic. Yet most people are still waiting for the right situation which will allow them to combine the best of both worlds in their lives. It won't happen that way! It never has worked that way; and it never will! They've got it wrong.

Talk about crucifixions…Your most powerful, priori feelings exist in relation to you satisfying the bio-survival needs of your physicality. You've got to eat, breathe, eliminate, sleep and reproduce or you won't survive. The more you fulfill those prime physiological directives, the more pleasure you feel. Spirit (if you would) genetically programmed those priorities into your nature. If you don't satisfy them you will feel guilty (no matter what you think). But, after hundreds of thousands of years of morally bullying people in order to socially harness the power of their working potential, you've been programmed to think you should feel guilty if you do satisfy those needs. Damned if you do, and damned if you don't— talk about crucifixions!

Still the life urge cannot be denied and we continue to reproduce ourselves. However, with the replay implications of modern technology, we can almost instantly scrutinize every facet of the performance. Whether you want to watch the televised hardcore fornications of the economic-based war machine, the graphic gyrational spurting of sexual suck and fuck gymnastics, or any emotionally suggestive variant in between, it's all there to justify, with mass hysteric reinforcement, the qualities of your own infatuation with frustration.

All animals are into some sort of courting ritual. For most of them these rituals are biologically structured to their metabolic chemistry. For Homo sapiens this process extends through emotional reactions into self-consciousness. Keeping in mind all the conditioning factors structuring our exchanges that we've discussed so far, let's observe how sexual barter continues to direct commerce in our modern world.

Now, it is the natural function of the woman to bring forth life. She is from that priori-based level, the true sexual aggressor. The complex, rich tapestry of feelings which constitute her personal inclinations (after the basics of physical survival-maintenance) are all structured along those lines. They orient her perceptions, activities, intuitive insights, and through the feedback of her involvements, orient the flow of hormones throughout her metabolism, in turn reinforcing the structural reactions of her brain chemistry. Now, she may be perfectly logical in applying herself to any given task at hand. But when making decisions concerning her own personal satisfaction, for the most part, she will be oriented on the deeper priori functions of her life-bearing psyche.

For the moment, excluding all science fiction projections of test tube engineered liberation, she is motivated to seek a man for the purpose of reproductive pair-bonding. This is not to imply that she is elementally limited to and controlled by these mechanisms. However, regardless of transcendent, transformational or avoidance disciplines, our psyches have been oriented from these basics. Because the way society is still structured to reinforce this process, the male represents power to matriculate this inherent drive in the female. He represents it biologically in the sperm he manufactures and socially in the economic structures he still controls. Even when a sperm bank usurps the function of the former, and an independently successful career cancels out the latter, he still represents the necessary power for completion of the feeling-based patterns in her psyche.

Nevertheless, man still needs his fix of tenderness. And for the most part, has not resolved the archetypal bogeyman fears which keep him from making full contact with and utilization of his own feelings. Yet he must be open with woman or go insane. So he approaches her with great longing and urgent need, overlaid with mistrust and fear of the nearness he must brave in order to open up and get what he seeks. All of which in this modern age is greatly ameliorated by the intellectual vicariousness of mass media. Though emotional patterns are not being defused, they are stimulated constantly by enough variations and associative releases to lessen the obviously pent-up frustrations of most of the populace.

So when physical, emotional and social circumstances bring together a man and woman with some compatibility, a romance starts. Remember, it is not what you do, so much as where your mind is at when doing it, that determines the quality of the experience. For some people, immediate sex may be easy; while for others, puritanically long drawn out courtly rituals of sufficiently modest embarrassment maybe necessary. But whether the standards are self-imposed and almost absent, or complicated social rituals of proper approach, the man goes offensively on the defensive. He demands, in whatever way is suitable to his psyche, certain acknowledgments to the superiority of his power.

If the woman is interested enough to consider the man a serious candidate for partnering, she goes after him. Supposedly, she holds the key to his satisfaction and fulfillment. She can lead him safely into and out of the feelings he so reverently denies. She proceeds to phychologically *mirror* the man: In whatever he is interested, she also shows an interest. However arrogantly he might pronounce his given right to do whatever he wants, she acknowledges him with understanding and some degree of complied acceptance. If he says he wants his freedom to date whomever he chooses, she may pretend (even to herself) to go along with his wishes. The modern equal-rights-type may cheerfully acknowledge her understanding based on similar needs and desires. The less aggressive woman may simply agree to go along with his desires while indicating she prefers to see just him. He's wary, yet longing. So he tests her, and she does whatever is necessary to register on his feelings the sincerity of her interest and fascination with him.

After however long this initial phase takes, he starts to acquiesce towards her. He becomes accustomed to the thrill of sexual-sensual stroking. He starts to experience steady access to the gentler feelings he longs for but is usually too estranged from to contact. He begins to feel the dependable comfort of companionship. Diminishing is the discomfort of having to project and defend his self-image. Ah, the luxuriating comfort of peaceful acceptance. The weariness of isolation and ego-compensation subsides somewhat. The healing joy of caring for and desire to give to another infuses his being. He acquiesces toward a rate of exchange which seems to more than compensate for the deep-seated vulnerability he tries to hide.

He wants to continue having these feelings. Maybe he was wrong in his initial assessment. Perhaps he should offer to share some of his power, kingdom and glory with her. So he starts to soften and accept her. He let's her know how he feels: "You know, you're really wonderful." When he acknowledges his openness to her, the energy suddenly shifts: "Yes, I really am a beautiful person. And just look how miserably you've been treating me." Now that he's pursuing her, she begins to reel him in.

This shift is hardly noticeable to the participants busily playing off each other's energies. They are merely performing the ritual they've been programmed to enact. The whole thing comes down to manipulation of power. To the socially sophisticated elite, this may seem remotely obvious. But what about poor Joe Schmo, working class? Or dear, shy spinster Mary McProper of the well-behaved school of good little girl self-denial?

These patterns I'm discussing are basic to everyone. I have yet to find a single exception dramatized even in any fantasy form of art or literature. They exist in the most primitive societies, as well as the experimental playgrounds of communal living and sexual liberation. These are emotional patterns based on compromise in order to access power. Power for what? On the simplest level, power to get out of bed, face the day and accept the psychological uncertainty of life. Power to afford distractions and social mobility. Power to turn on and explore those attributes in your personality which you want to nurture. Power to rationalize justification for unacknowledged dissatisfaction. Power through devious social manipulation, is a direct projection of the ignorant internal compromises we've made since our species first began to distinguish itself.

Some people, as children, have had their nervous systems so usurped by rigid structures, that their range of social responsiveness winds up being more stifled than their parents. They accept whatever they've been conditioned to believe. There is resignation to their lot in life; usually some religious projection of afterlife fills in the rough spots. If they accept the norm under which they've been raised as a willing yoke of social responsibility, they may remain relatively content. For them the fight is over. Some can't accept their indoctrination, and go to great lengths to break free. Not only do they denounce social custom, but go out of their way to act out rebellious patterns that they feel will prove the inadequacy of what they're escaping from. The vast majority shuffle between various gradients of these extremes, ultimately waiting for marketplace sanctions in the form of buyable commodities.

So woman has mirrored man until he can no longer settle for not experiencing the feelings he's been able to open up to with her. But this is an old game. For ages, he's been wary of her. He has had economic control until so recently that the changes are as yet barely accountable. He will reward her with favors and dispensations if...?

What does he want from her? It's not the sexual act per se. He can have that, buy it, yet still feel dissatisfied. He wants a more encompassing communion within his own consciousness (soul, if you like), without having to encounter the awesome isolation of his fears. He wants privilege without responsibility; validation without substantiations; shortcuts that take forever, and only lead him away from where he was going...where he's already at. He wants someone to take advantage of him, to justify his need for self-reproach and self-incrimination —he wants an *excuse!*

You can never get from another what you need to be for yourself. She knows that, but she is just as wary of his tendency toward self-deception. And besides, infatuations are short-lived unless they can be bound into the psyche of the other. Bind them with love? Love has no boundaries. No, they must be bound to that which he is so afraid to let go of—those deep-seated fears with which he tries to justify his usurping power...his expediency...his responsible lack of responsibility.

Now, we must take a moment to get something straight. When it comes to psychological manipulation, nobody can directly harm you—at worse, they can only con you into trapping yourself in your own emotional fixations! Perhaps someone is trying to make you feel insecure and uncertain. Verbally, they attack the quality of your being with harsh remarks and sly innuendos. Maybe they say something like: "You're a screwed up asshole who will never amount to anything." Now, if you break down those eleven words, you'll find that they mean only whatever you're ready to have them mean. Screwed up, asshole, amount, anything; these words mean millions of different things to millions of different people. Nobody knows exactly how you would associate them. From your mind, you, alone, supply their meaning. All the other person has done is present an image; you fill in whatever hopes or deep-seated fears by which you mentally characterize such things.

We talked earlier about the spiritual con game; how we've internalized it, and continue to run it on ourselves. Maybe someone says to me: "AM, you're a beautiful person." Now that sounds nice (maybe) and it would be easy to get a little lost in that. I could start thinking of all the reasons why the statement might be true, while basking in the feelings such emotional recall generates. Or I might stop and scrutinize the person addressing me, thinking: "What is it in you that allows you to see beauty?" Someone else might see something totally different. What I'm doing is not giving a charge to the words spoken; rather, I consider the source. In essence, I become a mirror. If I neither accept nor reject, then the intent of the words, the repercussion of their range of meaning stays with the other person. If I don't think: "Well thank you, that's nice." What's nice? If I don't defend myself: "That's not true, you're the one who..." Whatever I'm tempted to see doesn't have to manifest. Then there are no repercussions in my psyche; the other person obviously has been projecting their own feelings.

This is the true meaning behind the phrase *turn the other cheek...resist not evil.* Usually when someone (or your own self-image) lashes out at you, you defend yourself and may even try to counterattack. You have, of course, trapped yourself with your own definition just as did the other person. Nothing can be resolved this way. It is only another warlike gesture to power maneuver for one-upmanship. Both people wind up hurt, blaming the other for that which they've inflicted upon themselves. The expression, "turn the other cheek" is, in reality, a very powerful psychic tool (we're just evolving to where it can be used safely and effectively). On an apparent level, in terms of simply learning to heighten the sensitivity of your awareness, it is probably better to bear the abuses, slings and arrows (even unto death) rather than become as distorted and lost as the person aggressing against you. Just as on some level it may be better to spend a lifetime in devotional detachment from the pleasures of life to discipline your mind into perceiving at a more encompassing and self-directed frequency. Because such drastic measures are no longer necessary, I can now relate this to you.

Again (and again) remember: It's not what you do, it's the state of mind you're in when doing it! If someone trespasses against you and you assign no meaning to it and associate no feeling with what they're saying, then they are stuck with the state of mind they tried to trick you into assuming. Their negative intention weakens them, giving you power over them. For most people this is a power they really don't know how to command. It's like being given access to an incredibly advanced computer while not having the faintest idea of how to run it. At any rate, the person who trespasses gives you power. From a spiritual perspective you may retaliate righteously, even putting the other to death. But if you do so to get even, then you will bare the scars. Except in life-threatening situations, by simply not involving yourself in a negative thought-form, you will more than amply control the situation. With no way of being distracted from their own negativity, they become their own tormentor. Of course, this process was taken to an extreme when Jesus allowed himself to be placed on the cross. The height of rational social power (Rome) and socialized spiritual discipline (Judaism) came together to represent an immediate advancement into the future for our species. They trespassed against an individual who neither took it personally nor used his power to retaliate. Rather, he consciously had set out to gain power over the collective psyche so he might manipulate it to nobler and more evolved plateaus. By such representational trespass, humanity gave him that power and he formed a psychological logo which has greatly reshaped the structuring power of social exchanges to this day.

It's like taking a walk through an insane asylum. You've been informed that whether or not it's fair, all the people within are so mentally bent out of shape that they're no longer able to discern reality. And someone comes up to you and babbles something about making love to the President after they defeat the invading Martian Armada. Probably, you'd try and humor them; but it's unlikely you'd allow your feelings to get involved with anything they're saying. Too often the problem becomes, how to tell from where someone is coming without a socially institutionalized scorecard to keep you informed. At the moment I'm giving you a few basic insights that will guide you safely through your social interactions, 'til you've learned how to discriminate more quickly and reliably.

After all, we don't want to exist cut off from our feelings. To communicate interpersonally through our feelings is the poetic expression of the soul. If anything, we want to open up to our feelings as fully as possible. Optimally, we want the ability to move into and out of our physical senses, feelings and thoughts at will; to combine them in whatever degree is appropriate for our needs at any given time. Yes, that's partly toward where humanity is now transiting. But until you understand exactly how to process energy through your consciousness, don't fake it. That's why I'm giving you these safeguards.

How is it that we've locked ourselves into power competition? Viewing the male / female relation from the above perspective, it becomes relatively easy to see how woman has bound man to her needs. Woman feels that what

man wants has something to do with her. She could equate
it easily with sexual release, companionship, child rearing, housekeeping and an object over whom to lord his
uncertainties. Yet none of these more obvious capacities
are truly the answer. She can feel the answer in the isolated intimacy of their lovemaking when she takes command. She can feel his hunger to make contact with the
part of himself from which he feels cut off. And more than
that, she feels his dream-need to reexperience, in unceasing
escalation, the ecstasy of transcendence which once he'd
somehow, at sometime, touched upon in his past.

She suggests, in whatever way is appropriate, that she
can fulfill him and take him to these heights of feelings
with which he longs to connect. She implies and suggests,
drawing him emotionally into her. Always there is something more he wants; and she always let's him know there
is some condition not quite fulfilled enough for her to let
go and give him what he so pleadingly demands. Even if
they are ultra-compatible...even if she loves him most
dearly...even if she's a well-educated, economically independent, sexually liberated woman...even if she's willing
to go so far as to take mind-altering drugs and scurry
through psychic corridors with him...even if she wishes
she could consummate the utmost communion of energies they're capable of sharing, she won't let go. The first
reason is that she, herself, doesn't know how to let go and
bridge her own emotional toilet training. And secondly,
unless deconditioned, she resents him too much and trusts
him too little to open up fully with him.

Even if a man has been sucked and fucked half to death
by six different women, he won't be satisfied. It may exhaust him. But from a psychological level (baring higher spiritual attainment) there is only one way a man can
be sexually satisfied. That is, if woman, who is the nat-

ural sexual aggressor, let's go, gives herself over to pleasure and takes man on her trip. However, you can only have the kind of lovemaking that leads to sexual satisfaction between **equals** (each person having a self-actualized independent sense—not just a rationalization—of the inherent power of their birthright). Whereas, except for a few brief cultural peaks (experimental honeymoon periods before self-conscious economic compromise usurped the flow of human need) at the flowering of early civilizations, the double standard has made this all but impossible up 'til now. Because of the double standard, we've had sex-role confusion. Man has tried to extend his apparent external, physically aggressive inclinations into the internalized realm of feelings. It is there that his obvious inadequacy disorients him; and the female is able to skillfully capitalize on his weaknesses. Externally, she seems to go along with the man, giving him what he thinks he wants. Inwardly, she punishes him for his unfairness by simply refusing to be the psychological aggressor, and letting him feel inadequate.

Haven't most of you had some experience with this? Man and woman making love; maybe for hours; maybe for a found weekend...Perspiration, saliva, hormonal secretions, sighs, moans, groans, orgasmic climaxes, ejaculations, the works—an erotic encounter of the fucking far-out kind. Yet on some level man still wants something more from woman. Even if it takes hours or days before he could get another erection, he's still sort of snuggling, in some way intoning: "Yeah baby, you drive me crazy when you're so hot. Give me more, lover. Let's turn it up" A woman may give him a, "For Christ's sake, you must be joking," kind of look, while implying that the lovemaking was great and, of course, they'll do it again, but...But he wants something from her and he can't figure out what it is.

Remember those two types of women—*wives and sluts*—who socially characterized themselves when the male economically power-gridded society? Yes, the ol' madonna and the whore routine. The wife type learned to control men by *denying themselves pleasure.* Such denial is, of course, relative to the degree of social sophistication. A church mouse might keep her thighs clamped, only opening them under pain of dirty religious duty. While an international jet setter might go through every position in the "Hollywood Revised Edition of the Space Cadets Sex Manual," but still clench up tightly around the ego defenses of her somewhat cynical self-image. Because of this man must keep coming back to her, or someone like her, to get his fix. On one level, in the deep, feeling recesses of her subliminal psyche, she still resents the "prick" for having usurped power from her. On the other hand, she never really has been opened up to the quality of sexual release about which we're talking.

Seduction: If I can introduce you to a state of mind (and body) which is better than what you've previously experienced—when you realize that it is available to you—then never again will you be satisfied until that state becomes part of your normal repertoire. But if you haven't experienced such an existence, you'll be understandably reluctant to threaten the methods of your power base, no matter how dissatisfying they might be...until you're so threatened that you have nothing to lose but your discomfort.

The slut accepts Eve's condemnation (so to speak) and allows her consciousness to stay plugged into rapid-fire energy hormonal flows of her sexual psyche. This is what she barters for economic subsistence. She may have a truly loving nature and basically be highly inclined to sexuality. But part of what she's selling is her sluttishness. She takes the responsibility of aggressing from the man. She gets him erect by placing him in a frame of mind where socially conditioned moral indoctrinations aren't cued into his value judgments. She gives into her own pleasure circuits while simultaneously demeaning their value.

Woman needs to open both her sense of social aesthetics and sexuality to her own inclinations. When they are united functionally in the psyche of the female mind (a level of consciousness) the result is something totally different from the wife-slut split which for too long has distorted feminine nature. Denying herself pleasure and/or approval is mentally paralyzing for the female. It trips, unnecessarily, certain neuro-chemical hormones which distort her sense of spatial relation. These hormones flow in response to the state of mind which structures her range of potential interaction, to which she's been conditioned to feel she should be limited. If her intellect doesn't develop to where she can individualize her point of view, and / or the spiritual capacity to transcend the confines of her mental orientation, she separates from her mental ability to transpose spatial relations. She becomes depressed into not releasing energies, which in turn fills her with anxiety. These anxieties result in physiological self-sabotage as the unreleased tension turns inwardly against the woman.

But we do have to relate, however dissatisfying it all too often feels. Actually, out of ignorance in the way bonding is handled in the womb and at birth, most people inadvertently are conditioned to subliminally seek punishment. They are conditioned to feel pseudo-satisfaction with their dissatisfaction. Unfortunately, sexual barter under misplaced priorities of the double standard is how we've been relating.

Courting rituals are basically territorial. Through mirroring, woman comes to represent man's connection to his estranged feelings. In turn, man represents the means to fulfilling the child bearing / rearing needs which were conditioned primitively into her psyche. **Note:** Until otherwise deconditioned and reprogrammed, these basic structural patterns of the feelings continue to dominate people...even when a woman has no desire and / or physical capacity to give birth (e.g., a total hysterectomy); even when a woman to whom a man is attempting to relate is financially independent enough to have no need of his patronage.

Among the women who fall into the potential *wife* category, a sisterly conspiratorial arrangement takes place once a woman has singled out a man. If the women involved are friends, they will support their sister's efforts. The first stage of attraction between a woman and man revolves around sexual attractiveness and implied possibilities of greater satisfaction. To enhance their friend's attractiveness, the other women soften their own vibrations, making them more alluring. On a pure sex for pleasure level, the vibrational resonance of several women is extremely arousing to a man. The group support, with nothing specifically said, implies that by focussing on this one woman the others will become somehow accessible to him. Usually, the man is drawn into intensifying his exchanges with the initial woman. When he is sufficiently committed emotionally, her female friends retract their allurement; leaving him polarized (out of committed guilt) to the initial woman.

This is territoriality. Because most men have cut themselves off from many of their feeling processes, while being overly preoccupied with the validation of their belief systems, they too often choose to be blind to the kinds of declaratory exchanges that go on among women. Power (to live the way you want) is what they're seeking. When approached for partnering, man indirectly represents woman's emotional bid for her own fulfillment. She responds with almost deadly earnest that her chance for fulfillment shall not be denied. It is her slant on *possessiveness*. Man must be brought into a stage of emotional fixation (dependence) and committed responsibility (guilt-shackled obligation) before she can rest somewhat. If man doesn't want to make a commitment in the standard, openly accepted social form, then any other woman who is interested (sees him as an enhancement to her own power) feels she has the right to try and commandeer him to her own ends. Remember, on the feeling level there is no right or wrong; just getting or not getting what you want. To the contrary, woman views man's protests of independence as really not his choice.

Courting is hot. Woman let's go sexually to some degree to attract man. She feels (despite what she may think) slutty; but this is socially sanctioned sluttishness, which may be forgiven by proper conduct as soon as partnering is achieved. Once a certain level of intimacy and commitment has been reached, off goes another psychological time bomb. Propriety and controlled sexual distance sets in. All the feeling patterns imprinted on them as infants by their parents as to how a husband and wife relate, start to orient their accessibility towards each other. Along with all the fear, mistrust and resentment which still exists between the sexes, these feeling patterns inhibit their optimal closeness.

By simply thinking of the way in which it makes sense to live today, we've come to believe that we can control and eliminate these age-old patterns. But to the contrary, out of ignorance, most people wind up losing sight of the other person because they pay more attention to their own ideas of what they think the other person's all about, than they do the actual person before them.

Today the intellect has developed to a point where society can see its obvious compromises. With technological time and labor-saving devices, there are many persons mentally adroit enough to defy old patterns. They go off seeking new ways to fulfill themselves. But to do so, they must extricate themselves from the morass of emotionally-structured commitments in which they've felt stuck. In the first place, they don't understand how their nervous systems are attenuated to these social fixations. The standard pattern of so-called readjustment is denial of what they identify as their old image, while projecting a new image. It's like: "I'm stuck in this hole over here and I no longer like it. But I've got all these commitments to this hole. How do I get out of it? I know, I'll dig myself an even bigger hole, with even greater emotional commitments."

Commitments, fixations and avoidances particularly characterize the nature of relations between the sexes. The whole idea is nicely summed up in the expression, *falling in love*. To fall: to lose your sense of equilibrium and coordination. Falling implies lessening one's level of awareness in order to enter into a highly desirable state referred to as love. But love, my friend, isn't what you find when intelligence goes blind. Rather, you are conned by your own ignorance. You're led to believe that you must give someone else the power (your power) to give or take away from you what they never had the right (or ability) to give or take from you in the first place.

Instead of love you fall into *emotional fixations*. You're confusing where you got to with how you got there. You're confusing the state or mind accessed, with the person, place, or thing that seemed to catalyze you into it. You don't know of any other way to even temporarily expedite the compromises through which you narrowly limit (objectify) your awareness. As through your tunnel of objectivity, you can receive only those impressions which match socially indoctrinated criteria. At the same time, you keep wanting to avoid anything which threatens the basis of whatever power you have. And you feel threatened continuously; because you've denied—by falling in love—even the normal sense of mental clarity through which you usually operate. For what do you sacrifice your intelligence? For a chance to experience certain ranges of consciousness you don't know how to synchronize with at will. Ironically, those levels of consciousness are always there and the more you keep your wits together, the more they open to you. And just as ironic, the more you fixate and blind your reason to these emotional patterns of approach, the less accessible become the feelings you seek.

It is on the feeling level of consciousness that all approach and avoidance mechanics of behavioral conditioning take place. This is where you are conditioned to reactive patterns—which, unless otherwise consciously rerouted by you—will dominate the rest of your life. They are territorially inspired reactive patterns, which subliminally coerce you into avoiding anything which doesn't fit in with age-old established norms. It's often seen in the vehemently guarded attitude—"I don't want to think about what I don't want to think about." But you say it's not true. We've come a long way since the blind dregs of primitive superstition. Intellectually, yes; in the marketplace, yes; in our science and philosophy, yes...but in our interpersonal exchanges, no!

Rather, as our intellects developed we overlaid these emotional patterns with augmented social rituals. To illustrate, let's take a broad look at an aspect of modern socio-sexual bartering, where sublimated physical reactive patterns, overlaid by social ritual, have been intellectually bypassed by modern educated people. In the battle between the sexes, intellectual structures slug it out with feeling patterns. However, there are levels of consciousness which can empower you to transcend factionalism, enabling both participants to harmonize their perspectives.

Take the Jewish religion. It is a religion whose spiritual potency centers around and subsequently is enhanced by the relations of family. There is a kind of give and take equality in the home. Men, of course, usurped power and decided the tenets of basic social structuring. And women—by tone, gesture, innuendo, sexuality— manipulated man. By submitting to a sanctioned spiritual path, both sexes lived in relatively respectful harmony. Misunderstandings between the sexes weren't resolved, but men found enough strength in their spiritual practices to handle woman with less fear and greater emotional proximity. As long as this path was followed in the ordained way, relations were mutually beneficial. Because of events in their history, the Jewish people oriented most of their survival skills through refinement and expansion of their intellectual potency. This further deepened the internal split between the primitive based reactions of their feelings and the aggressive expanding possibilities of their intellect. As long as they subscribed to their spiritual path, this battle—though never ended—was ameliorated. But once they settled in the new world of advanced opportunity, there was a tendency for many to diffuse their spirituality. They didn't know how to maintain their spiritual potency while changing the patterns from which social interactions had been outlined to precipitate that energy. More and more emphasis was placed on intellectual adroitness. Without the spiritual connection—which needed to be updated in modern context—the resentments of the female and fear of the male resurfaced with a vengeance. With already highly developed intellects, Jewish women have run amuck. Emotionally, they're more adroit at manipulating the male; the modern colloquial vernacular, Jewish princess, surfaced to describe this phenomenon.

Of course there are many explanations which could (and should) be considered when making such statements. But for the moment, I'm simply illustrating these mechanisms. For instance, in Christianity, the Christed aspect of consciousness (with all it implies) is exemplified through the personality vehicle of Jesus. For numerous reasons, Jesus was not recorded as being a sexual lover. Now every woman raised under Christianity (at least, inadvertently) has been taught to look for the Christ in man. If she feels she's caught sight of this associative attribute of spiritual consciousness (so to speak) in a man, yet that man has sexual relations with her..."Then you're not the Christ. You're that damn man who stole my power" At that point, from whatever level she's socially relating, she'll attack him with those deep-seated resentments. As I said in the Introduction, angels (and such) have received a great deal of bad sexual P.R. on this side of the manifestation.

We could go on and on. There are seemingly infinite variations on these basic themes. Or more precisely, on these rates of perception and the levels of consciousness produced by the interaction of the human nervous system with its environment. What should be obvious by now is that so far, the ways in which we've come to relate to ourselves and others really have never worked.

Any woman who makes love with me is, at least, as fortunate as I am to be making love with her! Any man or woman could feel the same honorable way, if they took the time to work it through. Before the marketplace gestalts into something more inclusively in keeping with our potential, it must be steered into Space Age functioning at a far more efficient rate than it has to date. To do that, I'm willing to barter skills, knowledge, insights, techniques—just about anything, except my pleasure and the states of mind necessary to achieve it. I take pleasure in everything I do. Pleasure is one of my main geiger-counters by which I guide my movements. I show I'm grateful through my enjoyment...All of which leads to fulfillment and yet more new vistas into which I can expand.

We're about to discuss those new vistas and how to start attaining them. They can be achieved only without fear, doubt, confusion, anxiety, guilt, shame, jealousy and possessiveness. These aberrated states of processing our perceptions will not be resolved by man and woman. Rather they will be resolved by self-actualized, deconditioned creative individuals who will focus their consciousness through whatever equipment with which they have to work.

It is time to end sexual barter and begin sexual satisfaction!

5

Sexual Satisfaction

*I*t's time to make sex a Grade Double A Class Act of accepted sociability!

The time has arrived to stop falling in love. Intelligent open-minded, free-thinking individuals should be *rising in love*!

Wonderful loving is when you can't get enough and it's always satisfying!

It's time to start gearing our feelings to living within all the superlatives we're capable of imagining!

It's time to introduce you to sexual satisfaction. You've already been introduced to too much dissatisfaction!

How do we make this happen? Just let me differentiate what this book can and cannot accomplish.

This book is a discourse on insights and techniques of human sexuality; along with their functional integration into the human nervous system and their subsequent social implications—(Stone Age) past / present; transitional / future (Space Age). As such, like too many other wisdoms through the ages, it can be merely assimilated as more intellectual dragon shit to feed the infinitely voracious computer-like aspect of your mind. What I'm hoping is that you'll turn it into a guideline for accessing your own past performances and perspectives; as well as a means of validating some of the techniques and insights I'm herein offering to you.

Anything that one human can do, given strong enough desire and determination, another human can accomplish. Years ago, at a primitive village burial ceremony in the mountain jungle regions of southern Mexico, I met a man who seemed remarkably fit for his age. He was reported to be a hundred and one years, and his wife was a mere child of ninety-three. They'd just walked some fifteen miles across the mountains from their neighboring village to pay their last respects to the old woman who was being laid to rest. After the ceremony all the women were sent away. The men hung around the graveside to palaver. There in the midst of us all, this youthful old man squatted on bent knees cheerfully talking to all the men while downing some four hefty swallows of mescal (a stronger homemade brew from which tequila is later refined). Not that I wanted to live my life in the same manner as he; but before me was the fact that one could maintain strength, vigor and clarity past one hundred years. If he could do so, then I— relative to my own needs—could do at least the same.

Many times in my youth I've sought out exceptional people and situations to validate that such was accessibly achievable. Often I found people who excelled in some way, but didn't really understand how it happened. Of course, they had wonderful rationalizations about how their coordination with the outer circumstances of their lives had made this all possible. Yet beyond recommending to me (if they even were so inclined toward benevolence) that I follow their own particular idiosyncrasies, they really couldn't direct me according to my own needs and level of development.

That was okay with me. With conscious determination I'd decided at the age of four years—before anyone could have guessed what I was going to be up to—to figure out how the human mind works and find ways to alleviate the fearful inner turbulence under which I observed everybody was suffering. I've never met a person I didn't understand. I spent a lot of time learning how to extract the essential structures of consciousness from the idiosyncratic experiences of various individuals. These understandings can be made accessible to anyone interested, relative to their needs and level of integrative development.

One way of doing this is through the printed word. After all, I've found leads to many of the treasures I've tracked down in the written longings and inspirations of numerous literary compatriots. Measurable comfort can be found in the realization that someone else has gone through similar longings and considerations. Even the injustices such explorers and experimenters received at the hands of a subliminally hysterical public, vehemently denying that they have fears to avoid, have been a kind of validation to the accuracy of my pursuits. Of course, I regard all suffering and it's glorification as simply *misunderstanding*. One of my aims is to take you efficiently into ways of processing energy that validate by pleasure, rather than pain, your essential being.

I can not do this directly for you. However, I can help you do it for yourself. I can show you where the best water is. I can show you how to obtain it. If necessary, I can even hold it up to your mouth. But I cannot swallow it or savor its effects for you. This you must do for yourself. However, if it is possible for me, most certainly it is just as possible for you.

I've come to see that many people lack even the basic awareness of how the various aspects of their consciousness function. They keep reducing everything they experience, sense, and feel into associative, intellectually abstract symbols. To help them decondition their infantile social indoctrination and gain more inclusive control over their nervous system, I've developed some rather unique counseling techniques. These techniques are remarkably safe, efficient, penetrating, and non-regressive. They are methods in which I intend to train others. I mention them here because I want to remind you that just reading and thinking alone will not decondition and free your nervous system. Experience is the greatest teacher. And these counseling sessions (not psychological self-reflective analysis) are a very dynamic way I've discovered to help people achieve greater experiential awareness.

In the same vein I also conduct workshops. They are a way of psycho-experientially dancing with others. When you are truly experienced in something, you can convey that experience to another. Actually, that's all we convey anyway. The question as a teacher is how to make you aware in accordance with your level of development.

Let's say two people are making love. One has truly opened up their nervous system to where they can access degrees of sexual satisfaction. They can, by way of their being, convey this to the other person. The other person may not understand exactly how this happened. But once they've experienced through the other a degree of satisfaction, they know it exists within themselves. From there, they can decide how much of this experience they want to consciously actualize. They can read texts, take courses, and experiment until they can achieve the desired state of mind at will. Then they can seek for even more inclusiveness, or just refine the level at which they've come to feel most comfortable.

So when I give a workshop, I'm not simply exposing people to ideas and techniques. That I can do in this book. And I'm not just exposing them to their own psyche, while untying the conditioned knots in their feelings. That I can do in a counseling session. In a workshop I'm exposing you to aspects of my own dynamics and those of others, so that you may safely have an opportunity to probe extensions of your own potential in ways you may not have felt knowledgeable and secure enough to seek out in the past. Then without inner or outer pressures you may choose your own rate of exploration.

I recommend that *functional hedonism* become incorporated into the Space Age way of life. It is by no means the only consideration, or even the most important consideration. Yet by successfully incorporating hedonism into every individual's lifestyle, it would greatly help them to facilitate the wholeness of their potential.

Does that mean everybody should run about seeking continuous stimulation, distraction and gratification? No, most people are already half-crazed from doing so; and their lives don't seem particularly satisfying. What about when you get too old to participate in being sexual, or even care; does that mean your life can't be just as rewarding? What's such a big deal about sex anyway? Plenty of people do it; some try to do nothing but it. They don't seem to be that much better off. What about communicable diseases, exhaustion, unwanted pregnancies, and all the other social responsibilities that sex entails; how do we account for them? And what about the truly great individuals of history? Where would we be if they'd been so busy indulging in fanciful pleasures that they didn't take time to make the discoveries for the betterment of us all?

To be hedonistic means to pursue pleasure. Now you'd be right if you said pleasure is a subjective quality varying from individual to individual—and even more from circumstance to circumstance. Still each of us have some criteria where we make a fairly clear distinction between pleasure and pain. Let's make this distinction more explicit.

I've been telling you it's not what you do so much as the state of mind you're in that determines the quality of any experience. The state of mind most people are into is not the pursuit of pleasure. Rather it is getting away from the pain. What pain? The state of tension (insecurity, inner-doubt as to self-worth) created by the intellectual aspect of a mind running away with itself; along with hundreds of thousands of years of reconditioned patterns of outmoded feelings, constitutes the painful state of mind from which most people are trying to escape. Everything else is coincidental.

The absence of pain is not pleasure! But if you've been in a fairly continuous state of pain, getting away from it for even a while can seem like pleasure. Most people are oriented to pursuing the absence of pain, which they've mistakenly labeled pleasure. Since most of this takes place in the mind through the dualistic nature of the intellect, their very effort is what keeps them focussed on the pain. That is, in order to (mentally) get away from something that's causing you pain, you must hold on to it (the idea) in order to have something from which to escape. If, for instance, you doubt your attractiveness to the opposite sex, this contributes to a painful state of insecurity. Perhaps in an effort to counteract this pain, you purchase every kind of marketable fashion and product meant to give you confidence. For a while your efforts and fixation on these other considerations may distract you from the pain caused by doubting yourself. But the only way you can verify this is to remember why you bought these items and to measure how far you think you've come from the source of your anxiety. To make such measurement you must think about your uncertainty. As soon as you do you're brought right back into the pain of your self-negation. If there's nothing to fixate upon, then there's nothing to get away from.

Now, none of the above is pleasure...any more than the cessation of war is peace...any more than the opposite of God is the Devil. These turbulent repercussions of perception all stem from a basic misunderstanding of our own mental processes.

What then is pleasure? You say some people find pleasure in inflicting or receiving pain. There are many who seem to take pleasure in destruction. Isn't telling people to pursue pleasure giving dangerous license to such aberrant beings to further indulge in negative acts?

Such people are not finding pleasure. They're not even trying to escape from pain. Rather, they're trying to justify their pain as being pleasure. Obviously, they are not developed enough to deal from a logical basis; where at least, in the shadow of their ignorance they could reasonably convince themselves of the nobility in their suffering! Remember, when the intellect fails to take command and at least achieve a reasonable stalemate with its conditioned feelings, that person can justify anything by their feelings. Whereas the feeling body could be programmed to germinate only the highest of our ideals as proper, so far this has seldom been the case. But when such aberrant behavior becomes a psychotic mean, you find that even the normal social taboos are perverted in their infantile conditioning process. With such people pleasure is not even the real consideration.

You see, to get away from the pain of their own self-torment...to release the tension invoking anxiety of their inner-doubt, people will go to a lot of trouble. Pleasure is neither trouble nor even a bother. If it were, it wouldn't be pleasure. But many people unwittingly bow down to the dark gods of their ignorance-generated fear, in essence saying: "I'll eat this way, speak this way, pray this way, think this way, act this way, live this way—anything—just get me out of, and don't let me go back to this hung up, self-tormented state of mind." They are like the *child soul* screaming for comfort in the darkness. And they will get such comfort in whatever existing form that corresponds to their psychological level of development. They are trying to get away from the pain.

The *adult soul* is not in any pain. So it is, when you've come to understand and thereby take control of the workings of your own nervous system. So it is, when you've cleared out past conditioning and feel things more as you experience them in the present of any given moment. You're not trying to get away from anything; rather, you're trying to get towards a more encompassing, inclusive state of awareness which further expands your capabilities and the quality of your life. You're continuously seeking to up the ante.

Now let's look at pleasure and what is involved in the Space Age pursuit of pleasure. Pleasure magnetizes, it is a conscious lodestone towards a more promising LOGO. Promising what? At least that which you've currently come to sense is positive to your feelings of well-being. It results in at least that state of mind in which you feel peaceful, clear and validated. More than that, pleasure is the motivation even as it is the promise of the next step...the next more encompassing rate of fulfillment which makes you desirous to approach life. Pleasure—not absence of pain, release of tension, or avoidance of anxiety—is the most accurate way yet available to our present and near future levels of development to evaluate the correctness of our decisions and the quality of our actions.

But if pleasure is so good, simple and beneficial, why are we having such a tough time obtaining it? The pursuit of pleasure is declared and constitutionally sanctified as one of humanity's inalienable rights by the so far most humane and experimentally progressive country on the face of modern Earth. In other words, how do we as humans best go about obtaining—in joyous, delightful, satisfying, healing, invigorating great gobs of ever-expanding increments—pleasure? And beyond its obvious benefits, how can this be incorporated into our present activities of everyday traditional / transitional society to combine with, and enhance the other aspects of our life?

I didn't just say we wanted to be hedonistic. Rather I qualified our pursuit of pleasure with the word functional. We need to become engineers of functional hedonism. As individual adult members of a free-thinking society, we have at our almost instant disposal all the wisdom of the ages along with the technological capability to actualize any need we truly have. (We really don't have a need to radiate and ecologically poison our planet.) Society is not wrong, just out of focus from too many shortsighted and patchworked compromises. What we need more than anything else right now is a way to quickly and peacefully transform the imbalances in society. To do this requires higher and more integrated functioning of our planetary nervous system than previously have been available. Pain, tension, guilt, shame, anxiety, dissatisfaction and reactionary idealism—the up 'til now modus operandi of our social efforts—is an ineffectual way to go about facilitating quantum leaps in human intelligence.

Oh, not that we haven't had such breakthroughs with many an exceptional person. But even their brilliant contributions for the most part have been disjointed in their design and subsequent application by the unwholesomeness of their own distorted psyches.

Un-whole-some-ness: some of the wholeness of the operative unit isn't functionally interconnecting. Which means at whatever level of perception, the energies being channelled through our consciousness are imbalanced. Which means unevenness in thinking, feeling, sensing...being. Which means mistaken inner factionalizing where we war against ourselves to justify rationalizations mystically ballyhooed to take up the slack of our seeming inadequacies. Which means the externalization of that same war into self-righteously aggressive social factionalism. War—in any case, at any level—is a whole organism mistakenly trying to glorify one aspect of itself at the expense of another. All war is a no win situation!

We need to develop our individual intelligence to its fullest extent. This can be done only in relation to the wholeness of our human potential. Sexuality most certainly is an undeniable part of that potential. Yet few of us use our sexuality for little more than releasing various degrees of tension; as such, most of us are only being used by our sexual nature. Sexuality is one of the prime orientations of our physicality; which in turn makes it a priori conditioning factor of our true feelings. Its implications in helping to expand human intelligence go far beyond what we currently have suspected.

You see, sexual satisfaction (as with optimal health, peace of mind, enlightenment, creative artistry, athletic prowess, etc.) only can be achieved consciously. It is not a mystical, accidental, per chance process. Sexuality can be used as an extremely powerful tool for evolving consciousness and physical health. Like any means of conducting energy, it represents power. Remember, power has no intention of its own. As in the past, some of the people who have managed to open their sexual power too often have misused it to work their will over others, too often inflicting damage on their own sensibilities. Along with a lot of socio-political maneuvering there have been some very good reasons for keeping sexuality under psychic lock and key. However, in light of the evolutionary changes now taking place, such measures of safety have become detrimental to our current well-being.

You can have the desire for, and set out to achieve satisfaction along numerous lines of interest. But unless you make your efforts reasonably proportionate to your needs and circumstances, you won't achieve your goal (another gestalted level of integrative incorporation). For instance, you could set out to explore supra normal levels of your own consciousness. By extracting your awareness from all but the minimally unavoidable essentials of body maintenance, while diligently applying yourself to psychically realigning with higher frequencies, you can achieve states of consciousness far beyond the realm of what is available to the average person. What determines the extent of your expansion in this manner will be the degree to which you need to expand in order to satisfy the initial impetus of what motivated you in the first place. Plus, and perhaps most importantly, the degree to which the experiential insights you gain can be incorporated into the circumstances of everyday life. If you push yourself relentlessly past your need to discover and ability to communicate, you can become lost; swamped in energies which will dissipate your life-force. For a primitive mind this might take nothing more than rapid and fairly sudden immersion into a highly technological society. While for an artist-scientist-philosopher the circumstances would be far more complex. However, there are limits to being human (though these limits truly border on Divinity). And it is in relation to being human, our own needs for individual growth, and the circumstantial quality of the times in which we must relate that determines these limits.

In other words, whatever our endeavor, we must make it *function* in relation between the microcosm of our own individuality and the macrocosm of human potential. What we are concerned with making optimally function, as a point of internal guidance for our own evolutionary growth / spiritual unfoldment, is our ability to experience pleasure in the process of living. We are seeking to create an approach to our functions in life which engineers our efforts around functional hedonism. At whatever level of consciousness we're operating, it is our state of mind which will determine our success / pleasure or failure / pain. Mind—the wholeness of which our consciousness is an interactive part—plays itself through the Life Force, through which it animates all considerations of manifestation into activity. As I pointed out, the basic root structuring of the Life Force is sexuality. Sexual satisfaction is a prime ingredient to successfully optimize our human potential. And though there are a number of levels which supersede it, no one can successfully achieve them without consciously optimizing the sexuality of that part of their consciousness from whence they've launched themselves into higher realms.

Everything has limits. Those limits are structured by the resonating quality being considered in the dynamics of relating energies. This holds true from subatomic particles to the universal-dimension-qualifying archetypes emanating from the Godhead. When we consciously learn to experientially harmonize our life-force within a given structure, we come to understand its nature. In understanding we gain control over its workings. When this process has been incorporated in our consciousness, we transcend the limitations of that structure and find ourselves creatively able to work our will through the nature of its properties. This in turn opens us up to more encompassing structures along with the limitations and opportunities they represent.

As human individuals, our sexual nature too, is structured. For too long we've either ignored, debased, suppressed, perverted, or avoided our own sexuality. For those reasons we haven't learned to harmonize and take creative control over our sexuality and transcend it. The power that our sexuality can contribute to the pleasure of our well-being has rarely been achieved. By now we're painfully enough aware of our shortcomings. The times demand our species achieve its birthright; and as intelligent individuals so should each of us demand the pleasurable quality of life which will support the anciently anticipated evolution of our true human potential.

We will now consider those techniques—physical, feeling, mental, paranormal and social—which lead to sexual satisfaction. Along with which we will examine those enhancers—aphrodisiacs—by which we can endlessly vary the art of loving. All of which we must functionally integrate with the effects they will have on the quality of our consciousness.

Techniques

1. Structuring:

Animals are manipulated sexually by Nature. The nature of their metabolism is genetically structured to be bio-chemically cued into various activities by the quality of the environment in which they're living.

As a species, we evolved to the human state when our nervous systems opened up to self-reflective intellectual manipulation of thought symbols. We no longer simply responded to physiological sexual urges, but also began to direct the flow of energies into distinct patterns of social interaction. That was just the beginning of our human potential, since the rituals of sexuality which followed were still dominated by nature, coupled with the reactive feelings by which we were emotionally patterned to respond. For a long time, only by subordinating individual will to tribal effort could we survive. Eventually this group dependency expanded to where progress depended upon the group interaction of the community (religious/political). Yet each human has always dreamed of what it would be like to function in a realm of plentitude, with free access to think, feel, and live their life the way they wanted. Each human has dreamed of being a self-styled, self-actualized, autonomous individual interacting with the social whole of humanity by choice rather than conscription.

When acting as an *individual* you make conscious choices about the way in which you want to live your life. Neither are you coerced by dogmatic social pressures which seem out of touch with your needs and the appropriateness of circumstances, nor are you pushed about in an unending stream of subliminally conditioned emotional reactive patterns. You have choice, in any given situation to come, go, or just be still while waiting for understanding and / or inspiration to precipitate harmonious motivation through your nervous system. You have the power (energy given conscious direction) to live your life the way you want. As an individual human your power is directed through the intellect. Intellect is the switching station through which various levels of energies are consciously leveraged into form and function.

To love or not to love...to open up to pleasure or not to open up to pleasure...to be or not to be...upon what criteria do we intellectually base our choices? As free-thinking individuals it must be through understanding and nothing less. Still our intellects tend to decide things around our highest criteria for participating in the living process. So, if I were to ask you: "Why are you here? What is the purpose in your being alive? What is your reason for living?" What would you say? Perhaps: "Gee, I don't know...no reason really." Or, "To be punished for spiritual transgressions and be redeemed by suffering." Or, "It's all chance, a random, freak chemical accident of Nature." Whatever your opinion, this priori consideration of your intellectually generated self-image (ego) has a lot to do with the kinds of choices you make in your life.

It always works best to base your intellectual leveraging on the most encompassing criteria that can make sense to you. You could say the reason you made love was because you had this physical urge. Now, from what we know of bio-sexual functions that would make some sense. But if you try motivating your love life around such narrow criteria, your choices for the most part will leave you pretty stranded. There are thousands of criteria in the modern arsenal of psychology around which to motivate your choices. And we could run the historical-academic gambit from ancient to present times coming up with an almost endless selection of criteria, many of which directly contradict one another. What we need is the most encompassing criteria we can find that makes sense for us in this day and age.

I am going to lend you a *Prime Directive*. You are welcome to plug it into your conceptual framework and use it to distinguish all subsequent choices you make. Of course, you are just as free to think nothing of it. If you find a more inclusive Prime Directive that functionally works for you, by all means employ it. There are more inclusive prime directives. Remember though, if you try to direct your energies from a place you have no need or ability to function through you'll just dissipate your power. For the time being, at least, I believe you will find this applicable to all human needs of near future evolutionary progress.

I am going to make a series of statements. They are simple and direct; nothing tricky. Think them through. Agree with them in your mind only if you cannot find the slightest exception. If you find even one exception, then they are not true and should be rejected.

2. Prime Directive

1. **I realize that everything I do is for the quality of feedback that it provides to my consciousness!** (That is, whether having a bowel movement, going to sleep, eating, watching television, whatever; everything you do somehow effects the quality of your consciousness.)
2. **That the more I upgrade the quality of feedback to my consciousness, the more I evolve my awareness!**
3. **The more I evolve my awareness, the more I fulfill my spiritual destiny in life!**
4. **What I have to work with in order to accomplish this (my purpose) is my physicality, my feelings, my conceptual intellect and the experience of paranormal perceptions.**
5. **Where I make this happen is in whatever environmental circumstances I find my consciousness**

directed to be aware of at any given moment!
6. **Therefore, my purpose in life—*Prime Directive*—is to fulfill myself in evolving the quality of my consciousness by interacting as fully as I'm appropriately capable of, in every moment of which I'm aware!**

Now you know what you're here for. Everything, so to speak, becomes grist (*experience*) for the mill (*consciousness*). From such a perspective you'll find it relatively easy to order all other intellectual criteria which you will use to make your choices. Though this is applicable for any and every consideration, let's direct it to those choices we make about our sexuality.

To make love or not to make love...to experience the sharing of pleasure, or to forsake such experience...to follow the socially prescribed ways of interacting, or to seek out the potentialities of your own inclinations. Every intelligent person agrees that one of the inherent qualities of life is *change*. Even if you possibly could (which you can't) participate in the exact same conditions every day, for the exact same reasons, they would still continue to be different. Because the way you perceive—the basis which determines everything you consider—is continuously augmenting itself. This happens whether or not you consciously acknowledge this condition. From an intellectual self-conscious level the possible combination of considerations are infinite. And that's from where most people make their choices. Unfortunately, no matter how astute your choices, the primitive rate-conditioning of your feelings too often slanders your awareness. Still, for whatever its worth, you must make choices.

Ideally, we postulate the ease of continually readapting to the changes of life—going with the flow. And in functional actuality that is not as difficult to obtain as most people have been led to think. But for the time being most people are still stuck in intellectually structuring their activities and then willfully trying to forge them into actualization. Their choices may be as disjointed as their own self-image is functionally categorized in antagonistic opposition.

For instance, on one hand you may think you should be free to casually interact sexually with anyone, anytime it strikes your fancy; while on the other, you try to steer your sexual activities through social etiquettes, religious morals, positions of personal control, romanticized idealism, or a pseudo-need to act more competent than you really are. Or you may allow yourself to accept the structuring vestiges of some system to which you've been taught to give your power, and then without much further thought, graft that system's values into your own. Of course, the inappropriateness of the way you process experience will probably keep you continually dissatisfied. But, at least, you won't have to assume responsibility for self-conscious choice (you try to make yourself believe). As such, it seems that you can quite often get the thrill of aggressively releasing far more of your power than you might have felt you had the right to, if you'd first bothered to consciously reason out the situation. Along with the fact that while most such systems trade-off the right to decide for yourself (for the thrill of self-righteousness), they also advance the idea that stoic suffering is an heroic quality which denotes worthy participation in said system. Induction into military life (millions of people are) would be one good example.

Now even if your feelings are still primitively conditioned, even if you haven't scientifically, artistically, philosophically and / or in some competent manner as yet disciplined your intellect; if you're going to function as an individual you must have something upon which you base your decisions. If one of your decisions is to experience in your life the fullest and most satisfying range of sexual interaction, then how will you proceed? One thing you can do to help accomplish this is structure your choices and decisions from the Prime Directive. By doing so, sexuality is no longer a case of just rebellion, release, fulfilling expectations, denial, morality, status quo, romantic propaganda, obligation, biological drives, reproductive necessity, power manipulation, etc. Rather, it becomes a continuous part of self-fulfillment whereby all of your sexual choices will be made to help upgrade the quality of your life by expanding your consciousness.

3. Geigering

Okay, so now you can accept sexuality as an integral function of your own individual growth. Still, there are all these moment to moment everyday choices that must be made. And if you choose inappropriately, you remain dissatisfied or even worse. Or maybe you made choices that were absolutely optimal for a given circumstance. But then for seemingly no apparent reason the situation changed. Or the situation remained the same, but because of the way others, or even you perceived the situation, the desired feedback no longer satisfies. How do you know what to do, when to shift, how much to explore, etc.?

I mentioned in the Introduction that you could find it very helpful to learn to make a geiger-counter out of your feelings. There are three levels of consciousness *geigering*. And if you can learn to incorporate them into your criteria when evaluating your choices, they will enable you to become psychologically almost infallible.

The first level of geigering involves your feelings: If something feels pleasurable, move towards it (if you're so inclined). As soon as it stops feeling pleasurable, or you no longer want it—**stop**. Maybe you've been making love and it's orgasm city. Everything is exquisite. Suddenly the energy shifts. Something surfaces between you which doesn't feel harmonious. As soon as you feel the shift, stop interacting indiscriminately through the feeling aspect of your consciousness. No matter how good it's been, proceed no further until you understand exactly what is accounting for this shift. It may be something simple and innocuous. Fine, bring it back into alignment and go on. Or, it may be the quality of your interaction has released deep-seated subliminal fixations neither of you were previously aware even mattered. Whatever, when pleasure subsides, move away from feelings.

This is an appropriate place to discuss heart-break / ache and any other notorious repercussions resulting from allowing your feelings to freely and openly exchange with others. Let's say you find yourself romantically-sexually turned on to someone. After the sociosexual preliminaries of appropriate courtly response to each others coded signals, you proceed to commingle your energies. Given the basic attraction, exchange is fairly easy because you're not quite sure what to expect from the other person. In a sense, it is mutual psychological masturbation. Being in the realm of the somewhat unfamiliar you're able to avoid setting off the internalized censors programmed into you. However, as you start to become more aware of each other's patterns you will associate them with the inhibitory responses to which you've been conditioned. You will spend less of your energy consciously interacting with the other person. Progressively more of your consciousness will lock into factional internal dialogues concerning how the

images you're forming to categorize the other person relate to your ideas of previously determined social correctness. This all happens very quickly and usually
undetected. Whether real to the situation or just your own
associative projection, there will be numerous things that
will start to bother you about the other person.

Most people make the mistake of going much farther
with their feelings than the situation's level of communication warrants. This starry eyed imbecility is an emotional
pattern which has dominated sexual relationships for so
long that most people unquestionably have come to regard
it as peculiar to the magic of love. But, maybe there are
a few things that bother you, or something you wish you'd
taken time to work out and make clear. But the energy
exchange felt so good and you don't want to chance messing up the good feelings you are having, so you kept it to
yourself. You try to reassure yourself: "Somehow it'll work
itself out." Or you'll get around to it later. With each encounter more feelings are exchanged. Continuously, newer
discrepancies appear which you also half-heartedly try to
ignore. Soon you've accumulated such a complex of avoidances and misunderstandings, that even those harmonious feelings you'd exchanged at the beginning can no
longer get through. Now, with nothing much left to lose,
except for the pain of your dissatisfaction, it finally seems
time to get around to clarifying those few small inconsistencies. Except now they've become grievances charged
with anger. Anger is the manifestation of those feelings
which you didn't allow yourself to express when you felt
them. You suppressed them 'til you no longer could; then
they issue forth with all the pent-up intensity by which
you denied them in the first place.

Now you try and get it straight, but: "Who cares, I'm
not getting what I want anyway. So why should I put up

listening to this shit from you." Or, "Oh yeah, all of a sudden you don't like this or that. Why didn't you say so before, if it was really bothering you?" The answer to that most relevant question is you didn't know any better how to express and resolve your feelings then, than you do now. So you dance around each other looking for everything but direct communication and satisfaction. And when (whenever) you can no longer rationalize why you should endure your dissatisfaction ("Lord, have I suffered enough yet? Well, child, have you?"), your relationship ends.

Ah, the tragic splendor of heartbreak. ("Like I paid my dues. Yeah, for what?"). You mourn the loss of closeness— except if you'd been really close, you wouldn't have needed to separate. Well then, there's all that wasted time and effort put into the relationship. Outright mercenary gold digging not included, the only waste you made of your time was by not enjoying every moment to the best of your ability. No, all this outrage is a cover-up. I mean, if you couldn't admit your confusion and inadequacies and work to resolve them when you were feeling strong and in love, you sure as hell (How sure is hell?) aren't going to expose yourself when you're feeling weak and vulnerable. Then what about the heartbreak and aching emptiness inside?

They say Nature abhors a vacuum; that includes the human nature of our feelings. Everything in the whole of Nature exists within a dynamic counter-balance of relations. If you change the focus on one aspect of the whole, then everything else must proportionately rearrange itself in relation to this change. If you take a certain intense aspect of your feelings and fixate them upon an object or person, then if you suddenly lose them as the object of your energies you have an emptiness. Something will have to take its place. If another person or situation isn't immediately available, then you will fill in that space (of consciousness) with exaggerated variations of whatever feelings you're currently processing. By the time most break-ups occur in a relationship, you're processing rationalizations to substantiate everything you consciously or subliminally avoided looking at in the first place. What causes pain is not the loss of the other. Rather, it is all those places you compromised and didn't look at. You took twenty steps in with your feelings when the degree of communication might have only justified one or two.

As you start to understand the implications of what I'm telling you, you'll see that there are no shortcuts. And that you'll never have any real satisfaction until you learn to be honest with yourself. So the first step is to create an emotional geiger-counter out of your feelings. No matter what the problem, even if you haven't the faintest idea of how to approach it, as soon as you experience any negative turbulence in a relationship, stop interacting with your feelings. Hold the line on what you know works between you but proceed no farther 'til you've learned how to resolve the misunderstanding. When you understand how to resolve it, you have a choice. You can further expand the quality of exchange between you and the other person through your feelings. Or the understanding may give you insight that says the relation isn't suitable to proceed any farther. Whichever may be the case, if you don't push your feelings past where the quality of communication keeps them clear, there will be no heartbreak; no deep aching loneliness inside. And if by insisting on clarity before feeling, the other person doesn't want to relate, it will be no real loss to you.

Remember, there are distinctly different levels of perception (consciousness) through which you may base your interactions. We are talking about taking control of the nervous system so you can choose what combinations will best suit you at any given time. To intensely open up the depths of your feelings can be like an intersection with Heaven. But you don't have to relate through your feelings. Without denial, suppression, or any other kind of avoidance, it will be best for you when you can pick and choose at will.

The second level of geigering, which I've already touched upon somewhat, is the basis from which you can safely exercise intellectual judgment. It is *Understanding*. Any time you are experiencing any emotional distortions...any degree of fear, doubt, confusion and / or anxiety, there is simply something you're not understanding. While at the same time you're insisting that your opinion (rationalization) is an understanding. As such you spend so much time defending (locking yourself within the confines of) your opinion that you no longer have the presence of mind (ability to sensitize your awareness) to see the reality of what is actually taking place. You feel forever pursued by your own need to be correct; and simultaneously are denied a sense of correctness by the pursuit of your justification. You wind up locked within the dualistic infinity of your rationalizations, cut off from the vitality of the living process which ironically (from such a level) never stops taking place all around and through you.

So should you, or should you not: get too emotionally involved...commit yourself to working out a relationship...be monogamous...experiment with drugs and sex aids...have children...let the other person know how you truly feel...? Most certainly, you're entitled to your opinions; they give you something to think about. Admitting you really don't understand what's involved in any situation won't necessarily guarantee you the answer; you'll have to earn that. Certainly, it will keep you out of psychological trouble; while at the same time, it will place you in the best position possible to reach an understanding—open, honest, sensitively attenuated receptivity.

I always say: *"You can't screw an honest person. You can only make love with them!"* What worries you about your relationships? That somebody might learn how to take advantage of you; manipulate you to their own ends; leave you expiring in the dregs of your own ruin? Are you fearful, doubtful, confused, anxious about how to handle things in life? Then ask yourself in any given situation: What am I not understanding?

If you're confused about how to respond to your partner when making love, then you don't understand what's involved in making love. Are you doubtful of your ability to physically satisfy the other? Then you don't understand the sexual nature of the male-female physicality. Are you anxious that you'll never be able to really share the joy that is in your heart? Then you don't understand upon what to base communication that's appropriate for you. Are you afraid to go your own way and explore the interests of your own inclinations? Then you don't understand the workings of your own consciousness.

If you don't understand, you don't have to—at least inwardly to yourself—defend what you think. Which leaves you free to *pay attention*...which makes life more interesting...which gives you more pleasure. By being honest with yourself in this manner, how can anyone psychologically harm you? Maybe someone sets out to seduce you for kicks. Maybe they're a sexual scalp hunter, into heartbreaking. So they get those juices flowing in you and tell you lies to rope you in: "You're the best. I'll love you always. Do you think anyone could be happier than us?" Well, maybe you emotionally buy into those statements. You like the attention, the physical sensations, whatever. Then you find out the other person was being insincere. You're not sophisticated enough to completely decipher their patterns. You've been made to feel dependent, afraid of loss, committed, guilty—Damn it; you never should have taken a chance and opened up your heart to being hurt again (and again). Right?—Wrong!

What to do? If you ever get so hurt that you're afraid to open up and feel, then no one could do you greater harm than you've done to yourself by cutting off your awareness from the most precious of gifts—*Life*. The first thing you do is recognize you're experiencing turbulence and emotional distortion. Which automatically should register that there's something you're not understanding. Now you can stop feeling desperate about justifying what you allowed yourself to be led into believing. Alright, now that the pressure's subsiding, what don't I understand? Well, let's see: "I like being sexual, but I've never felt comfortable about how that should or shouldn't obligate me to another person. I'd like to feel good about myself (self-accepting), but I've always thought that means I have to prove myself so other people accept me as being good. I don't want to lose this person; gosh, we had some good sex. But I don't seem to have that person anyway; guess I never did. Damn, I just don't understand how to get what makes me happy in this world."

We'll get into understanding that which can give you control and help you change in just a bit. First, let's examine our friend's predicament. Right now this person is starting to realize they're in a dilemma that probably they've always been in, and still don't know how to resolve satisfactorily. Right now we have them dissatisfied, but not making matters worse by trying to justify their misunderstandings. It amounts to a cessation from pain. But that is not pleasure. And still there remains that gnawing pain-like craving to move into the experiential feedback which produces real pleasure.

Next we turn to the *third level of geigering*; of repolarizing yourself towards pleasure, instead of just away from pain. In the first two geigerings we've talked about being honest with yourself concerning the quality of your feelings, and the completeness of your intellectually oriented understandings. So we have a sense of guidance about not getting involved with what we don't want. But how do we start to open ourselves up to experiences that will expand and satisfy us?

What you do is simply: *Make the best you've ever experienced the least you will accept!* Like: Make your ceilings your floors, and new ceilings will continue to open up to you.

We've all known, to some degree, moments of mental acuity, high physical stamina, inner calmness, clarity of mind, health, sexual enjoyment, etc. If you've had such a moment, even once, then the reality of your nervous system operating at that level of competency has been made available to you. If you've had it even once, then you can come to integrate such rates of awareness into your everyday normal repertoire of perception.

The problem is that most people tend to confuse where they get to (state of mind) with how they got there. The associatively identify the externals of what coincidentally was happening in their lives when they achieved some breakthrough into more inclusive functioning of their awareness. Let's say when making love the circumstances, persons involved, and degree of inner relaxation was prevalent enough to allow someone to experience pleasurable sensations they'd never before had. Perhaps this person has made love with the same person, in the same manner, in the same environment numerous times before, yet had never reached such fulfillment. The person will want some way of obtaining such feelings again.

Obviously, they don't understand how to hook up their sexual circuitry to the conscious control of their nervous system. They probably will inventory what seemed to take place when they were experiencing pleasure, and hope that by sticking fairly close to those coincidents they somehow will be able to experience it again. It becomes a mystical approach of using ritual to try and evoke attitudes that can sensitize your receptivity to receive what you normally press from your mind. Certainly in higher goals of transcendent lovemaking, such an approach can be most valuable. But regarding sexual responses that are basically within the reach of everyone, such an approach to obtaining pleasure actually can drive you away from it. It can lock you into a narrow defensive form of self-justification. When the pleasure doesn't come, you become even more defensive and secretive. Of course, all this means is that you don't really understand; and you're too busy defending the opinions you've tried to substitute for real understanding.

Now I keep repeating that it's not what you do, but the state of mind you're in that determines the quality of any experience. Obviously, adherence to the exact same formula within the crucible of human consciousness will not always produce the hoped for or expected results. Whereas, totally unrelated circumstances under unfamiliar conditions may evoke responses similar to what you've experienced in the past. To achieve pleasure (or just about any other state of mind you desire) at will, you simply have to understand exactly how your consciousness is processing the energy. You know it is not so much a matter of what's going on externally; but more a consideration of your internal rate of perception. Using the third form of geigering, you start to identify with the rate of perception to which you're interested in having willful access.

Let's say in making love you experience for the first time a state of mind where you feel totally attenuated to the other person. It's as if without thinking your every movement and touch seems to be synchronized. You feel exquisitely connected to sexual pleasure, while at the same time you are remarkably detached and clear. Energy is not just raking your groin like a volcano ready to erupt, but is circulating throughout both of your bodies. Okay, let's say just for openers, you know you can go on for hours playing like this, you've reached at least that state of communion. Instead of seeing it as some superlatively mystical how-can-I-reach-it-again state, you should view this ceiling of what had been your previous rate of sexual perception as a new floor. Let's walk on it.

You've had it once; that rate of perception now is available to you. You can have it whenever you really want. How? You make it the least you will accept. In the above example, you only seek to resonate to, at the least, whatever rate of perception you were in when having these experiences. You move only towards those feelings that are similar, regardless of external activities. As soon as it starts to move away from that level, become mentally still 'til you can see what's involved. Only base your intellectual ideas on those exact understandings you acquired when in that state of consciousness. Soon you'll be able to distinguish how your relation to external stimulus either draws you away or enhances your rate of perception. You're beginning to understand exactly how to reference your mind at will in order to open up your nervous system to experience such energies. Then you can experimentally realign circumstances, artistically varying your experiences as part of your ongoing exploration. In turn, this leaves you free to discover newer ceilings of perception.

You've begun operating from a more inclusive level of consciousness. Responsively, you're conforming your actions to your insights and creating appropriate intellectual structures. Whereas before, you were coming up with ideas, trying to erect intellectual structures to leverage your rate of perception, and conforming your actions to your dualistic notions. When the dualistic nature of the intellect dominates and directs your share of the life-force, your actions too often can be in precarious stalemate between pleasure and pain. When you add to this the primitive emotional fixations of our infantile conditioning, you can find yourself too often working against yourself in a continuum of self-negation. From this more centered perspective: When experiential insights produce understandings which enable you to control the expenditure of energies through the intellect, you find yourself continually expanding with self-acceptance.

Geigering from the third level deals with the experiential level of consciousness. As experience is more inclusive and happening at a faster rate than the intellect, it is a transcendent level of awareness. It transcends the dualistically associative cross-referencing of symbols which is the intellect. It is a transconceptual state which is entered when we go from contemplation through meditation. When you can consciously enter into this rate of perception and begin acting from it, you start to move into what has been called the realms of spirituality and you must deal with the psychic and paranormal structuring of energy. Sexual love is one legitimate way to do this. But there are a lot of warning / danger signs posted along the way.

Before we get to that, let's understand the composite of this geigering—which can keep you psychologically safe and intact through whatever configuration of energies are involved. You are being honest with yourself; regardless of what the necessities of survival dictates you must tell others. If it doesn't feel good, stop until you can understand why and gain control. You know that all negative inner turbulence is ultimately a state of your own misunderstanding! You move towards the best you've ever felt by distinguishing what rate of perception it has produced in you. You settle for nothing less. Which means when you don't know exactly what to do, don't fake it. Hang out with it 'til you do understand. When its under your control, do what you like, while remaining receptive to how your experience can further expand your awareness. As such, there is no wrong or negative. You're either moving towards pleasure, or seeing turbulence as an opportunity to undo some past psychological obstruction (misunderstanding), which is also a pleasure. *It is through pleasure that you geiger yourself into fulfilling your Prime Directive!*

Does it seem perhaps too simplistic? Within the pattern of any activated energy configuration there is a calm center (e.g., eye of hurricane; center of cyclone). If you get caught outside that center, the forces involved will toss and tear you in various directions. But from inside the center there is calm, order, and opportunity to control the power of the energies in flux. So it is with the center of your awareness; that balancing point in the complex interaction of rates of perception which composite human potential. And you will find that the closer you come to attaining that center, the more balanced, simple, direct, and controllable become all the energies at your disposal.

4. Individualism

Geigering can keep you safe in your explorations of consciousness. It also allows you more succinctness when tuning into newer possibilities which can add to your fulfillment. At some point, at least for the sake of your own peace of mind, I highly recommend that everybody learn how to decondition their feelings, and how to re-program them at will. It is not within the scope of this book to discuss the processes involved in deconditioning and/or reprogramming. Yet I feel that you should have an idea of how these processes could add to the quality of your life.

You consciously wouldn't sit down and reason out that you should pick on yourself, disqualify your own validity, make your own body sick with guilt and shame, or any of the other ways we perpetuate our own self-torment. Yet most people's awareness is absorbed in the negative, self-castigating contingencies of just such a process. Deconditioning the feelings means regaining conscious control over the range of choices you have in responding to any stimulus. It means bringing the flow through of energy involved in that level of perception back under direct control of your intellect, instead of the representative intellects which conditioned you before you could intellectually defend (scrutinize / discriminate for) yourself. I have identified three major blocks in the early stages of maturational development which I feel horribly inhibit human potential on this planet. I've found that once these locks are deconditioned, they stay permanently deconditioned. After which it is fairly easy to teach anyone who wants to actualize the process, how to discern and release any residual blockages in their feelings.

Then comes reprogramming. Once the feelings are

within the dominion of your own intellect, how are you going to structure them? Certainly, you want to keep this an open-ended process and be able to reprogram them anytime you gain more relevant information. But up 'til the point of deconditioning, most of your intellectual processing has involved holding at bay the negative feelings conditioned into you, while trying to outmaneuver them. You're accustomed to thinking away from the negative; not towards the positive. You're used to thinking defensively offensive; strategizing like a soldier in a war zone. And you have been and will continue to remain perpetually at war within yourself, until you're neurologically liberated.

Suddenly, however, the war is ended. Your feelings will go wherever you direct them. Energy follows consciousness; where you put your awareness will become how you're able to perceive. But all you've known is war and cessation. How do you convert your thoughts to peace? How do you learn to think like a lover instead of a soldier? That's what reprogramming is about. What you think and do with your life is your own business. Though I'm usually happy and often interested in offering suggestions (I enjoy interconnecting and sharing), my main concern is providing you with tools for your own self-actualizing.

But consider for a moment what deconditioning and reprogramming can mean. All the energy and conscious awareness that has been drained continually from you, becomes available again; to do with as you see fit. Your sensitivity heightens; your energy increases. You are finally catching up with yourself—not only resolving your own past discrepancies, but as a representative of humanity, healing and resolving the evolutionary legacy of our species. All the social forms of interaction which have preceded you up to this point are yours to combine intelligently in any proportion you need. You are, of course, part of humanity (probably more so than ever); but you're also a free-thinking, decision-making entity, responding to the conscious awareness of your unique perspective (Nobody else can be you!) of life. You're now ready to operate the mind's machinery along with its Space Age extensions which we've technologically created. Welcome, you've entered the future the only way you can—as a self-actualized individual.

You can't give something until you have something to give. If what you have to give is a mind full of ideas, then you'll share and hopefully stimulate those who can open up to them. But if they are ideas that you haven't as yet actualized through the individual awareness of your own experience, even if you've somehow imagined the ultimate truths of life, your ideas will not convey those truths; only the imagery of them. *In actuality, we communicate only what we are, to whatever degree and level we've integratively individualized an experience.* You do no more for another than you do for yourself! The more you fulfill / actualize your individuality, the more you do so with that part of God, Life, Spirit, Nature, Universe...whatever you want to label the part of the Life Force that's manifesting in this time and space as you.

So that's what you bring to your relationships—your individuality. When you make love, that exchange of sexual energy has the capability of conducting between you and the other person all that you individually represent. History, art, crafts, cooking, environmental designs, love of nature, theater, cinema, music, exercise, spirituality, heritage, genetics, skills, work, education...the experience of everything that has ever impinged upon your nervous system, plus all the subtle realms which may supersede your present awareness while shaping your sensibilities far more than you are yet ready to let yourself imagine. All of this can be exchanged during sex. It all becomes alchemicalized in the crucible of your consciousness; and if harmoniously inter-blended with the other, it can produce exquisite releases of energy capable of advancing the evolution of your being. All of this...conveyed through touches, stares, smells, tastes, sounds. All of it dependent on what each individual brings to the sexual act and how ready both are to harmonize it.

You see, now we're talking about freedom, choice—to be with someone because you want to be, rather than because you're afraid not to be. Your individual right to come and go, interacting as much and for however long it satisfies. It is by choice that each individual exercises their power. If you have no options, the best you can do is hang on and try to learn from a situation. When you can come, go, or be still, as you please, then your actions are full of power which you can direct according to your awareness. For instance: In a sexual love relationship, if you can only express your feelings if certain social formulas have been adhered to (commitment; declaration of love; promised support; acknowledgment of indoctrinated moralities, etc.) then all you can really do is conform your responses to prescribed patterns of acceptability. However, if you can either express or not express feelings, to whatever degree you honestly feel motivated in any situation, regardless of context, your feelings will bear great potency and truly carry your inner awareness into consummation with the moment. When all choices lie open to you, it ultimately will not matter if you act in one particular manner to the total exclusion of other possibilities. As long as you always feel freely that you can exercise any of your given options, your acts will be full of power.

The basis for healthy relationships—in whatever forms

they are expressed—must be the consciously purposeful commingling of actualized individuals, who are consciously in control of whatever apparatus with which they have to work. Now we're just about ready to bring these individuals together so they can creatively conjoin their energies into ecstatic realms. First, let's consider upon what individuality is based.

An individual is one who utilizes all aspects of their physicality, feelings and conceptual abilities in accordance with their own unique perspective. If your mind is not responding automatically to subliminally conditioned patterns, then you must respond to the consciously evaluated dictates of the moment. You cannot augment the moment directly. But you can consciously augment the responses of your nervous system to the moment, thereby taking on a co-creative partnership with the moment. The moment of which you're a part—regardless of the quantum of time and space it may contain—is any whole of experience through which you relate. It is what's been often called (and almost as often misunderstood) the *spiritual dimension*. It is where the human heart—that mediating integrative center of awareness—pulsates, poised between the physical, feeling, and mental attributes over which we've been given dominion and those decidedly supra normal motions of consciousness which have dominion over us. Most of the problems now threatening the existence of our species stem from trying to motivate our interactions from the third level of conceptual intellect rather than the *fourth*, the *Heart Center*. When you can functionally actualize yourself from the heart, accepting the privileges and responsibilities which it entails, then you truly become an individual.

It is not man and woman who will resolve the conflicts and confusions between each other; that is like two re-

volving mirrors circling each other in search of an image
to reflect. It is the creative individual taking control of
whatever physio-psycho-sexual equipment with which
they've been endowed, who consciously directs their
energies through it with skill and purpose. As an individual you're operating from a more inclusive range of perception than any combination of the particular
considerations you're functioning through. Being able to
move in and out of your senses, feelings and / or thoughts,
at will, or being able to remain centered in the experience
of the moment, exquisitely aware, without having to label or react is the anchorage of each individual's true
security.

We're looking to create more rewarding, fulfilling and
encompassing levels of intimacy between one another.
What should we base them on? You can easily access our
historical track record to see how we've failed in satisfying this need. Inner security: a firmly rooted sense of
connection extending to, and focalizing awareness from,
a rate of perception transcendent to any of the limitations
of physical form, emotional fixation and conceptual du-
alism. From the heart of things we're all the same. But how
many people relate from the heart? It is from the heart that
we recognize unity in all things. It is analogous to the dark
side of the moon. The bright side of the moon is the quality
of the sun's focussed reflection, as the subconscious is at
times brought into focus by the emanations of the whole
of human potential. The sun's illumination on the moon
is so bright, that on the light side you can only see the
immediate focus of your attention.

But from the dark side, both you and the surroundings
are barely differentiated. What becomes far more visible
is the quadrant of space to which your positioning has
brought into view. The light side of the moon reflected

the immediacy of your orientation in viewing it. Even so, aspects of your subconscious (feelings) are continuously drawn into the conscious scrutiny of your individual perspective as stimulated by experiential circumstances. But when subconsciously inhibited feelings are scrutinized by the self deluded intellect, patterned associations are triggered, and your interactions become entangled in the compromised distortions of your personality.

There are appropriate techniques through which you can bridge through your subconscious feelings, enabling you to start accessing some of the more inclusive aspect of wholeness of mind which, when compared to the perspective of the reasoning intellect, becomes super-consciousness. From the illuminated perspective, you're awed by the brilliant awareness of your own self-consciousness. From the dark side you are transported into the vaster transformative aspects of which you're but a part. The dark side of the moon is the gateway to the stars—our evolutionary destiny. The unapparent side of our subconscious is similarly the gateway to our hearts.

When you're insecure you hold back (on yourself). When you are secure you open up to the most dependable inviolable aspect of the living process—*change*. Change with awareness produces growth. Consciously accepted and acted upon this leads you to exploration and experimentation with your human potential. It is through the heart (a quality of consciousness—not the physical heart pump) that all aspects of the dimensions we call spiritual enter into human consciousness. In our attempts to make these insights relevant, we've leveraged them through our intellects into the appropriate religio-socio form and function. Yet, because of our compounded legacy of past misunderstandings, we've diminished their potency; perverted them to justify the pain-charged avoidance patterns of our past. By such an inverted process of interpretation, we've come to equate human sexuality and its erotic fulfillment as somehow being antithetical to spirit. As even in the same breath, we've elevated the aggressively imbalanced rationalizations of our misunderstandings to the central dominant theme of social progress—war.

People have had it backwards. More correctly, you could say: *The more spiritual you are, the more sexually erotic you become!* The more you open up and integrate self-actualized conscious control over your neural circuitry, the more lavishly will life's energies flow through you. To successfully control that energy you must understand how it processes through you. You must understand the workings of your consciousness so that you may choose how best to interact with the Life Force at any given moment. Understanding is an awareness of how something works; to that degree (and only to that degree) will you have control. Control—without the emotional turbulence of doubtful, confused, fearful, anxiousness which too often has impaired your judgment, you will do only what feels pleasurable to you. Such awareness is the product of experience. When your consciousness is absorbed in experiencing, you have entered the level of perception which is the true demarcation of the individual human. From here you are centered within a higher, more encompassing rate of perception. You directly experience communion with life through that part you are representing.

To learn to operate from such a rate of perception is the only true security for any individual. It is from such awareness that the war between the feeling and the conceptual aspect of your mind can be ended; and the victim, your metabolic temple, can be healed. Such a level of perception goes far beyond pleasure; *pleasure being only a conscious tracking device to the heart.* It is where paradoxes conjoin. You are alone, yet according to what you're ready for, totally interconnected. From here it becomes easier to resolve the problems of men and women. It is a center of power that no person has a right to give to or take away from you. Secure, you are ready to really communicate as intensely and intimately as you desire.

5. Communication Skills

Some say: *Fuck them if they can't take a joke.*
I say: *Fuck them only if they can!*

If someone accepts you in a place where you shouldn't accept yourself, what will you do with them when you're no longer there? Suppose all the emotional and / or social compensations for which people have been sexually bartering suddenly were made available without any further compromises. Under such conditions, how would you relate with the object of your affections? As I've said: *You can deal with whatever you look at; you cannot deal with what you refuse to look at.*

We do not want to continue automatically interacting through the emotional structures established in our Stone Age past. We need to establish structures in keeping with the Space Age proclivities of today. They must be open-ended, flexible structures that we may augment as we see fit. No more of: "That's the way it is, because that's the way it's supposed to be." Or, "I don't want to think about what I don't want to think about." As intelligent free-thinking individuals, it is time to openly approach one another and straighten out these particularized misunderstandings.

I've talked with you about the power of being an individual. Each of us must learn not to succumb to overly identifying with the perceptual rates of our physicality, feelings and intellect. Rather, we must center our awareness in a perceptive rate from whence it becomes relatively easy to see how these levels of consciousness process. The more you can do this, the more fully you can utilize and enjoy these tools of consciousness. There is importance in being able to be alone with yourself. Suchly, you will discover what you have to utilize. When neither compensation nor fear is present, you're naturally drawn toward doing what you like. If as yet, you haven't discovered what that is, then in silence it will announce its presence to you. As while waiting in the silence of your thoughts, there is nothing to make you uncomfortable with yourself. The least you should accept is that peace of mind. Anything or anyone that draws you into relating must be at least as pleasurable as the peace you already have...at least!

As individuals we are each a unique wholeness unto ourselves. That, however, is only part of the picture. We are each individual parts in the wholeness of being human. To be human is to be related. Obviously our abilities to relate the information formulated through our individual experience is what has enabled the evolution of our species. For we seek through each other the extended expansion of ourselves. Thus it has been in our past; so it shall be in our future. But the way in which this must take place is changing in our present. We now must take conscious control of the machinery as well as the responsibility those privileges breed. As such, the old structures by which we related are obsolete.

Conscious individuals, secure in their true identity within their hearts, must now create the levels of communication that will enable our species to continue evolving. Since the old ways are no longer adequate, we, as representatives of this transition in human development, are charged with the task of finding more appropriate forms of communication. The consequences of failing to respond by ignoring this are now making themselves painfully clear. The Armageddon mentality is a suicide pack with ignorance. Realize there is no past to make up for; no mistakes for which we must compensate! As soon as you change your level of awareness / state of mind / rate of perception, all things change with it. And once you've started to act upon such understandings within your own psyche—ending the warfare therein—it becomes time to expand the process by extending yourself through *relationship*. The next step is to appropriately augment the rates of perceptual exchanges between man and woman.

So while we're holding off the aggressive inertia of fear-ridden, institutionalized social compromises with one hand, we must forge ahead into exchanges based on individual understanding. In the meantime: "God, do I need a friend...a lot of friends...as many friends as I can make!"

Friendship is an excellent vehicle for human interactions. In fact, friendship is more important than being lovers! No matter how attracted to and compatible you are with someone, you can't always be lovers. Being lovers is a very high, but exclusive exchange of energy. Its delicate rate of interaction must be fed by every other consideration of your consciousness. It is an art form, a creative expression, an act of worship; it is one of the highest promises of humanity fulfilled. However, there will always be times, even between lovers, when that aspect cannot surface. Either the preoccupation of integrating and adjusting to other considerations will take precedence; or the focus of what your consciousness is ready to explore will move you beyond such expressive limitations. From the human perspective, love is limitless and all pervasive. But the rate of attenuating your nervous system with others to mutually share the experience of love is definitely limited and structured according to the nature of the consciousness involved.

You can't always be lovers, but you can always be friends!

I can always care about you, try to help you, want to see you fulfilled. In the course of our relating I can accept the fact that personal changes at times may diminish the active exchange of our affections. As a friend, I can acknowledge your space and help in any way that seems appropriate. Personally, I've found it genuinely helpful to act from the conviction that: "No woman has to make love with me for me to care about her and try and help her as another human individual!" I will barter for almost anything in a free and open marketplace, except my personal pleasures in making love—on that, I put no price.

What I'm strongly suggesting is that each person learn to deal with others from the more encompassing considerations of *individuality*. Stop giving your power away by blaming the other. Obviously, not all commingling will immediately yield the kind of response by which you hope to be acknowledged. You don't have to take the other person's attitude personally. Friendship is not feeling you must be friendly. Friendship is not an obligatory state. When ineptness in communication skills oblige you to relate, respectful courtesy can carry you easily through the intricacy of social commerce.

Alright, what is so holy about friendship then? You must choose to be a friend; friendship is a relation of choice. It is by choice that the strength of a relation is measured. Upon what do you base that choice? If you think that friendship only means finding people who will be your friend, your choice immediately narrows to what will support the rationalizations by which you've chosen to compensate for what you avoid in your own self-awareness. *Hate is communication only with your own excuses.* (Think about it!) Even those who are hateful look for those whom they can call friends. That amounts to mutual conspiracy. You can never get from another what you need to be for yourself. However, until you've experienced that reality, you will continue to search for validation.

In truth, you cannot choose someone to be your friend anymore than you can tell someone else what to do with their love. Is a friend someone you can buy, coerce, bully, shame, or trick into caring for you? Certainly you can gain followers, conspirators or undertakers of some sort to respond to your demands in such a manner—but would you call that friendship?

I've called many a person friend. Quite often they were people I hardly knew; people I might never expect to see again. Often these people couldn't understand me. My sense of self-assurance produced uneasiness in them, although my intentions towards them were genuinely sincere and honorable. Still, I called them friend. That was my prerogative. A friend is something you can only choose to be. How many truly benevolent individuals, on both personal and magnanimous levels, have chosen to be friends (often representative of humanity at large)...have proven their sincerity by the quality of their actions; yet have been slandered by those to whom they were friendly? Why it's enough to make a less centered individual turn into a self-justifying cynic. Oh, but when two or more people choose to be each other's friend, then...

Upon what does an individual, who has decided they're your friend, base that choice in order that it qualifies as true friendship? Remember, you can do no more for someone else than you can do for yourself. Let's say you've reached the level of integrative awareness where you're no longer reacting to subliminally conditioned inhibitions.

Rather, you're continuously reprogramming the possible ranges of your responses to the stimulus impinging on your first three levels of consciousness. You're directing those rates of perception from the more encompassing vantage point of your actual experience. All your choices add up to fulfilling your Prime Directive. In terms of your evolving conscious movements, all interactions must, at the least, facilitate the best levels of consciousness you've known. In order to fulfill yourself you must continuously expand the range of your human potential. To a greater extent, that must be done through your experiential interrelations with other individuals. The basis for your discriminations about whom will best enable you to do this can be easily facilitated through the three levels of geigering we've discussed. In other words: *the same considerations upon which you successfully establish your own individuality must also form the basis upon which you establish your friendships.*

This is not mere morality we're discussing. When you choose to be an individual's friend, you're choosing to see them as a means to your own fulfillment; which is the fulfillment of humanity on every level. By so extending yourself, you base friendship on an interest more encompassing than family, economics, business, religion and socially pressured etiquette. Thereby you recognize in each person who comes before you another individual soul passing through this plane of existence. In your heart you honor them for that part of the whole they also represent. But as I said, not everybody (though far more are ready than most suspect) operates from the heart. Your experience with the other person will determine to what degree and the ground rules by which you will relate. Only to the point that they honor themselves can you outwardly honor them. If their level of self-awareness is inhibited by social indoctrination, then geigering will enable you to discern whether or not exchanging on the feeling level will even meet your basic criteria. You may choose to help them in many ways, but still retain a sense of personal detachment. When there exists sincerity and a willingness to grow, you can experiment with the other. Your geigering will keep you safe and informed about the possible range of interactions.

We're talking about sensing, feeling and thinking to any degree of possible combinations and gradients therein, between yours and other's nervous systems. You may choose to be a friend based on a clear awareness of how the interrelations fit in with your own growth and fulfillment. The other person may not yet have developed the strength of understanding to consciously make such a choice. It is better to give, than to receive (just as it is better to serve in Heaven than it is to rule anyplace else!). Still, you can't share more of yourself, than the other person has as yet developed the ability to receive. When your cup runneth over, then, by all means, spill some of it out. Until then, whoever is in need must be nourished; must receive. It is false pride (the kind that it hurts to swallow) which will not accept a sincere offering when needed.

Yes, you can be a friend to anybody; it is your inner acknowledgment, not their acceptance which determines this. When two or more individuals—*acting from their most inclusive perspectives*—mutually choose to be each other's friend, and truthfully acknowledge the basis of their choice to each other, then a friendship is born...a friendship which, in the light of day, can bear the scrutiny of others.

So now there is friendship. Through an inter-conscious recycling of energies, you enable each other to actualize more of your uniquely combined respective potentials. And certainly one of the major considerations is the sexual nature of your friend. That other individual may represent a sexually compatible circuit of energy which can combine with yours. When such is the case, part of your friendship will extend itself naturally through the relation of being lovers.

Being sexually intimate, with all the corresponding pleasures and advantages that go along with it, is one of the most rewarding states available to us as humans. Everybody, no matter how much they protest, wants the rewards of close sexual bonding. It is by far the singularly most pervasive subject matter of our art, literature, social merchandising, and even formalized religiosity. And now, due in good measure to our technological advances, the means of participating in a sexually fulfilling lifestyle are available to large segments of the population. So what's the problem? Why aren't people enjoying their hard earned freedoms even more? First off, they've never before had the option so functionally open to them. They're not sure what to do with it; like warriors, who have been battling all their lives, are told there no longer will be a need for such battling. But that's all they know; what do they do with peace? Secondly, there's a lot of debris from the sexual barter approach that must be cleared out before energies between lovers can flow rapturously. Deconditioning releases the fixations of the nervous system; but they must still be consciously replaced. Only through the active dynamic communication skills of the individuals involved, can the fixations that deal with and are cued in by sexual relations be handled.

Not to be ignored or rationalized, understanding must replace the emotionally reactive, moralistic patterns currently present between man and woman. To what degree are commitments functional; and when do they change into psychological bondage? Privacy...everybody needs it;

to what degree should sexual intimacy allow you to intrude upon the other person? What do you do when you've committed yourself, but still feel you're not getting what you need? How do you transform the possessiveness and jealously by which we conscript each other's movements, thereby defeating the closeness being sought?

Let's run a scenario: Each individual—as long as they're geigering in complete honesty within themselves—has access to a centered placement of inviolable perspective from whence they are invulnerable to any of the so-called destructive forces of this world. Let's say that you've now become experientially aware of this. You've had it proven to you beyond a shadow of a doubt. From this state of awareness everything feels pleasurable and anything can be handled. Whereas if you lose your anchorage, everything you encounter makes you painfully aware of your imbalance. No matter through what circumstances you're psycho-mentally interacting, never settle for less than this wholly *centered* frame of referencing your awareness. Subsequently, your individual choices are always molded around what enables you to maintain and expand your center. It is your true security; and with it you feel much more at ease to explore in depth and to the heights the multitude of ever-unfolding possibilities, which you potentially represent. Knowing how to discriminate among the various rates of perception, you can easily readjust your center, regroup your understanding, and forge ahead as it suits you.

Within the frame of human reference through which your consciousness is centered, the means to self-fulfillment *Prime Directive* involves your interaction with others. You know if you lose your center, your interactions will become dissatisfying, embroiling in factional, hostile compromises that have little to do with what you're really after. Also you know that no relations can be any better than those qualities of the consciousness that formulate them. If you lose sight of yourself—regardless of intentions—your relationships will be proportionately forfeit. Therefore, your choices by which you extend yourself through your relations will be an active amplification of the same geigering ground rules by which you normally relate in your own mind.

You meet another individual of the opposite sex with whom you find a genuine attraction and the potential for a highly functional compatibility. Like yourself, the other person similarly knows they must base their actions on the individual integrity of their heart. You are both directing the various movements of your consciousness from the heart of things. You want to be each other's friend; so a friendship is formed. Each of you have learned to take control of your own nervous system. You've both cleared out former subliminal conditioning, replacing them with suitable programs. But neither of you have ever tried to make a vibrantly open, sexually impassioned love relationship work from this basis. In fact, the only thing you know in terms of relating as lovers is the standard arsenal of manipulations which has up 'til now characterized the battle of the sexes.

At first, without needing or meaning to, for lack of a better way, you both trot out all the male and female trips and begin running them on each other. You have sex. It is hot and heavy, but far from really satisfying. However, you each experience enough of a connection...enough pleasure to waken the hunger of your priori feelings to want more. On the chance that you can make this happen, you start to fixate on and cater to those aspects that are turning you on in each other. By so doing you tend to ignore other considerations which are surfacing. You don't know where to draw the line on your privacy; nor do you state the conditions by which it is acceptable for the other to approach you. You were socially programmed to feel you won't have really deep meaningful sexual relations with someone until a certain level of intimacy is "properly" reached. That intimacy is supposed to be evaluated by the depth of commitment. The basis for such commitment always has been engineered around marriage (or mutually exclusive partner-bonding). Marriage has always been an affair of power economically filtered through the ownership of property rights. Supposedly, you'll get what you paid for (messing with the goods, darling), but then you have to live with it. You have to accommodate yourselves to each other's presence. And where there's forced sacrifice, inevitably there's retaliatory resentment.

Because you're not sure whether this arrangement is going to work out...you're not sure whether it's going to satisfy and help fulfill you, you hold back from expressing many of your feelings. You want to have the upper hand in case you have to make a getaway. You're overly cautious about becoming committed and stuck to something with which you won't be happy.

You're both saying, in no uncertain terms, how you're accessible and anxious for sexual exchange. She's waiting for him to do his big strong man thing and take her. He's doing his big strong man thing and fighting off the nagging suspicion that he won't be able to satisfy her. None of this is conducive to what they're after. But with such close sexual proximity to one another they start to feel stuck. Inadvertently, they each want the other to somehow reassure them that their time spent is worthwhile. Not knowing how to give or receive what they want, they instead take conformational homage from the other by placing more demands on the other's attention. Neither has as yet taken the responsibility to admit they don't know what they're doing.

More and more they're placing demands, while narrowing their range of interactions. They both start to resent this infringement, and besides, even that occasional jolt of passion is dwindling. Compensations? Hardly! What can you substitute for satisfaction? But still there are commitments. They each said something, at some time, to supposedly justify some proximity of feeling they felt inclined to express. But they each viewed it in their own way. And while thinking the other person remembers and will judgmentally hold it against them, really they are only holding it against themselves. So they try substituting innuendos. The hinted promise that if such and such was to happen, then what you're hoping for in me will materialize.

Of course there's no security in this type of being. Out of insecurity they become jealous and possessive. Each feels resentful that they're not getting satisfied. After all, they're making a sacrifice of their time, energy and awareness. And after paying such an exorbitant price, they certainly aren't going to let someone else collect on the fruits of their labors. Let the other mildew in unfulfilled promises. At least they have the memory of when there were some moments of beauty, gentle tenderness, excitement and love, to hold onto.

Bless the pain...! Their relationship may not be working, but at least their individuality is. This mishmash of tepid castigations and fettered feelings is certainly not why they wanted to get together. Obviously, they've proven that this isn't the way to go about relating. Who needs dead, stuffed-trophy memories hanging in some game room museum of your youthfully misguided vanity? Especially when there are warm, pulsating exquisitely alive, luxuriously endearing exchanges being continuously born just for the opportunity of taking place. No! Considering the dismal track record of alternatives, they've got little to lose and much to gain by making their own way.

They pull back and re-center themselves. Independently, each examines the turbulence that their attempted commingling precipitated in their consciousness. Each of them goes back to when they first encountered such energies, 'til they see how, out of ignorance, they mishandled those energies. They see where they avoided examining the things that bothered them; where they closed their minds to other possibilities. They see how, by compromising with what seemed expedient at the time, they locked themselves into a position of defending what they'd faked themselves into believing. As they clearly look at the confusion from which they initially ran away, the cramp in their consciousness diffuses, leaving those energies involved ready to follow any direction they might. The pain and confusion is gone. Again they move forward and approach each other.

They acknowledge that their friendship must be based on helping each other to fulfill themselves. ***Love cannot exist unless there is truth!*** They must honestly discriminate. That if they really care, they have to know when to kick with love (pull back) as well as hug and kiss (come forward). That if they don't kick when necessary, it can be as detrimental as not hugging and kissing when needed. That they may hug and kiss through their respective sexual natures. But all necessary discipline must emanate from their individual heart centers, from whence the injustice of prejudiced excess is not possible. That when they can't mutually channel love, at least they can respect the individual that the other is.

Now they want to work out the male-female recycling process so it is as mutually satisfying as possible. How to proceed? They borrow their format from that most holy of scientific concepts—*experimentation!* No longer will they be moved by emotional commitment. They'll discern the quality of their movements with each other relative to their own personal geigering. It won't be: "I feel stuck in this commitment and I want out. I know, I'll stick myself in a deeper hole of emotional commitments to justify getting out of where I was. Problem is I feel more stuck than ever." Nor will you want to base your intimacy on commitments like: "Well, the reason I'm having sex with you is because I'll love you forever." Whoa, who knows what you'll do forever, or even tomorrow, as circumstances and your rate of perception alter (which is their continual nature to do). At such a pace your social interactions are too ponderous, too primitively inhibited to compute the Space Age, omni-dimensional assimilation you were born into this stage of evolution to express.

Experimentation: I woke up today. I have these qualities of energy pervading my consciousness. I feel a lot of sexual energy. I'll run an experiment with it. I hypothesize that if I combine my sexual energy with your sexual energy, I'm going to have a pleasurable time. Now that may or may not be true. But there's only one way to know; I run my experiment. Now it may have been terrible, total rejection...etcetera. Or it may have been multiple orgasms and ecstatic rapture. Whatever, when the experiment is over—and it's over whenever I pull back and look at it objectively—I analyze the results. Maybe I found one aspect was fine. Then this other aspect was so important that it could never have worked even remotely as well without it. Yet another aspect over here almost ruined it; and it should definitely be deleted from the process in the future. While this other aspect, I'm not sure what it's good for; so I'll keep it on file in case it becomes more relevant in the future. Now what? Do I want to run it again, change it, bring in new variables, whatever? I'm back to center, relatively unencumbered psychologically. Ready and capable of recombining my energies any way my consciousness geigers it to be fit.

Okay, so these two individual friends of the opposite sex now have a basis around which to explore their sexual interactions. They know how to say *no*...which means their *yes* will count for much more...probably so much more, that other people will not be anxious to force them to say no. They're strong, full of options, secure, and know how to always take their own space. Now they want to engineer the means for deep enriching sexual satisfaction.

They're rising in love. It is the fullness of their awareness that they bring to every act. They want to be able to sexually express their feelings unconditionally. While they do not yet understand exactly how to do this, they do know that if communication breaks down between them, they'll never have the opportunity. Now whenever there's contention between them, they automatically realize there's something they don't understand. They pull back from the male-female aspect of their sexual nature, re-center themselves and, detached from their feelings, come together as two intelligent individuals to sort out the confusions of the man and the woman.

They've stopped expecting from each other and begun paying attention. There are no guarantees they can make their relationship work. There's only working it out. At first their passions seem to cool. Even so, the proximity of ease and relaxation is making it easier to touch and respond to each other's rhythms. They respond only as long as it feels good. What they want is the excitement and attention of when they were first courting. In their lovemaking they want the bottom line to be the more than pleasurable connection of orgasmic osmosis. In every way they want these intensities, but with the leisure and control which allows them to savor and assimilate. No more fleeting glimpses of merging pleasure ricocheting through disorienting, disproportionate moments of sacrifice; they want to make love to the maximum...to discover and fully express their range of respective sexuality...They want to transcend themselves and together explore beyond the limitations of sex.

Keep them courting! No longer comfortable with complacency...nevermore accepting less than the experiences that give them control, they both have activated their too long repressed sexuality. Woman must learn to sexually aggress, stretching to the limits of his desires. Man must learn to receive, opening his feelings to oceanic depths of her ever-surging connection to the rhythms of Nature.

Into all of this they've geigered. So many useless shells of psychological warfare have been discarded. Nothing negative holds them together. They're each strong independent individuals who can come and go as they like. They can be alone, but they see an opportunity for greater fulfillment in combining their energies. All the energy formerly usurped by emotional fixations has been returned to their consciousness. They're on fire within the moment, but don't know how to burn.

They're ready to get it on; to explore the full range of their sexuality. Let's help them out.

6. Making Love

On the lover's banner of peace reads the motto: *Scrape them off the ceiling!*

The first rule in making love is: *Please yourself!* Please yourself, then make me part of your pleasure. That's the only way you can really please me, anyhow.

Making love is not being sexual for the sake of pro-creation; nor is it a distraction to release your jammed up bio-psychic energies from the tension caused by a frustrating day. It may accomplish such results, but this is not its true field of focus. In the human form you have complex organic biochemical units capable of consciously directing energies for the sake of self-maintenance and improvement of its own operating capabilities. Everything you do is ultimately for the quality of feedback it provides your consciousness! When so efficiently directed, sexual loving is one of the most pleasurable means of elevating your consciousness through interaction with another human being.

One of the great obstructions to this lies in a basic misunderstanding into which the man has been conditioned. He's confusingly come to identify orgasm with ejaculation. He's bio-emotionally timed them together, so that the only time most men experience orgasm is for the brief, hardly discernable, eruptive few moments when his penis is spasmodically ejecting sperm. Ejaculation and orgasm may be sequenced together; however, they are two discernable, distinctive modes of experience, with very different effects.

Maybe a man is in the midst of sexual intercourse. His muscles are tensed, he feels powerful; he's wide-awake, absorbed in concentration; he's supporting himself on his hands, driving his hips into the female with flexible insistence. Suddenly he ejaculates. His arms grow weak, his body drops down; and quite often, oblivion calls him into sleep. If he does this often enough, day in and day out—depending, of course, on his age and physical condition—he will start to feel drained and physically exhausted. This can and often does lead to ill health, which only serves to increase man's fear of woman. He attaches ridiculous insinuations of vampirism to her; in his mind she's robbed him of his essence. Or more generally, it creates a subliminal hysteria about fears of impotency and his inability to sexually satisfy the woman.

Looking at the male's ejaculatory mechanism as a means to orgasmic potency, we find wide discrepancies in experience. Sometimes with ejaculation comes a peaking of consciousness carrying him into a startling transcendent intensity where the fixation of his self-image is arrested and bludgeoned into irrelevance. For a moment his consciousness hangs suspended in a feeling which seems sufficient unto itself. Ah, if only that moment could go on forever...Actually that moment is always on, it's just that relying on ejaculation is not a conducive method for experiencing much of it. Limiting one's sojourn into the realm of orgasm to a few spasmodic contractions of the penis is about as fulfilling as trying to savor the quality of a gourmet meal while vomiting it from your mouth. And even if he's convinced himself that this ricocheted clutch at ecstasy is the best he can hope for, the ejaculatory method isn't very reliable. Sometimes it's wow; other times it's like nothing, and he despises himself for even bothering.

The reason for ejaculation's seeming unreliability is that it's not the orgasm. But let's examine its function in relation to orgasm. Obviously, ejaculation for the male is

the means by which he fulfills his part in continued procreation of the species. As he evolves the conscious utilization of his nervous system, his choices in satisfying
his bio-sexual urges become more studied. He structures
them through memory of whatever pleasure he might have
previously received. The pleasure is, of course, Nature's
way of seducing him into the procreative process. From
that level it is the pleasure of release. As the potency of
sperm level builds up on the testicles, the connected pleasure usurps his concentration. It releases hormones which
activate states of mind and levels of energy, muscular and
organ tension. A kind of psychic vortex is created, drawing
his attention towards the buildup of this groin-centered
intensity. He is driven to need to release this tension
through ejaculation. But it must be ejaculation with absorption of his consciousness into the process. Under more
simplistic circumstance (i.e., meager sociocultural ambi-
tion) this absorption is easy to achieve. Just as you eat to
satisfy hunger, sex is taken in order of need and availability.
As consciousness via personality plunges ever deeper into
the complexities of culture, its natural rhythms must be
continuously reestablished according to circumstance. If
this is not done accurately (and obviously it hasn't been
done so en masse up 'til now), then the ability to connect
with and control biological processes is diminished. Which
often means that man can't put aside those many things
to which his thoughts are attached sufficiently enough to
absorb himself in the ejaculatory mechanism.

To reestablish this connection he may resort to all sorts
of complex situations and accessories. He tries to distract
his mind from the stimulus-response ratio long enough to
let the pleasure circuits of his sexuality take control and
redirect him towards orgasm. Extremes of this nature can
be seen in sadomasochism. There the pain (giving or re-

ceiving) jerks consciousness into concentration. In the momentary intervals between pain, pleasure can slip in. The pain is not the pleasure, but becomes the only way the person can find release from the constrictions of self-denial. The pleasure appears simultaneously with the pain. At which point the pleasure (mostly in the sense of release) plus release of responsibility (power of control or being controlled) catapults one into the bio-sexual mechanisms.

At this stage of sexuality man is looking for orgasmic potency. For both man and woman the orgasm has a number of functions. On the more mundane bio-psychological level, the orgasm functions to bring the system into, at least, a temporary balance. You might view it as a reward for spending so well. The well-spent part is the bio-physical procreation aspect. When operating mainly from that level, biochemistry between the male and female draws them into a concentration which should result in orgasmic procreation. The orgasm, at that level, is the release and the relaxation of all the tension built through the physiology to pinpoint focus, leading into procreative activity. Then all the energy concentrated into the sexual center releases, and backwashes biochemically, psycho-mentally and homeopathically through the cells of the body. This serves to quiet, heal, nourish and rebalance the system from strains of the procreative act.

However, our lives are far more complex today. Our nervous systems have been opened to complex associative correlations that take us far beyond the rhythms inherent in the natural environment. Which in turn has both magnified the amount of sexual current available through our systems, as well as making connection with the release of orgasmic potency a greater effort to obtain.

If a man isn't having sex "to get his rocks off," then what is the purpose of the action? The penis is the dumb animal part of the human body. It's fairly easy to condition and redirect the performance of the penis. For a long time the procreative urges of nature, along with the need for momentary tension-breaking transcendence beyond an inner-persecuting self-image, did the directive conditioning. But this mundane orientation of penile functions can easily be rerouted through conscious effort by any individualized man who has reached a certain level of self-awareness.

Now, there is a rhythm to ejaculation which varies from man to man according to age, health, level of activity, state of mind, etc. (We'll get into how to determine that rhythm later.) When there is the need to ejaculate, it should be done freely with all the release, nourishing, and rebalancing akin to that level of orgasmic potency. But it is not necessary for a man to ejaculate every time he has sexual love! On the contrary, it is far better on all levels for a man to have frequent prolonged sex with less spermal ejaculation.

If man is making love but doesn't permit himself to ejaculate, the level of stimulation keeps building. Many men have learned if they can manage somehow to prolong the moment of release, when they do "cum," the ejaculation is more likely to have that violent eruptive orgasmic potency they were seeking. From that perspective it seems like the pressure keeps building in their testicles 'til they're half delirious with the need to explode. The pressure building in their testicles is certainly not from more and more sperm being pumped in beyond the level of containment. It takes time for the body to manufacture sperm; it does not materialize instantaneously. Rather, the approach towards, and slight pullback from ejaculation serves to focus the consciousness into that vortex connection. This focussing is necessary for the pressure to build. If, instead of such focussing, he just lets the penis ejaculate through simple arousal and tactile stimulation, the man will often miss the orgasmic potency which can carry him beyond that threshold. At such a point the body is not nourished, the self-image is unabated and exasperated, and an aggravating sense of futility can set in. However, when the man nears orgasm and pulls back, he must do so consciously. Doing this a few times totally draws his consciousness into a releasing unity with ejaculation.

You can start to visualize this by looking at man's past ejaculatory experiences. As pressure builds to ejaculatory-orgasmic potency, it is not the sperm in his testicles uncontrollably anxious to explosively erupt. It is actually the rate of perception drawn to the nourishing immersion in a more transcendently inclusive state of mind. As for a few violently disorienting moments, if the consciousness has been sufficiently drawn into the ejaculatory mechanism, he reaches beyond himself (self-image) and gets an all too brief, tantalizing glimpse at the energies inherent at that level of consciousness. This draws him far beyond the experience of a beginner's state of self-transcending meditation because the biophysical energizing that accompanies very high psychic states already has been activated. But it is almost simultaneously shut down by the backwash of release through the ejaculatory mechanism of orgasmic potency.

Now, without getting involved with all the seeming paradoxes of consciousness this might bring to mind, let's look at the function of the orgasm from a more advanced perspective. Once man's consciousness is connected through opened energy centers of the genital region, the pressure on his consciousness builds within him toward release. Once he manages to do this without ejaculating, that energy will continue building. Soon enough it reaches the resonance that should normally be associated with orgasmic potency. And sure enough the energy starts releasing through the man's body and psychological self-image. If this is a new experience, it can be extremely intense and disorienting. He will start to get initial pulsations of energy expanding upward from both the sacrum region of the lower spine, and the lower abdominal region in front. The energy is not to be denied. It will push through both physiological blockages in his body, plus subliminally suppressed psychological fixations.

In the past, other more esoterically mystical approaches—have handled these upward surges of energy piercing into higher consciousness by devotional rituals and stage by stage initiations of discipline. My own experience, both personally and as a teacher, has enabled me to see that these same blockages can be more easily and succinctly integrated into the Space Age needs of our neurology by deconditioning the feeling body; returning it to the control of your own intellect. Then through open-ended self-reprogramming of your feelings, however it suits you best in any given consideration, you learn to move at will into and beyond all levels of accessible consciousness to any degree and combination you desire.

So, by letting his psychosexual energy build beyond the normal ejaculatory release mechanisms, man enters consciously into the realm of orgasm. The energy has not diminished; it keeps amplifying. Suchly, there is now time in which to orient oneself. He can savor and relish the sensations and activities in his body, as they affect his levels of perceptions. Of course, a lot of things he encountered when first experiencing sex—before they were swept up in the currents of his avoidance patterns—again become accessible. It is easy to see the way by which he's neurologically structured his sexual energies up 'til this point. As he presses on, much of what are called psychic and intuitive processes present themselves for his possible involvement. Obviously, to keep building the psycho-mental energies through sexual priming requires a new kind of structuring.

Man is now in a position—like woman—to have multiple orgasms. On a physical level, how does this affect his body? What techniques, physical and mental, can enable a man to do this? And what is the nature of the dynamics between man and woman when sexual love is being processed from such a state of mind?

However long this sexual communing continues, man may or may not have a need and / or desire to punctuate lovemaking with ejaculation. After a certain point, the reason for which most men think they are making love has been resolved and surpassed. The tensions have left body and mind; both have become supple, relaxed, invigorated, alert, glowing and content.

Most men go through life sexually far more dissatisfied than satisfied. Despite their efforts and rationalized beliefs to the contrary, their search for relief in masturbation (self-manipulation and / or pay for play rental of available female equipment) usually leaves them feeling worse. In a world where one has been conditioned to feel dissatisfaction and suffering is somehow a positive indicator, "going for what you know" and "taking whatever you can get" seems to make sense. For most men it is bad enough that their dearest longings seem destined, at best, to inconsistent chance flirtations. As for most, the prime time graffiti on the cesspool walls of their rationalized consciousness is: "God, I'm so horny! If I don't come soon, I'll go insane!"

On top of which I seem to be suggesting retention of that pulsating, hypnotically consuming sperm. Won't legions of testicles turn blue; while barely constrained masculine egos escalate into orgies of unrestrained macho-aggressiveness? Two things to remember: (1) Master the classics before you aspire to the abstracts. For the man, orgasmic potency, achieved at will, with all the inherent benefits already mentioned, is the classic. (2) When you understand how something works, you control it. What must be understood experientially, not just intellectually, is the bio-psychic nature of sexuality.

If the only relation a man has ever established with his genitals is possible procreation and / or release of emotionally displaced tension, then retention of sperm could indeed be somewhat damaging. As you start to transcend and redirect the biospheric rhythms of nature which have instinctively (reactively) dominated your actions...as you individualize, you synchronize the rhythms of your physicality with the unique perspectives and subsequent demands of your conscious interaction with circumstance. If instead of trying to release the tension (absence of pain), you start to cap it, increase it, and tap into it at will, using it to nourish your physical systems, it will aid the evolution of your neurological efficiency (pursuit of pleasure).

It is not a man's balls turning blue (so to speak) because his cup runneth over with sperm. The body has ample mechanisms to handle the release of such a buildup. Besides which, a man should always feel free to ejaculate while enjoying it to the max. What is, however, irritating to a man is having his consciousness and the dynamics of his bio-psychic energies limited to mere physical sexuality when there is no actual need for release of sperm. Also, when there is no real need to release sperm, yet the man feels stimulated, he has reached a point of individualizing his potential which demands he take conscious control of redirecting his energies.

Acting from these considerations, a man's approach to a woman as a lover, takes on entirely different sexual tones. He no longer seeks to conjoin with her because he needs to release physical-sexual tension. As he individualizes, he no longer depends on her to access the depths of his own feelings. Since there is nothing to be afraid of, he does what he likes. Pleasure is his geiger-counter. While he appreciates being alone, he can see that a number of his own assets and potentials have been designed to activate only through sexual relations with a partner or partners. As through their physiologies, by wielding their feelings, accentuated at will by their intellects, the direct experience of ecstatically rapturous energy becomes accessible.

Acting through her sexuality, from a more encompassing perspective of individuality, woman is equally qualified to channel and benefit from the conscious transmission of bio-psychic energies through her neurology. Let's say she's already been deconditioned from the primitive inhibitions placed on her feelings. She no longer feels anger and resentment towards man, because she has access to her own power; she too, can come and go as she pleases. The good and evil split is dissolved; she no longer feels the least bit negative about letting go and sexually opening up full throttle. She's begun to take conscious control of her feelings, redirecting them at will. For her too, by design, there are certain aspects of her own system she can only activate through psychosexual communion with man.

No games of one-upmanship power manipulation...no lies, no avoidances. We have a male and a female, two individuals seeking to sexually play with each other for the maximum of possible benefits they can achieve. They are now naked, together in the privacy of their room. The preliminaries of biochemical attraction, sociocultural acknowledgment, and psychosexual cuing responses have already taken place. They are here, now; with nothing else to occupy their attention except satisfying themselves through each other.

There is no mystery to fuel their desires. Everything has already been openly declared between them. He is a bit self-conscious about the dependability of his erection ("Suppose it doesn't stay hard...!") Yet he knows better than to try and stimulate himself with fantasy images. He is here to experiment with the reality of their potentials. Remaining calm, he allows himself to absorb his attention in her. If she really wants him, she'll call him forth. She'll stimulate him to erection; it will be as if his penis is part of her nervous system, and he hardly has a choice but to respond to her desires. If his performance isn't aroused, then it's not so important at the moment. He wants to play with their energies. When she does call him forth, he'll be virtually indefatigable.

Simply at ease, he feels no need to be more than the moment asks of him. This takes the pressure off him. Relaxing, like an adventurer about to be entertained by his own explorations, she has become the territory through which his awareness will roam. In her Earth Nature she mirrors his spirit into a conscious aspect for him. Relaxed and alert, the more he let's go of the considerations of his self-image—focussing into her—the more he comes into himself. His penis is at a pleasantly irritating half-mast. Energies are tingling in undulating ripples through his body.

She is moody, not so sure about whether the connection will really take between them; or even if she really wants it to. In the past she might have pretended; she'd have felt obligated to perform and service him. But not so anymore. She no longer has to be sexual. And if she's going to be, she'll settle for nothing less than a fulfilled transport of pleasure. Gently surprised by her own power, feeling comfortably secure, she finds it pleasant to be with him. He seems to be rolling and flowing with her, yet making no demands. It's a quality of feeling which is very present, very clear; one she usually has been able to share only in comaraderie with other women. It makes her giggle inside. She is there to be sexual, yet has no real sense of what that means. But there is joy in the sharing which attracts and draws her closer to him.

They talk in breathy little words. They touch and stroke and kiss. They are not trying to find arousal; rather it is finding them. It draws them. She has watched his penis become hard, then relax a bit as they talk. She can feel him waiting for her; she can feel the fire building. He sees the light and strength in her eyes. He feels desirous, open...malleable. He floats on the luxury of being centered enough to let down his guard completely. What he wants...has always wanted...is to taste her power as she actively demands of him what is her right. Yes, he must have been crazy to think he wanted to dominate her. Demanding she acknowledge him in passive tribute only reinforced his own uncertainty. It had made her seem dull and uncaring, while alienating him deeper into his own separateness. But now he craves to become immersed in her strength. He wants to nurture it...encourage it. What will she do with it? How will she touch him? What hidden parts of himself will finally be revealed? He feels so alive; so entranced by this wonderful human being who is choosing to share with him.

She smiles at the look of delight in his eyes as he watches her nipples harden. Her vagina has begun lubricating. She's looking more lustrous and beautiful by the moment. Gently she touches him, and returns the earnestness of his kisses. Purposefully, she weaves her hands over his body. They brush half-absently over his thighs and around his buttocks. His body shakes and ripples. She is careful not to stroke his groin. She wants the ache to build in him. She'll feed his passive gorging on her own desire, 'til it transforms him…'til he rises up with his power, demanding that she must want him—undeniably—before he'll fill her with his presence.

For both of them, there is no goal to be achieved. In a haze, feeling the vortex of his groin sucking his consciousness, he feels his erection—he is the erection. It no longer matters. But God, the pleasure. He tastes her. He wants to set her on fire, just so he can bask in the heat. He kisses, licks, and caresses her everywhere. He feels when she responds. Feels her body flow with his touch. And he feels when she momentarily loses contact, flowing into associative thoughts. He pulls back; waits for her to acknowledge his gaze. Then silences her before she can wonder why, with his delight in their sexual exchange.

She has become a container of pleasure filled with the elixir of life. He bites lightly over her body. At first she responds unthinkingly, wanting to reward the source of her pleasure with an increased fervor of desire. Low purrs and animal-like growls take the place of words. These sounds released from deep inside, bring forth the long suppressed absorption of two shameless creatures responding in confident abandonment to the animalness of their nature.

His mind is clear, yet thoughtless. He wants her to touch him…to run her fingers and tongue lovingly and hungrily over and around his straining erection. But she hasn't She wants to be made to want to…to be made to want to drive him over the edge and into the heartland of his soul. He complies. He sucks and licks her nipples 'til she can't turn her awareness away from the sensation. His tongue darts up her neck, tasting, squeezing every pore with his lips. Like an angel with a vengeance, his head moves in triangular rotation between her nipples and mouth, drinking in her many nectars. She moans in silence. Her body molds in synchromesh to his every movement. Her thighs part easily, deliriously with distant reverence as his own thighs caress the length of her soft flesh.

He pushes his thigh up between hers, 'til the lips of her vagina part and drape their wetness onto his flesh. The pressure is building; she wants release. She wants him hard, throbbing and erect inside her. He can feel it. He pulls back and shakes himself into concentration. The question of an erection has long since passed. That desire to ejaculate potently pulls at him. He laughs at himself. He greets her questioning half-open gaze with a smile of power. She wants him. She wants man...she wants the god-like male animal to satiate her beyond desire.

Good, he'll give her so much pleasure she won't care. She reaches for his penis. He shudders as her hand makes loving contact. For a moment he luxuriates in a sensation that could drive him into quickly spending. Then he pulls back. His penis moves beyond her grasp. His body backs away from her; his tongue leaving a moist trail of saliva. With excruciating deliberateness his tongue savors its way down her body. Down to the ends of her thighs, licking at her knees. He's read about the erogenous points of tactile stimulation—every part of the body should be able to climax. Now he's licking, purposefully biting back up her inner thighs. He is conscious of her every reflex, as she gasps and twitches. Several times his tongue grazes across the lips of her vagina. Then the tip of his tongue fleshes, expanding itself in a slow meshing turn, directly over the swelling pulse of her clitoris.

Knowing what it is, and what to expect, she still can never mentally prepare herself. With the contact of his tongue her body convulses into itself. The wonderful pleasure of the shock of contact momentarily brakes the drawing concentration of her build to orgasm. For a moment she can feel his mind again. Again...how empathetically telepathic they've become; she can't stop—doesn't want to stop the direct, thoughtless transmission that's synchromeshing their awareness together. And how deliciously he wants her.

For a moment he raises his head and finds her eyes. He smiles forcefully into her. There's no fear or resentment in either of them. He wants her to know how consciously ecstatic he is, as waves of lustiness wield his primitive animal power between the extremes of finesse and passion in the supra conscious mind. Then his tongue plunges her back to the hilt of her feelings. Her mind reels towards orgasm. His mouth rhythmically supping on every drop of vaginal elixir and every staccato pulsation of building intensity. His hands are steering her like a fine racing car. With fingertip control he massages sexual release nerve points along the pelvic girdle on the front of her abdomen. Currents are extending in deep waves of relaxation over her belly, even as the mounting tension to release builds incessantly through her womb. Nipples stroked, pulled into tautness; breasts squeezed in violent tenderness. His fingers softly, tantalizingly probing her mouth. She reaches to suck them reflexively, like a joyous spasmodic, only to have them pull away; as they caress their way back down over the curves of her neck and breasts. Nails raking gently down and over her belly, drawing magnetic spasms of electrical current shuddering through her. And always that tongue, even as his nails purposefully rake nerve cells of pleasure along her inner thigh.

Her whole body is a pinpoint of focalized concentration. She feels like she's coming from somewhere to meet herself. Now his fingers are releasing nerve points at the tail of her spine; then she feels the light, insistent massaging of her rectum. Everything has become one synchronized movement. She can't resist; doesn't want to resist. And spurred on by his unmistakable devouring joy in her, she convulses, with her body sailing off through the first bliss waves of orgasm.

For a few moments he leaves his head between her thighs. Eagerly, he swallows the health-generating liquids flowing into his mouth. A few times he flicks his tongue with slow, exaggerated gentleness over her swollen clitoris. Her body involuntarily jerks back; her clitoris being unbearably sensitive. Satisfied that she is ready, he moves on his knees between her. It is the act of an invading lover. She's still revelling in the solitary release of her first orgasm. His erection is so fierce he can afford to detach from it. His eyes are wide open, his concentration is effortlessly focussed on every facet of what he's experiencing. There is all the time in the world to soul-fuck through timelessness.

He moves onto his knees, positioning himself between her thighs. She hardly notices; for the moment she doesn't want to think. With his hand he places the darkly swollen head of his penis between the intoxicated lips of her open vagina. He rests there, feeling her gladness in the recognition of their contact. Then slowly he slides into her. She is so wet there is no blocking friction. He concentrates on feeling every millimeter of descending sensation; even as his consciousness, channelling through his sex, sucks her awareness deeper into each pulsation of pleasure. Totally immersed in her womb, he lies quiet for a few moments. He is revelling in the last spasms of current from her first climax.

Her intensity is slowly subsiding. But she barely has time to savor their new connection. For a moment there is the teasing hint of contentment. There is a connection which meets in a void beyond feeling. She cannot distinguish between her womb and his member. Where does one begin and the other leave off? She can't perceive the difference. The backwash of release from the potency of her orgasm seems arrested. Suspended between oblivion's transcendence and quiet joy, her senses are drawn into an empathetic awareness of his demanding presence. All this she feels for a few short moments.

Feeling their contact, with every muscle in his body responding in unison, he arches back in a sudden non-violently aggressive movement. She gasps; jerked back into awareness of her own sensations as she feels him pulling out of her. He stops as if he's reached the limits of withdrawal at the end of their tether, with her labia wrapped around the head of his penis. Her eyes reach up into his. He remains still, smiling with his glance 'til her own look returns the understanding. Then he starts to move, gyrating his hips in a wide circular arc. He can feel how open she is to him. She feels like he's teasing her—ancient dreams of being filled, swim snake-like in a unison of remote wishes—but how can this be a tease? Her fingertips trace the controlled power in his hips as they hover above her. Then suddenly he plunges up to the hilt, and grinds for a few moments, driving her through corridors of energized passion.

Before she can scream "yes," he's extended himself all but out of her again; torturing her like a sainted deliverer with precession titillations at the entrance of her sex. Demandingly, her thighs open to their fullest; as she digs into his buttocks, drawing him into her. No longer is she suspended. She doesn't want or need relaxation. She wants the build, the passion; again she's cresting on energy waves towards orgasm. "I want you," she half garbles; both proud and shocked by the sincerity of her admission. "You already have me," he laughs with challenging mischief.

A vagina in heat possesses incredible agility. He feels his penis being drawn in and sucked at as she molds to him. Yet within the same sensation he feels as if her insides are expanding, drawing him beyond the physical dimensions of space. It will take a while before he can switch into that place of control beyond the ejaculatory mechanism. Already he is moving too close to spending, while he can feel she's just starting to warm up to her hunger. She's urging him deeper. His mind reels in a weakening deliciousness. But what if he were to release his sperm now; how bored and disappointed they'd both be.

Pulling out, fighting for control, he was playing it a bit too close to the edge. Poor technique, as he can barely manage to shake his attention away from the sensations building within him. Just a moment more of stroking within her and he would have exploded. Instead the build is interrupted; two dry involuntary contractions throb through his urethra and the ejaculatory mechanism slightly subsides. Then he realizes his breath is coming in quick gasping gulps.

She reaches for him. She feels the fire burning like a phantom fever through him. Hardly thinking, she fingers his penis, drawing it back into her; aching to feel his sperm drip from the veins in her womb...aching to feel the male animal capitulating in luxuriant fusion into the seeming unquenchable power of her inexhaustible female capacity. Half pleading, with a concentration equivalent to relaxing an oncoming headache, he stops her movement. Huskily he asks her to be still, to wait, to give him time to adjust.

"I want to play in you for hours; just feel and exchange with you. I just have to get used to you," he half advertises. She's not sure what he means. She doubts if he, himself, knows. But she's used to frustration. At least there's something curiously amusing in his seemingly ineffectual effort to control himself. It makes her feel so much surer and wiser than the man-child floundering before her.

His tip is just resting in her vagina. More than the contact and sensation, now he feels a magnetism pulling at him, entwining, in pulsating waves, the current running in myriad strands through the limbo-void in his testicles. He forces his eyes wide open; though they want to stay hazed in languid distraction. Slowing his breath, he inhales deeply, and holds it; releasing it in conscious slowness, he waits 'til his lungs need the oxygen again before he inhales. The pain of the pleasure diminishes. Moving her hips a little, she squirms wantonly in response. All the way into her he plunges. He stops, holding his breath; still too close to spending. His body is rigid. Desperately, he's sort of ordering her not to move. He's got to get his mind out of the sensation. Shaking his head to clear it, a convulsion runs through him, spasming out into a clarity of release in his mind. Having felt the pathway it took, he inhales sharply. Contracting into his stomach, feeling the clenching release shoot up his spine. Suddenly he finds himself shaking like a nympho-epileptic. From the base of his spine up through his head it's as though he were one huge spasmed penis, convulsing as ejaculatory bliss waves shoot through his mind and out into the holy ether of God's goddess mirror. What has he discovered? No longer does his penis feel too close to spending.

Now they're gyrating intensely together. Sensitized to each other's every movement, they move in a give and take unison. He plunges deep into her sucking hunger. She moans a bit; opening up, moving in a hip-thrusting angle to draw him even deeper within her womb than she ever realized she could. He stops again, convulsively shaking as he redirects the immediacy in his groin into clear-seeing in his mind's eye. Then rising up to arms length, he pulls out 'til only the penile head rests in her. Arching his back, with his head extending to top the bow-like curve of his movement, 'til his forehead is perpendicular to the ceiling, he clenches tightly on his rectum, clutching pressure over the nerve center at the base of his scrotum. Then, with a deep, slow, deliberate inhalation, he wills the energy centered in his groin to up-wash its way through his nervous system. While at the same time he opens and relaxes all voluntary contractions in his penis, letting the subtle vibratory essences of the vaginal juices he's soaking in draw up into him. To aid this he sucks in his stomach, as though it were a pump. His body ripples; he feels alive, joyful; there is great scintillating clarity dancing brilliantly at ease. Totally sensitive to her; intermeshed into every sensation with her; he feels clearly detached from the ejaculatory mechanism. While he simultaneously feels like he's become part of and consciously attenuated to the orgasm—it's just another state of consciousness. One he's touched on and ricocheted through many times. But never with such easy, clear and constant access: "My God, Life is the coming thing!"

Suspended, for a moment she literally experiences a sense of her own sensations slowed, stretched, and enveloped by his intensity. For the moment he seems to be outstretching to somewhere past her. While at the same time their connection is both more intense and gently mellow. Dancing waters of vaguely familiar feelings emanate wonderfully seductive sensations from the archetypal recesses of her female psyche. As voluptuousness magnetizes her consciousness into the gentle warmth in her womb, omni-dimensional quivers overwhelm her feelings. She'd purr like a contented little girl, except the painless searing of their connections demands too much respect. Instead, the pressure of orgasmic release hovers like a comforting torture, sucking her concern into pinpoint genital expectancy. Struck curious, by the oddity of the sensation, she feels him pulling her energy up through him. But rather than draining her, she experiences a quickening, a livening of vitality, as though she were awash with an incoming flow. His psychosexual inhalation of her essence only seems to stimulate even greater replenishment of the same, surging in through her. Like an erogenous sluice gate between two dimensions, she feels plugged into some vast inexhaustible reservoir, personalizing it into a golden elixir to nourish this resplendent god-child melded within her.

He knows he's reached the point of clear separation. Now he can abandon himself to the wildest frenzy of erotic sensation without ejaculating. He smiles to himself, thinking of the disappointment of the old ways: One moment surging with godzilla-like power. Then a sweetly bored, demanding voice saying, "I want you to come, baby." Then exhaustion, mental disorientation, leading to oblivion. But with nagging frustration vexing his heart as she half assures him with contemptuously distant condescension that: "Oh sure, it was wonderful." Thank God that pattern of constricting his experience—that type of (devilish) ignorance is now behind him.

What is happening to her? She's building again to orgasm. But this is no surface release of pent up tension. It's more an affirmation; like a budding flower bursting forth to the enrapturing power of warmth and light. She doesn't want to be drained of anything. No, she wants to be filled...drenched...satiated beyond the capacity of her imagination. Her movements rising up in triumphant joy to meet his; only to feel him effortlessly increasing the connection between them. Always in the past, she's felt the man holding back, tense in his seemingly futile effort not to give into the voluptuous void into which she beckons him. Hardly would the fires begin to build in her when...Her mind gasping, mentally wheezing at fading reflections, as undeniable waves of pleasure draw her beyond the puny confines of her self-image. It's never been like this before. And he's relentless, as he genitalizes an unceasing barrage of pleasure through the core of her being.

So relaxed; even as his body gyrates with precession receptivity to her every response, inside the fully erect throbbing core of his penis there is a sense of total relaxation. There are various nuances to telepathy; and he feels definitely plugged into several of them. There is an incredible amount of energy circulating around and between them. Their communion is altering the quality of their physical perceptions. The blending of their mutual secretions envelopes them with an intoxicating odor. Gone is the self-consciousness of their differences. Replacing it is an intensity of leisure in which every pore in their bodies are open and magnetized through each other.

He'd crested with her last orgasm. Now he can distinguish. As her womb began contracting orgasmicly, he once again felt himself drawn back towards ejaculation. Some quality of her inner attraction amplified as bliss waves rolled them both over their desires. Incredible sucking connection; they both opened their eyes and looked deeply at each other. It didn't diminish their transport at all. In fact, they could both feel several levels to which they were simultaneously connected. Streams of unmouthed conversation flow in understanding between them. At the moment she no longer cared about anything except the coalesced consciousness into which their senses are diffusing. As with mutual awareness they both glide into responses they intuit will accelerate the rhythm creating them.

Pleasure, her right to be in the fullest, most gratifying capacity of her femaleness. "If Eve had only really known." Whatever, now she's become a shameless woman; unencumbered by the inhibitions of ignorant minds. How she wants to reward him with her. She hurls her neural openings into the amalgamation which more than encompasses both of them. Their bodies continue to intermesh with each other; but now—beyond the aesthetics of sensation—they're dancing on frequencies of energy. How familiar, these pulsations. They were always there, but usually kept indistinguishable by the deadlock of their fixations.

He feels the energy spreading into her womb again. Her muscles so relaxed, the tension blown away. This time her convulsion into the orgasmic reflex is deep, rich and sustained. Letting go of his concern, he telepathically soars with her. The sweet throbbing suck of her vagina around his penis is the deliciously heightened response that every man believes he's hungry for. Yet how inconsequential it seems compared to the pure recycling magnetism of the energies they now feel. With all its beauty and lusciousness, their bodies are merely lascivious leverages pumping their awareness into gossamer threads of sub-atomized pulsations. Pulsations, how translucent are these aggregates of energy which take human form. It's like dropping off into sleep, but without losing consciousness. Into and through the dream state. Radiating archetypal images shooting primal codes of remembrance through their synaptic relays. Garden images...vast inter-spacial tabloids of gods and goddesses, plants and flowers all pulsating through spirals of scintillating aliveness.

Again there is the pull towards ejaculation. Instead of backing away by using physiological techniques to stem the tide, he rides with it. She feels his consciousness sinking towards release. She has a trajectory magnetic lock on his consciousness. Unmistakably, on some level, she telepathically feels him reaching with his mind, telling her to climb and pull him up. She wills it; she feels his rate of vibration rise towards her, even as his need to ejaculate recedes. There's no resistance left between them. Again she orgasms and so does he. Their nervous systems convulsing in simultaneous synchromesh of tantric fusion, spurting their sense of concern somewhere over the rainbow.

What has happened to time? They have absolutely no sense of how much of it has just passed. They continued their sojourn, as flash peaks of ecstasy coalesce their awareness through sub-quantum doorways, peeling away laughter into vector coordinates, glimpses of the universal simpatico, the vibratory flux they're experiencing.

Past charity, beyond greed, the only reason left is the ecstasy they're swimming through. Their fingertips and tongues gyrate over the landscape of each pore. Now their positions have inverted them. His head oscillating between her thighs, his lips and tongue lovingly drinking in every

drop of her. While the whole flat of her tongue tantaliz-
es sensations from the base root below his scrotum, lus-
ciously enveloping his testicles, then running up his shaft
where she finds utter ease in almost swallowing the length
of him into her mouth. Their movements so slow and
deliberately aware of each other's responses. Again her
body spasms in orgasm. Juices sluice their way down his
throat. Their smells had blended and reblended as each
wave of energy alchemize their secretions into life-regen-
erating elixirs. Their smell is like food as they sniff in each
other. "Anything you want," she rhapsodizes. "I'll do anything to please you!" He pulls his head up to gaze deeply into her eyes: "More!" he says with the power of complete loving tenderness.

She turns him onto his back; sucks lovingly on his
penis for a moment; then straddling him, sinks, in peals
of ecstasy, down around his fullness. Bringing his feet
together, his knees going inside, he arches his hips up to
meet her. Suddenly she feels him consciously taking them
through a transformation of directional energy flows. From
the way in which he synchronizes his thrusts with her,
she feels like the penis is emanating from her and she's
sinking it deep into his more than willing vagina. It isn't
a mere momentary sensation. As they continue juxtaposing
orientations of energy she's experiencing what it's like to
feel her genitalia as a male sex organ thrusting into a female. "That's right," he knowingly smiles at her, "you do
want to know the raging cunt inside of me." Oh yes she
does! Gears stripping into superfluity. "Yes baby," he moans
in a purr so seductive that she feels as though there are
testicles attached to her about to be sucked dry..."Yes baby,
drive your luscious cock deep inside my cunt— fuck me
baby!" She does; and as she's doing, he suddenly reverses
psychomotional positions with her, so that with the next

thrust she feels him totally swollen up in the depths of her belly. As with the thrust after that, her consciousness shuddered, throbs and orgasms beyond belief.

She collapses onto him in grateful disorientation. Pulsating through each other, he clutches her lovingly against him. His hands roam purposefully over her back and neck and shoulders, massaging them and stimulating nerve points of release. She's amazed that she can even care, much less be turned on again. But he sits up with her in his lap, their legs lightly circling each other. Now he's swaying his hips, sending her rotating before him in a gyrating circle that continuously scoops through every possible angle in her womb. Only for a moment does she have time to wonder if it is even possible to come again. "Yes," he breathes in her ear as his tongue slithers into her auricular opening, "more...!" "You're driving me crazy," she gratefully inquires, as his hands mold her breasts into abandoned wildness. "I'm driving you sane!," he responds. "I'm driving you..." Her orgasm is short, hot, hard and intense, like a penis forced to ejaculate again when there is nothing left to spew forth.

"Just for the fun of it," he intones, asking for a needless confirmation; as he lays her back down without dislodging himself. She has never before felt so totally satiated. It is not her body that can't go on; she just no longer feels the need. Yet he still continues plunging deeply up inside her. His mouth nibbles, sucking gourmet-like at her uncontrollably responsive nipples; as she feels them yield some nourishing substance into his mouth. His hands reigniting nerve points over her buttocks and inner thighs. Reaching her hands between his thighs, both pairs of her fingertips lightly encasing and massaging his testicles. The connection is electric, as he moans in pleasured response. His body stretches out completely on top of hers. Only his forearms and hands are touching the bed where they cradle her head to his. Their mouths fuse in a rapturous synchronization of the same movements intermeshing between their thighs. Perspiration, alchemized in the crucible of their mutual lovemaking, drenching the skin between their bodies. It makes the movements ecstatic as their bellies and breasts move in undulating deliciousness against each other. Swimming through sensation; beyond the senses of their mind, they've totally become the experience of the moment.

It's a balancing act. Need and desire have lost their relevance. Experimentally beyond the necessary, the excess in which they're indulging somehow seems an appropriate precedent-breaker. "Please baby, I want you to come!," she pleads with honest-to-God sincerity. He raises up on his arms; their bodies gyrating like uninterruptible recycling dynamos. Their eyes are locked together. "No sweetheart," he commands, "you come!".

She does; and though he retained his sperm, his consciousness flew with hers. 'Til in satiated wonderment, they mutually surrendered as equals to sleep's nurturing womb.

This being the least they'd ever accept—so much to explore and experiment with—they make ready for Life's next teachings of human love.

Recreational Ecstasy

Heaven is not where you have the least sex.
Heaven is where you have the best sex!

$\mathcal{B}$ut while we're here—anchored to and operating from our earthian womb of material manifestation—we want to be able to experience the best sexual feedback available through our corporeal forms. We are going to examine how different environmental circumstances and sociocultural attitudes have coincided throughout the ages to produce quality approaches to sex. Mostly, we want to discern what is appropriate for enhancing our sexual enjoyment today.

> Sexuality is basic to our nature.
> But making love is a highly refined art.
> I'm going to make an artist out of each of you.
> You will learn how to make your love life into an erotic masterpiece.
> And that's just for openers.

Those situations, substances and / or techniques which can arouse sexual desire and further accentuate your love life are *aphrodisiacs*. There are four true aphrodisiacs which we're going to examine in this chapter. They are: (1) Intelligence; (2) Health; (3) Variety; and (4) Belief.

1. Intelligence

Intelligence is the ability to ascertain/obtain what is optimally beneficial to you in any given situation. There are those sensations and feelings available to you through sexual experience which can be uprightly satisfying. Besides being its own reward, satisfaction can pave the way to expanded insight, thereby leading you to even more fulfilling levels of satisfaction.

Now that we've cleared out all the vagina / penis teasing, market merchandising ballyhoo which has distorted the public from satisfying sex for almost too long...Now that we know what we want; how do we go about making it an attainable reality?

By now you must have come to realize that pretty looks, pedigreed underarms, witty conversation, and commando-computerized bed systems for educated consumers are not the answer. They can be an embellishment—as can almost anything. But without access to controlling the sexual functions of your own nervous system, they barely do you any good.

> *When you're hot,*
> *you can do miracles on a shoestring!*
> *When you're not,*
> *the whole power of the church-world won't do it*
> *for you.*

Unfortunately, most people have either been taught to drench their inner heat into dampened insipidness, or to inundate it with ineffectual insignificance. The power of the Life Force moves through you; even as you move your consciousness through it. When it is focussed, there is heat; biologically driven hypno-genital reproductive body heat. This heat may manifest as fiery passions of almost unassuageable longing to immerse yourself in the complimentary fulfillment of relationships; the worshipful brilliance of ideas to create vehicles of greatness which connect you to the mind of humanity; the transcendent illumination which burns away the shadows of a world-weary mind, redirecting your feelings to an inner reality. Fire...!: The Christed game of Promethean compassion. Particle-wave, fusion-fission; yin-yang lovers in eternal dalliance through form and function, into complete self-awareness. This motionless pursuit of motion...the slippery friction of genitals deliriously intoxicated with sensation...this fire, the vibratory flame of compassion "moltening" up through inert matter, into animated flesh, consummated by spirit.

Fire: What do you do with the need for self-fulfillment burning through you? Many have been taught to fight their fire. They nobilize their self-denial by consigning the divine spark to some two-bit pit in the shadow room of their superstition. So they try to drown the fire with cheapened secondhand emotions. Some try to fight fire with fire. They fixate on a mixed compromise of transcendent techniques and self-righteous justification, 'til the energy of their awareness is stampeded into an impotent blaze of senseless glory.

Don't fight fire...! Transmute it into the vibrational ether of the mind. Then reformulate it and apply it as it best suits your purpose (Prime Directive). From such a perspective, this *Life Game—the male and the female connected through the Earth, reaching for each other through Time and Space*—becomes more interesting. You've come a long way, babies, from being whirlpooled through incomprehensible forces of Nature to within reach of re-stylizing the motions of Nature, itself.

Talk about power (energy given conscious direction), the girls are just crazy for it. And the boys being equally crazy for the girls, will do almost anything to obtain some of this impressive stuff. But blinding Ignorance, my dear friends, is the Death Game. The cost is too high; Ignorance is never satisfying and it subverts your fire into a meaningless pseudo passion—like: "I must be getting close 'cause I feel so uptight and anxious inside."

God, what reflexes you explicate through us; omnidirectional conscious rebalancing of almost unlimited choices (there are always limits). It makes you realize that Pac Man and the hydrogen bomb are just social excuses for psychological nose pickers.

Alright, so you're convinced: You can't do more for anybody else (humanity, the world, God...) than you can do for yourself. How to do it for yourself. In consideration of maturing and harnessing—at will—the incredible reserves of energy which can be leveraged through your sexuality, what will help you achieve the state of mind you want?

Intelligence: What to do; for how long; to what degree; in what combination; and any other considerations relevant to you optimizing an experience. Should I unleash "the animal"? Should I "talk dirty"? Should I utilize the teachings of various erotic systems of approach?

I will answer the above questions enough to give you an idea about what's involved. These are but a few of the many considerations we could enumerate upon in far greater depth. This should give you a basis for understanding and further exploration of the turn-on, aphrodisiacal properties of intelligence.

The *animal*; in its dark unreasonable persona of destructive passion, scapegoatedly referred to as the *beast*. Left to its own devices, this beast will drag you into the slavish pit of your baser instincts. There it will lord it over you, deceiving you with lies of your own self-importance; binding you into binding yourself in chains of desire. Deadlocked within a perspective too narrow to encompass your evolutionary potential, the divine spark will diminish in you. Consequently, you will suffer in a lightless heat that burns you with the unassuageable loneliness of being cut off from the fulfillment of your own potential.

The animal; the limbic system feeling responses of the midbrain. Here, responses to pleasure or pain commandeer the intellect into etching emotional patterns which satisfy biological necessities and their subsidiary wanton urges. As when these patterns come to dominance in an ineffectually disciplined person, savagery and bloodlust may wreak havoc on the unsuspecting.

Afraid of our own power-potential, we've been waging war on our own desires. Now, that's not very intelligent. People suppress, repress, and deny their animalistic nature behind elaborate and complex sociocultural rituals of commerce. They bargain for proximity, and then race intoxicants and supposedly taboo images through their psyche in a desperate attempt to savor the pleasures of their own vitality.

Poor little animal; maligned little beast. You know folks, your body (and its functionally component attributes) is the first thing you're given when you enter this world; and it's the last thing you'll leave behind. It can be your temple (where your living, pleasure-loving spirit dwells) and your vehicle, taking your consciousness where it wants to go. Or it can be your prison, cutting you off and stifling your contact with the living process.

I suppose it can be pretty frightening to be afraid of something that's already frightened of you. Animals in the wild are instinctive. They respond to the rhythms created in them by nature. Their lives are relatively simple. Their passions, even destructive rampages, are not unethical. They don't have a broad range of choices because the limited development of their nervous systems narrow their reactive patterns to bio-survival contingencies. As humans, we do have choices—freer will than the animal. Still the animal remains at one with our other more developed aspects of human consciousness. And what have we done to our animal nature? To compensate for its own inadequacies our self-imaging egos have scapegoated our animal into an excuse for just about every screw up known!

That's not very intelligent. As it has been said: *A house divided (against itself) cannot stand*. When you can freely access the physical consciousness of your nervous system at will, that denotes intelligence. When you can do so, you're less likely to go around trying to act sexy in order to convince yourself that you are. You know exactly how to bring out the animal part of your nature. You learn to harness that beast and make it work for you. This, the beast will gladly do, because you take the pressure of decision-making away from it. The beast really doesn't know how to cope with decisions and responsibilities that transcend biological needs in a natural environment. But it does know how to party and have a good time.

Growl a little; purr...groan, moan with pleasure. Stretch

your body, feel the taut supple energy bristle across the muscles along your spine. Lick, scratch, rub, taste, sniff—abandon yourself to sensation. By all means, when you've mastered yourself (gained functional understanding) you will be master of the animal. Then turn that libidinally toothsome id loose and teach it to perform tricks. Feel the warmth spreading through your loins...the electrical sensitizing of epidermal cells in fleshy sensual relay. Dig your fingers in; let your nails make contact. Nails that can rip flesh apart, kept on the exciting, pleasure side of that borderline of contact. Let your teeth sink into the skin. Teeth that could rend flesh from the bone, kept within non-piercing proximity, declaring by their proud curtailment of a far more satisfying use.

Harness that beast to your art of making love. Teach it to fetch for you. It will become an energy-strata vehicle through which feelings will be telepathically communed. The animal will be thrilled to be put to service. It's wild unbroken nature utilized to the maximum...utilized in response to your higher demands, far beyond anything it could have responded to on a mere biologically induced level. As a working part of your relationship, these incredible feelings which channel through the animal will nourish its physical nature. New levels of vitality will make its skin healthier and its eyes lustily glisten. The animal will be ennobled. The beast will become a noble, regal countenance—a suitable vehicle for the true state of human consciousness—when it is cared for and inspired by your love of beauty (the centered harmonization of your awareness with your circumstances).

Talking dirty...?: Unclean, soiled, foul, besmirched; demeaning and debasing the value of your sexuality—is that intelligent? If so it must contribute to optimizing the experience of making love.

"I want to suck on your tits, 'til your nipples are swollen and hard. Then I'll eat your pussy 'til it's so hot you're moaning with pleasure. And after I've swallowed up all your steaming love juices, you're going to suck my cock until it's so swollen and throbbing it wants to explode. Then I'm going to shove my hot hard cock deep up inside your luscious wet cunt, and fuck you 'til you're out of your mind with pleasure. Do you want that baby? Yeah? Then say it. Tell me what you want me to do to you."

Alright boys and girls, why is this erotic, impassioned cryptic declaration of intended pleasure usually considered talking dirty? Animals play in the dirt. Animals suck, fuck, lick, sniff and taste each other with wild sensual abandon. You can't really enjoy sex without the animal. There's no heated bio-conductive, recycled transport without the animal. But you've been taught the animal is degrading to your spirit. It will distort your judgement; you'll lose your ability to reason. You'll lose control and the divine spark of humanity will be cut off from you. *Listen kids: It's about time you realized that you can't offend God with your genitals!*

If the only way you can maintain control is by following some avoidance ritual of self-denial calculated to frustrate and debilitate your basic (God-given) nature, then you never had control in the first place. Well, out of ignorance, as a collective society you weren't supposed to have individual control. You were supposed to be frustrated so you'd be malleable. Remember: All those things that would put you into the driver's seat of your own soul, you were pervertedly conditioned to feel were demeaning to you. But mumsy and dada, that's where the fun is. Where? Down in the dirt where you implant with your nature, then grow towards the sunlight of your spirit. So when you get tired of suffering (supposed goodness by self-denial and deprivation) and you want to enjoy yourself (supposed badness by self-interested amplification of awareness through pleasure), you got to let go of your tin-god dogma, and take a ride on your nitty-gritty animal sensations. Funny how you get to feel so good while doing it, and so lousy when you try to figure it out.

Of course, not understanding the nervous system, most people are mystified about almost everything. They need a ritual to get them into an attitude conducive to what they want to experience. So they leave the clean stranger behind, get down, and grovel with the dirty familiar. They grab for taboos, and voila, they feel sexual.

For the sake of colloquial nostalgia, you might still want to call it *talking dirty*. But instead of rebelling against convention in defiance of your toilet training, try rerouting your erotic nomenclature through different perspectives. For instance, when you say: "I'm going to fuck your hot cunt with my cock." Or: "I'm going to fuck your hot cock with my cunt." Or, whatever...Don't just say it with shocking defiance, like you're sharing a sneaky conspiracy. Start to be aware of what you're communicating. Urge each other with subtle nuances of greater intensity.

Take simple phrases like "I love you" and "fuck you." Think about what they could mean. Say them out loud. Start to look at how many variances of meaning you can give both phrases by the way in which you say them. Now make them interchangeable so you can convey the same feeling and intention with either phrase. Take the sexual parts of the human anatomy and convey their most lewd,, sexual images with very "proper", even scientific words. Then use what is normally referred to as "dirty talk" and say it to describe the body as if you were an elegant poet praising divinity through lovemaking as a worshipful act.

Words are symbols...often with associative emotional charges of feeling. As I said earlier: You want to be able to access at will, combine and recombine to whatever degree you want, any or all of the attributes of your nervous system. Words operate from the third, or intellectual level of conceptual consciousness. Used intelligently, they can leverage your sexual energy into a high-voltage launching pad of ecstatic bliss.

Intelligence says you do whatever enables you to gain that which is most beneficial to the optimally expanding fulfillment of your wholeness. And there have been some rather intelligent approaches to sexuality during various cultural peaks throughout history. The problem has been, as with all approaches to human fulfillment up 'til now, that these approaches usually had a sociocultural bureaucracy built up around them. So that only if you wanted to subject yourself to the corresponding life-style could you gain access to the benefits of these approaches.

Obviously this isn't in keeping with the intelligence of our present development. Our current view of physicality has become quantum. Obviously, our psychosexual outlook and "in-feel" must follow suit. We want quantum sex. But as I said, before harnessing the abstracts, you must first master the classics. Intelligently, we want to be able to incorporate the beneficial aspects of such highly viable erotic approaches as are found in Tao, Tantra, and Magic, without all the related bureaucratic structuring that would lock us inappropriately into an outmoded life-style.

It is fun to plug into the techniques of these or any other integral systems through which we functionally process consciousness. The easiest, most efficient and safest way to go about this is to already have access to the state of mind which these systems can open to you. Then you can experience these techniques as an adjunctive means to varying your own awareness. Let me illustrate this for you as regards to sexuality.

Most people have never learned how to manipulate their own sexual energy. The repercussions of which have gone a long way toward creating sickness in the body, distorted emotions, and aberrated states of mind. When we talk about a person being psychic, we are simply referring to one whose perceptions and activities operate more from the fields of the mind. This is neither in opposition nor in contradiction to Nature, where the biological processes influence the rate of perception; rather it is just another realm extending beyond the bio-survival considerations of animated life forms. A person having sex in a deliberate conscious way, say to achieve an altered state of consciousness would be a psychic process.

Being psychic can be as basic as doing simple arithmetic or learning to speak a language. In both cases the fields of psychic activity start to overlay and leverage the natural. However, when we say someone is "psychic," most people associate such a person as being sensitive to the natural forces of the world which they may be able to manipulate through a projection of their mental will. Now, there have always been people who could do such things. Actually, these paranormal attributes are in the process of becoming something quite common.

In the past, reaching psychic states have been achieved through a variety of methods and / or substances. And the above mentioned systems were very aware of how sex could be used to deliberately channel energy and consciousness. It is not my intention to explain these systems in depth in this book. Deeper sexual methodology will be covered in the second volume of my treatment of the erotic arts. Rather, I want to bring these systems into modern context so you can safely enjoy exploring them.

Why safely? The taboos which exist around sexual considerations had to do with more than a profit-guarding morality of the ruling elite. The level of consciousness being sought could neither flow through a body muscularly armored with tension, nor could it function in a personality matrix distorted into a caricature of its own avoidance patterns. But the techniques used were powerful. Once previously dammed up sexual energy was released, all blocks and distortions were forced to surface in the aspirant's mind. If not carefully monitored and transformed, these energies could ravage both the mind and the body. No matter what the orientation, methodology, techniques and substances employed, they all invoked an approach to order, structured around some greater, more encompassing, supra natural level of awareness.

In Tao, the force was Nature, itself, and the Spirit which creatively animated it. The methodology employed was that of *harmonization*. In Tantra, the force was archetypal images of mythologically idealized personae. By *identification* with these personae one gained access to the same qualities they represented. Thereby one was able to *transcend* and gain control over the phenomenal limitations of apparent material manifestation. In Magic the aim was channelling the forces of Nature by discovering how they worked. Not how they worked in the modern scientific sense; which also sought to channel the forces of Nature. Rather, the ego-matrix of the developing rational mind became the overlaid graph by which phenomena was mentally categorized. Symbols and ritualistic gestures were used to guide and fixate concentration. Actually, anything which could strengthen the mental focus of an ego-objective was eclectically converted into a magic prop. As such, the forces of Nature were but supra normal extensions of the qualities of the person perceiving them. To understand how Nature works, the seeming strengths and weakness of your own self-image must be understood. Then you can eliminate activities which induce weakness; while disciplining your actions to strengthen certain attributes. I deal with psychic aptitude and application in my books on consciousness.

Harmonization, Identification, Transcendence, and Channelling: Remove the formal sociocultural bureaucracy from these concepts and you have some incredible fields of activity through which you can amplify your sex life. Let's consider one illustration among many possible variations on the theme:

You're centered and are thereby extremely conscious within the moment. That moment is prescribed by the unique interblend of forces into which you're immersed. Your own self-consciousness makes these forces more than just natural. The fields of mental activity which have combined to shape your inclinations are orienting your awareness into all the possibilities optional to you. The *human gift* of choice (free will) operates through the *ego* (self-image) as it works to leverage energies into relatable form and appropriate function. If those energies are experienced as discordant and painful, then your choices are inadequate. One of the astounding things about life is that you're always living it. That is, unless you're lost in your thought process; with your awareness cut off from the flow.

So we have a man and a woman—two individual perspectives processing the same spatial potentials—who feel an attraction. There is pleasure. Part of it is biochemical. But the corresponding factors in this attraction operate far beyond mere biological urges. As such, many of the reasons for your mutual attraction are psychic. It is your choice as to whether you both want to pursue the potential rewards of this attraction. And if so, it is your choice as to how you will go about doing this.

For the moment (whatever duration of time that may turn out to encompass), you both acknowledge and decide to pursue the attraction. Economics and related social amenities is not a concern. What's important is how much your coming together (this part of your lives) can enrich your consciousness, increase your health, satisfy your needs, and fulfill your potential.

We're working past convention. We'll say you're both competent lovers more than willing to explore. You start off making love. You want to *harmonize* your sexual energies into a mutual recycling flow; so they can build and open you up to even higher realms. You're arranging your responses to each other not just as they feel pleasurable. Rather, you're noting what is giving you pleasure and consciously pulling back to discuss and vary your responses. Like breathing in and out, you're revealing yourselves to each other through juxtaposing positions of sending and receiving. By aligning your movements not only to each other, but also to all the impinging feelings the moment is positioning you to perceive, no other moment will be exactly like this ever again. The harmony your experiencing is the conscious wholeness of this moment processing through the both of you. You two, as focal polarities of energy, conduit the moment into a flow-through of relatedness. So that every touch, look, embrace, gesture, and word that passes between you is also the experience of you being processed in relation to the moment. The more you harmonize awareness through each other, then the more you will gain through access of the moment. So that all the potential energy formations which will become spatially manifest in this extended (gestalted) realm of your consciousness become yours to play with.

Don't try to intellectually nail it down. I'm leading you there.

Harmonization is a balancing process around a center. Male and female energies intermesh to form a new and more encompassing depolarized center. This can only take place between consciously willing participation of both partners. Additionally, it can be extended, in various proportions, beyond the initial male-female blend. You may experience many variations, realizations, pleasurable diversions and extensions of your basic center by sexually experimental play with members of the same sex. But you cannot extend the range of your center of consciousness into a new gestalted level of higher psychic fields through sexuality unless this basic male-female dipole is created. Of course, there are ways to achieve higher states of consciousness either singularly or en masse. But they are through esoteric processes other than human sexuality.

Once you've achieved harmonization around an interblended center, where do you want to direct your consciousness? You can now access any frequency within the wholeness of your expanded awareness by varying the tempo of your interaction. And when ready, you can access dimensions of spatially energized relations into the greater wholeness of which your awareness is but an aspect. This is done through *identification*. You can identify with your biology; with sociocultural rituals and patterns (accepted and / or outlaw); with objectified processes of scientifically experimental exploration; with religiously sanctified relationships; psychologically colored deifications of archetypal images; or just about anything else you're capable of imagining.

Whatever form with which you identify must carry a certain range of potential itself. This is its function. The form of two mesmerized horny people certainly connotes a different functional range of experience than, say, identifying with two silver screen sex symbols in a sophisticated romance. Of course you want to be careful as to that with which you identify; and there the geigering discussed in the previous chapter will be of inestimable service.

Understand, this is not psychological masturbation in the form of "wouldn't it be nice" fantasizing. Rather, you're centered. As from this center you become aware of far more than is usually accessible to you, and to some things which you could not normally access on your own. This is an accelerated high-energy state. Were you to identify with sickness and evil from this perspective, you could do yourself some serious harm. However, to attain a state by way of the orientation I'm offering you, should preclude such negative possibilities.

What you ultimately identify with is the essence of maleness and femaleness. You could do this as mythological deities; as Judeo-Christian gnostic logo points; as sci-fi postulated Homo superior species of humanity in the future; or any variance you wish. When you actually do this—not just intellectually speculate upon it—you enter into a realm transcending the normal fields to which biology and sociocultural conditioning usually conscript your energies. Depending on how much you've actualized your individual potential for evolutionary development, will determine the privileges you access and the responsibilities you must accept.

Transcendence allows you to encompass a far greater perspective of the territory on which your awareness is anchored. You *harmonize* with your own and each other's energies. This brings you to where you can access more of the energies around you. And with the right *identification* you can process those energies in such a way that you see things through more than normal eyes. This lets you *transcend* the mundane patterns which seem to lock you into repetition, boredom and frustration. Now what are you going to do with what you're discovering?

Making love is a highly evolved art. In art some people find a viable doorway through which to glimpse realities beyond the mundane. Some have found ways in which to live at the rate of vibration implied by those more encompassing perspectives. Those who have, utilize their art to channel their perspective through some medium into a viable commodity. *Channelling* involves taking your insights gained from experience and transposing them into the reality of your living situation.

You both *harmonize* while making love. The energy, along with heightened sensations and pleasure, becomes electric within, between, around, and through you. You identify through each other the highest qualities you desire to experience. The space around you flows into your *identification*. Energies, looks, and feelings become appropriately transmuted in both of you. Your bodily sensations are synchronized in a trajectory which turns you into a gestalted recycling dynamo; your consciousness becomes free to *transcend* the limitations with which you were normally conditioned to identify yourself. From such a perspective you can *channel* these newly experienced energies into form and functions which will further enrich your life...which will allow you to expand still farther.

I could write volumes detailing the multitude of ways this process could be utilized. And there are many other processes in addition to this one. Quite different from just fucking to relieve biophysical and *psychomotional* (indicating, any and all levels, the fluctuating total range of interactive motion which the workings of the psyche are able to process in any individual) tension. You can strip your gears and rewire them any way you wish. Quite a turn-on! Intelligence...without it, you're just a dumb animal unaware of your spiritual potential. Whereas the right word, look, or gesture can make or break your loving.

2. Health

There are many ways your intelligence can be used to enhance your sexuality. Yet no matter how you approach sex, one of the prime considerations will always be the quality of your health.

There is certainly a place for romance, beautiful surroundings, and even substances which may alter your perceptions. But too often, such adjuncts are used to obscure your real anxieties about not knowing how to open up your sexuality and relate with it.

First of all you have to *get ready for love.* Your body is the instrument through which you transmit your feelings. You may be the most passionate person in the world with a genuine capacity for sexual fulfillment. But like any current you're trying to transmit, if the conductive filaments are deficient, they won't be able to carry the charge. Sexually, your body is the conductive medium of your consciousness.

I'm going to give you a beautiful image with which to work. Say to yourself: "I want to luxuriate in my physicality!" Unfortunately, most people aren't very familiar with their bodies. They operate mainly from their mental outlook. Their bodies are like a garment that they slip into and out of according to circumstantial needs. In the process of which some do or don't keep them clean, pressed, shaped and fashionably stylized.

I want to luxuriate in my physicality. But that's hard to

do if you're stiff and tense with sore, aching, knotted muscles. Energy doesn't come easy when a body is nutritionally deficient. It's a chore to be sensitively receptive in a body stewing in the juices of its own toxic congestion. And if you're uncomfortable within your own body, how can you be sensitive to the exquisite potentials in another person's body?

Let's start to move your consciousness into control of your body. First of all, there is the efficiently healthful operation of the metabolic process, itself. The body, as a biochemical machine, converts fuel into energy, which it uses to power its activities. And as such, it gives off waste which must be eliminated from the system. When these two main processes (digestion and elimination) are operating efficiently, you have the beginnings of health. That's right; just as the absence of pain is not pleasure, neither is the absence of debilitating symptoms optimal health.

Once your body is digesting, assimilating and eliminating with unencumbered efficiency the next prime consideration is adequate nutrition to supply its demands. Just as when you put the wrong type of gas or oil in a car engine, it will become sludgy and reduce or halt performance capability, so too, our bodies can be reduced to subhealth performance by improper and inadequate nutrition.

Sadly—in one of the most horrid rip-offs ever perpetrated against the consuming public—most people have been misled into existing in metabolic states far below what is actually accessible to them. Understand, there are two basic ways you diminish the genetically programmed, self-repairing apparatus of your metabolism: The first is to not get enough of the right quality of nutrients into your system for it to adequately perform. The second is to get substances into the body which it can't handle and eliminate, which rot and toxify your system.

When your body is inadequately supplied with appropriate nutrients, it borrows from its reserves. As this condition continues, depending on the demands for energy placed on it by various activities (e.g., exercise, mental concentration, emotionalism, creativity, sex, etc.) it will strip energy and nutrients from one aspect of its functioning to supply what is being demanded for output performance. This imbalances the body. To compensate, most people usually wind up substituting their willpower to do what their bodies normally should be doing for them. In turn this rips off mental energy which could be more profitably used for creativity, recreation, and calmness of mind. Many people think they have a problem with having too much energy. Rather, they have too little energy; and to compensate, they've mentally revved themselves up so tight that they can't unwind. When you have an abundance of energy, it is just as easy to cool out and relax as it is to accelerate into high gear. A lack of adequate energy makes life far more difficult than it needs to be. It is one of the main factors contributing to an excess of emotional instability currently plaguing the public.

When your body is imbalanced, it does not digest, assimilate or eliminate well. It's not what you put in your mouth and swallow—it's what you can break down and assimilate that determines how well you're "nutritionalized." Inadequate digestion not only means poor nutrition, it can also mean impaired elimination. Some things are hard for the body to handle. For instance, if you want a binding paste which can be used in making papier-mache, just mix some white flour and water together; which is like most of the denatured products that we've grown up eating. Or take natural oils which should be lubricating to our systems; extract them at high heats with chemical solvents and they become binding to our system. Unfortunately, the list goes on and on; as does the list of highly processed, chemically adulterated foods our bodies aren't designed to handle. When you add to this the combining of more kinds of food at one time than the enzymatic process can adequately respond to, plus food poorly chewed from eating in a hurry, and under tension, you see our beautiful bodies being inwardly polluted.

This pollution is mucus-forming and creates a breeding ground for unfriendly bacteria to attack our systems. Toxins which stay in our bodies interfere with normal metabolic processes. Our cells are constantly replicating themselves. If they are forced to do so in a toxic environment, it can often lead to abnormality of the new cellular tissue, rendering it less capable of adequately performing. Our bodies must eliminate toxins. It is a basic biological law that no system can survive in an environment of its own waste. Undigested waste is designed to be eliminated through our colons (large intestine). If you weren't having bowel movements, you'd be dead. But distorted as most metabolisms have become, very few have adequate elimination. Excess toxins and waste become hardened fecal matter which may wind up accumulating in the bowels for decades. Then the internal organs of elimination (liver, kidney, spleen) can become overtaxed trying to handle this recycling toxicity. Which in turn throws off your endocrine system. All of this, if allowed to persist, will create debilitation in our bodies. Depending on how these factors combine, along with the kinds of stress to which you're subjected, and your mental orientation...all of these factors can bring about breakdown and its apparent symptomatology which has been medically classified as disease.

The above is a nutshell summary of what I enumerate upon in far greater depth in my book on health. An undernourished, toxic body is not very palatable to the consciousness which must dwell therein. Its odors become excessively strong...often offensive. Internal putrefaction sours the breath and bitters the taste of sexual emissions. The body often retains excess fluid. Brain function and related neurology is impaired. Emotions become exaggerated. Muscles and joints stiff and swollen; the body increasingly inflexible. Putrefaction lines the gastrointestinal tract with gas—you can't belch and fart your way to ecstasy! The skin loses its luster and becomes dry and scaly. How unappetizing—is this what you want to offer your lover(s)? Is this the altar upon which you commune with your spirit?

Now let's talk about *luxuriating in your physicality*. You want to be comfortable within your body. At the least, that requires a system relatively toxic-free, hormonally balanced; with adequate nutrition and good elimination of wastes. It also means your skeletal-muscular system must be kept flexible and toned.

Alright, let's say you've begun to actualize your birthright—health. You're feeling light, flexible, full of vitality, clearheaded and calm. How can you amplify this to increase your sexual enjoyment?

First of all, health is an aphrodisiac because high sexual capacity is an inherent part of being healthy. Most of the substances people ingest—from intoxicants, old home remedies, special foods, vitamins, whatever—are meant to gently coax or dominantly command your metabolic system to current into a place where you feel sexually stimulated and responsive. Whatever changes you make in your physicality simultaneously produce corresponding changes in your feelings...and vice versa. Sometimes ingested substances work directly on the mental-emotional fields, temporarily breaking fixations so that the body's physiology once again feels responsive.

Human physiologies may be poured from the same mold. But their functionality is idiosyncratically particular to inherited genetic dispositions, environmental circumstance, upbringing, mental activity, diet, and performance demands of individual inclinations. Let's say you've recognized what's optimal for your body type to adequately perform according to your daily needs. And you've decided that one of the arts you'd like to successfully cultivate in your life is sexual lovemaking.

As far as your food consumption goes, you want high-energy, easily digestible foods. It is highly inadvisable to try and make love on a full stomach. When you attempt to digest a full meal and have sex, neither function will be performed very well by your metabolism. Also, sex performed on a full belly will keep your sexual energy locked into your physiology, unable to transmute and nourish its other aspects. In turn, this can place undue stress on many of your internal organs. This is not to say you can't eat. But eating should be light, delicate, tidbit morsels; pleasing to the palate and easy to consume.

Juices (especially fresh) and pure water are excellent to drink. Fruits or delicate pastries go down well. Caviar, small amounts of pate, vegetables and dips; cheeses, morsels of seafood, chicken salad, or the like may prove suitable. But don't over combine. Narrow your choices. You must become sensitive to what your body needs at any given time. Don't eat out of habit or from mental fixation. What will best energize you and how much will satisfy without impairing the flow of your sexual energy will continue to vary. If you're really hungry, then eat a meal and relax for a while. But if you sexually want to trip the light fantastic, then I suggest you have mainly fluids, and only eat tidbits, if really hungry in the period before and during lovemaking.

Now there are a number of safe, legal substances which can enhance your bodily health into a higher and subsequently more sexual capability of performance. If you are not very knowledgeable, I suggest you seek out the competent help of a health professional who can explain to you in full detail exactly what they are; how they work; why, for how long, and in what combination these substances would be safely advantageous for you. If they arrogantly pooh-pooh nutrition, attempting to make you feel small for asking, then you're obviously dealing with an educated ignoramus. If they have volumes of wonderful things to tell you, but do not, themselves, appear to be practicing beneficiaries of what they expound upon, they are incompetent to guide you. You will find capable teachers and healers along with blustering charlatans in every health care system. It is not the system (no matter how socially sanctioned or verbally discredited it may be by a currently entrenched bureaucracy); rather, it is the quality of the person who utilizes the techniques of the system which determines competency. Like making love, health is an art. It is not a science; it is far more than a relatively reliable system of measurement and classification. When you are healthy, everything is enjoyable (even the struggles). Without health, even the most bountiful and elaborate is a lackluster effort.

As far as vitamin supplements go, what is most beneficial for you to consume depends on your degree of metabolic balance and the expenditure of energy required by your activities. If you are cleansing and rebuilding an imbalanced system, it will be different from maintaining or expanding on the capabilities of an already healthy system. And even though various manufacturers may distribute products which are labelled with identical ingredients, the quality of these ingredients, how they're handled, processed and combined, and (believe it or not) the state of mind and intention of the manufacturers will all go into determining how well your metabolism can utilize these products.

Beyond basically excellent health there are intelligent ways of safely amplifying the performance capabilities of your sexual system. The adrenal glands are involved in energy building and the production of numerous hormones, including sexual hormones. Pantothenic acid and Vitamin C are two vitamins extensively used by the adrenal glands. The adrenal glands work in a relay reflex between the *pituitary* and *hypothalamus*. The pituitary is the master bodily gland regulating endocrine functions throughout the entire metabolism, including the release of sexual hormones. The hypothalamus mediates between the intentions of complex thought processes and the pituitary's ability to put them into application. As such, the hypothalamus is thought to mediate stress and its subsequent reactions in the body (e.g., appetite control; sexual desire). As you progress into more inclusive states of self-actualization, the pineal gland—which recodifies metabolic activities according to individual ability to receive light emissions (not just visually visible)—starts to redirect sexual functioning.

There are tissue supplements—quality in material and method of processing is essential—which can strengthen all of these glands. This includes the testicles and prostate in the male; as well as the ovaries and uterus in the female. Of course, there are related vitamins and minerals which must be utilized concurrently, according to individual needs. For instance: Do you remember how they used to tell little boys, if they masturbated they'd go blind? Well, moralistic hokum aside, there is an associative degree of reality in that statement. Every time a male ejaculates, he uses up a little over two milligrams of zinc. Zinc is a mineral; one of its more important functions is to enable the eyes to visually focus and perceive images. Though I'm sure it would be rare, on a zinc-deficient diet with an excess of neurotic ejaculation, a young man could conceivably so deplete his body of zinc, it might impair his vision. Of course, other factors would enter into it, but this is just another way of reminding you that your body's machinery must be kept supplied with adequate nutrition to compensate for its expenditures.

There are herbs known to stimulate sexual health...ginseng being the most infamous. It is an over-all glandular toner. If the whole glandular system is performing at peak, the sexual glands (being part of that system) will obviously be enhanced. But there are different kinds of ginseng. Even more, there are different needs. The same needs in different people may require different approaches and supplemental factors to correct them; while seemingly unrelated physical conditions may both respond to the same treatment.

Herbs are used to enhance metabolic activity. They are a study in and of themselves. Then there is homeopathy, which reduces substances to their vibratory sphere in order to create health-giving resonating frequencies in the body to which the physical metabolism can respond.

Increasingly there are high-powered extracts from high-energy nutritive sources (e.g., algae products) coming onto the market. And now that we're starting to become fairly proficient in analyzing neurotransmitters (which are the metabolic cuing signal factors of all enzyme, hormone, and nerve activity), we're starting to discern which amino acids, in what combinations, can stimulate what activities. Amino acids require no real digestion and used properly can greatly enhance your metabolic vitality. But then again, to be effective they must be taken in the right combination of vitamins and minerals.

The right combination? Eggs are a complete protein. If not overcooked, they can be a real sexual-energy food. That is, if you digest them well and they're what your body needs. Non-polluted seafood is usually high in many qualities nurturing to the sexual system. Raw nuts, especially almonds, provide protein and essential oils. The list is as long as there are good, wholesome, natural foods eaten in combination and proportion to what will optimize you.

Are you confused? Were you looking for the magic substance—the grand panacea? There ain't none; there's only health and extended superlatives! Health is an art. The application of all these factors should be reasonably precise. While at the same time you should realize the body and its needs must be continuously reassessed and readapted. Although there will never be a time when your body won't need maintenance, once you achieve metabolic balance, it is fairly easy to maintain.

Now look at the bright side. With a few briefly smothered historical exceptions, for the most part, people have been, at best, oriented to staying away from or curing disease. That is to health what getting away from pain is to pleasure. But now we finally have the ability to think of health as something we move towards—nutrition, herbs, homeopathy, exercise, manipulative touch-techniques and their amplified application through advanced computerized future technology. Through the applied art of health, using the best science can offer, we can now safely accelerate the functioning of our metabolism.

You'll come to understand how the substances you do or don't take effect your vitality; mental concentration; clarity and focus (which will, of course, include your memory); your emotional stability; and your overall aptitude for pleasure. Which will mean you can increase your functioning capabilities as you truly desire (need). You see, too much energy in a system that has no need to expand it can be detrimentally overtaxing. An invaluable key to health lies in developing relaxation skills...to feel confident, or rather, confirmed in the comfortable dependency of your operating unit...to luxuriate in your physicality.

Control of your physiology—isn't that a turn-on! Increased vitality and a greater sense of ease through the years when you most need it, so that maturity ceases to be a crystallization into a caricature of how you thought you felt when you were young. Rather, it will become a chance to utilize that energy with greater personal insight...and so on. You know that's the real ball game of the future. Just realize the possibilities that could mean when applied to say, one area of your life, like sexuality.

Many people are becoming inclined to explore and integrate within the wholeness of their being, the potentials of their sexual nature. And I know that a simple, fairly explicit, how-to instruction book on health practices of diet, nutrition, herbs, homeopathy, cleansing, and building your sexual vitality would be very helpful. That is a large part of just such a book which I'm now preparing. And in addition to discussing how to balance and fire up your sexual vitality through your metabolism, it will also deal with exercising, breath control, beautification, and touch-techniques, for adding to your control of your own body and the ability to share / communicate with other persons through your sexuality.

You see, in order to become healthy, you have to understand how to take control of your body. Once you have gained control of that vitality, it is up to you as to how you'll use it. It is your choice. You will decide how to shape and use your body. Certainly those choices will vary.

The kind of body that would be optimal for a sword-wield-ing barbarian would certainly be inappropriate for a ballet dancer, or computer operator. The key word there being optimal.

What about for lovers? What type of body will serve you best? In this modern day, according to the demands and opportunities of our life-style—what does it mean to be *built for love*?

True health is always a question of balance; where you stay centered and in control of all your potential capabil-ities; not overly identified or fixated on any one aspect to the lopsided detriment of others. From this center you may choose at any time to accelerate and accentuate various aspects. For instance, in martial arts, you could use breath to hold and focus energy within you, bringing the body's skeletal-muscular-reflex system into a contracted, exces-sively hard, tight muscularly transcending state of unified action. Or you might choose to let your body's energies expand into their barely sustainable metabolic aspects; relax into seismographic, psychic receptivity, you become attuned to psychic energies from more than normal fields of activity—Meditation. For either of these extremes to be effective, a center of awareness must be discovered, and a flexible balance between this center and the require-ments of an everyday life-style must be obtained.

Today we have machines to do many of the dull, wea-risome, drudging activities that up 'til this century occu-pied most of our time. This is freeing us to concentrate more on the kinds of activities that give us pleasure and develop us. Looking good and feeling fit have become common pursuits for most people. What does that mean? When greater freedom emerges in any given area, we al-ways tend to go after—usually in excessive gobs—what we previously felt had been denied.

There is a healthful difference between *tone* and *tension*. Tension—which most people carry far too much of in their bodies—jams the natural flow. In our muscles this means impaired access of oxygen and nutrients to the tissues, and poor elimination of wastes. In turn, muscle tissue congests. It becomes swollen, stiff, sore, achy and brittle, as accumulated toxins wear down the cellular tissue strength. When active in such state, muscle fibers foreshorten, or irregularly elongate; which can interfere with nerve fiber transmission. Some people say no pain, no gain. That's not necessarily true. If managed properly, the body can be accelerated into high performance without the tense, painful congesting of muscles and undue stress on bones.

Now what are we trying to gain? As lovers we want light, flexible, strong, vital, very sensitive bodies. We want both a functionally efficient ease of movement and a high degree of sensitivity. Oversized, sore, knotted muscles are cumbersome when making love. There is a balance which must be struck. It can be best approached by conditioning your body into being toned enough to more than easily handle daily tasks.

Aerobics can be beneficially stimulating to your system. However, sexual ecstasy is by far an easier, more enjoyable way to stimulate those "make you feel wonderfully high" endorphins. Balance involves ease, relaxation, a flow-through around a center which can control the movement of energies. When in *balance* you're continually charged by the recycling of currents through which your consciousness interacts. There are cycles within cycles; each one having its own apparent center. One such center you can place your consciousness within is the balance between sexuality and health.

Undoubtedly, health contributes to your sexual satisfaction. Even so, high-amplitude sex can go a long way toward making you healthier. On the physical level there is movement of the body; extensive stretching and toning of muscles being flexed. All of which takes place in a positive mental attitude which is rewarding to the body. Blood and lymph circulation is stimulated. The endocrine and nervous systems synchronize through the physiology in an exhilarating focus of energy. And this healthful acceleration of the metabolism happens in a counterbalance of deep relaxation. Your feelings become sensitized to the sensations of the moment. Tension dissipates as your intellect stops imaging itself. With the highly charged resonance feedback between feelings and intellect, you gain greater access to supra human images which can guide your body into newer states of health.

Sexual healing can be uprightly stunning: drinking each other's saliva and sexual emissions; bathing in each other's dipolar energy fields; learning to nourish your vitality off each other's recycled energy flows is not a haphazard byproduct of sexual give-and-take. *It is a conscious, willful intention of give-and-give.* If such practices are not approached with specific purpose and knowledgeable understanding, then they will not have any great effect on healing and accelerating bodily vitality into longevity states.

And while we're talking about how to achieve more sexual pleasure through health, let's consider touch. There are nerve centers that connect to all the organs in your body located in your feet, hands, and ears. Your body is a complex of systems connected through a number of pathways. Even more so, it is a bio-cosmic resonator, usually far more aware of its surroundings than is your intellect. These inter-connective, bio-chemical, electric systems can be stimulated by various kinds of touch.

To learn how to release your lover's muscular tension...to know which nerve points will release and stimulate sexual energy...to know specific areas of exceptional sensitivity to tactile stimulation...to know a variety of ways to touch and combine the effects of these areas...and what substances (oils, herbs, etc.) can be applied to produce a diversified range of erotic sensations, all of which can enhance your pleasure.

Then there is touch extended through water. Water, the element said to correspond to our feelings, has the power to cleanse disruption in our emotional fields as well as our bodies. Hot bubbly water to soak in; where your sore achy tensions can be relieved. Playing geisha for each other, you can scrub each other with loofas, brushes, and cloths. Learn to surrender to each other's touch; to trust and be healed by it.

Powerful, youthful, agile, lithe, flexible, supple, sensitive body vehicles which you can wilfully control. Bodies coordinated to adapt and expand to the direction of quality energy you channel through your psyche. Inter-blended conduits of dipolar recycling energy in erotic synchromesh—*Health*. Health is an aphrodisiac; health is feeling wonderfully alive and connected; and that is a turn-on!

3. Variety

> *If I were a musician*
> *I'd play to every ear*
> *as if it were a desirous vagina...*
> *—said the magician as he approached*
> *the spiritual womb of each heart.*

You can never imagine how wonderful life can be. But you can (find out)—live it!

It's been said that variety is the spice of life. It would be more accurate to say variety is one of Life's main characteristics. Life is change; it varies from moment to moment / from perception to perception. Life's pulsating richness stimulates and vitalizes you whenever you're attuned to it. But Life can be a boring, repetitive letdown when you only deal with your ideas about it. So that instead of experiencing and being charged by the ongoing flow, you feel cut off from it. Trapped inside a sameness—which is simply an overlay of the perceptions that you've opinionated and projected like a tollgate of expectations to your awareness. How people long for something pleasantly unexpected which will make them pay attention to what's really happening.

For instance: You meet someone and find yourselves sexually attracted to each other. You both would like to nourish on the pleasure that your harmonized commingling could produce. You court each other, appreciate each other, sensitize to each other's cuing signals, cater to each other's whims—you pay attention. You're excited, aware and spontaneous as you adapt to each bit of feedback. So that even if the sex lacks the artistry and bliss wave action of fulfillment, it's still somewhat satisfying. However, maybe it's exceptional. Let's say you have the experience, passion and chemistry to crash into a found weekend of epicurean lovemaking. To whatever degree, there is a newness which excites and enables you to feel connected.

How come that diminishes for most people? Of course once you've tasted sexual pleasure, to whatever degree, barring psycho-aberrant toilet training, you will, of course, long for more and even better, if possible. Why does an act so thrilling, along with a lover so desirable, usually lose attraction for most people? Most people would say they've gotten too used to the other person, and they'd be correct. But what does that mean?

It means you've labelled and categorized your reaction rate to some stimulus; so that you no longer perceive said stimulus, only your preconceived notion of it. It means you've run out of ways to stimulate, repress or distract yourself away from how you've locked into normally perceiving that stimulus. So that lips which you once hungered to kiss no longer excite you. You've kissed those lips for all kinds of reasons, in many different ways, in a variety of situations. The repertoire, the sensual range that those lips can offer has been exhausted. So that every time you kiss those lips, the sensations and feelings they create are already familiar. Soon, by the pattern of cuing signals you've come to associate, you know what sensations will be elicit before you caress those lips. Now those lips hold little interest; because even when kissing them, all you can perceive is your past reactions.

So you either resign yourself to diminished returns; accepting that your days of rapturous lip-kissing are over. Or you start looking for lips attached to a person and / or situation whose potentials for interaction aren't already completely mapped out and filed away in your mental categories. If you feel constrained and obligated not to find newer more exciting stimulation, your sex life feels dull and bland; you become indifferent. If you pursue stimulation for its own sake, you eventually run out of new possibilities; you're jaded (so to speak); you become indifferent.

Now there are two basic ways to go with variety: One, you either keep changing the stimulus to keep it interesting. Or two, you learn how to operate from a level of consciousness where your preconceived projections don't overlay and cut you off from the vitality of every unique moment. Actually it is best to combine both of these perspectives.

With regard to changing the stimulus this can, but in no way has to imply changing sexual partners. (The nature and range of relationships will be covered in the last chapter.) But let's take a look at what is pretty much within the range of every lover:

Variety—*"Lover, it's always different! I never know what to expect. So I don't expect. Or if I do expect, it's nothing I can't easily let go of and change as the situation motivates me. But then again, I do kind of expect I'm going to enjoy myself as much as is humanly possible every chance I get."*

Variety; according to our *Prime Directive*, we have available for possible interactive combinations anything and everything that can affect our awareness. There are all the sensorial receivers and decoders of our physicality; along with every nuance and qualitative shading of the way we feel (respond) about what's going on within and around us; any kind of thought-imagery we're capable of structuring; along with all the paranormal, transcendent, psychic fields of more inclusive or symbolically dimensional activity we can channel. Then there are all the environmental circumstances in which we find ourselves—some seemingly dependably stable, yet all of them always in rearranging flux—each one carrying its own range of potential cuing factors to elicit responses from our nervous systems.

The whole ball of wax as you interpret your relation to it—your ego, which catalyzes the degree of your self-image that you're ready to let interact with others around you—your *personality*. In turn, psychically balancing between your awareness (conscious and unconscious) and the creative intelligence that is continuously animating through you—*God*. Obviously, the whole world is a stage. Did you ever consider for whom you're performing? "Lord, you see how grateful I am. I'm enjoying (revelling in) every resurrecting psychic-sexual sensation you've provided me the means to play / immerse my awareness within." Variety—nothing up my sleeves except the Universe!

You can simply respond to it (all) as you become aware of each moment. Or you may wilfully set yourself to perceive it through particular states of mind and systems of thought. All of which can be alternately recombined through numerous techniques. For instance, you can learn the actor's *inner monologue* ability to juxtapose into character types: If I were this and you were that (e.g., madman, nun, average, dedicated, naive, innocent, premeditated, sinner, socialite, folklore cliche, etc.), and the circumstances were so (e.g., tropical, laboratory, politico, religious, business, surreal, extraterrestrial, unexpected, status quo, etc.), I could cue into an already established range of personality responses. This, then, would enable me to emote reactive patterns which are normally beyond my range of direct personal experience. You can even attune to some deity, genetic evolution, futurism, or archetypal attributes as your capabilities match with your inclinations.

Variety; how do your surroundings impress themselves upon you? For instance, Nature certainly carries a different charge than a high tech computerized mind-designed environment. Do you allow each factor in your surroundings to operate different attitudes and sexual stimulations for you; or do you only respond to situations that cue you back into the original environment you were conditioned to associate with sexual activity?

Environment encompasses everything from your state of health to your external surroundings. Vary the combination or intensity of any of these factors and your sexual sensibilities will be altered to some degree. What stimulates your sensuality can often depend upon the stimulus to which your senses are exposed. Color and degrees of light illumination have direct effects on your senses. For example, bright yellow will stimulate mental activity; deep red can draw you into the blood and its associative lusty passions; tropical greens can be energizing in a slow healing way. Angular objects have an intensity of purpose; while softly curved, flowing designs can dissipate intensities. Beats, tempos, rhythms—depending on the order in which sounds reach you—induce particular responses in your nervous system. At times the blaring of city traffic may make you smile with whimsy; the gurgling sound of running water could irritate; the driving amplification of rock music might relax you; at other times, perhaps the opposite.

Spicy tastes can excite the nervous system; sweet tastes could tranquilize you; or they might not. The tastes and odors of your lover's secretions—depending on their quality and your mood—can amplify your attraction, or repel you. It may be so hot and humid you are turned off sexually; or the same weather may wildly excite you. Blank, bleak, barren walls in a room with only a broken-down mattress could draw you into a bohemian jubilation of primal, poetic, sexual torching. A sumptuous silk, satin and lace boudoir might overwhelm and pacify your lusty desires.

Television might distract you from sexual interest. Or it might relax you to a point where you can become interested. Reading to each other; especially sharing deep esoteric passages might peak your energies so high, you want to make love as an acknowledgment of the space you share.

Hair swept up at a new angle; different style in the fit of your clothes; the flushed exhilaration of having just exercised; the sleepy, half ethereal look of snuggling into wakefulness under your blanket; a flower brushed in half-innocent seduction across the lips...**Appearance**—*It's not an illusion; it's a rate of perception.*

Massage sore achy muscles into release, then a mind too tense (trying not to acknowledge it's physical discomfort) is suddenly able to relax. Nerve endings rechannelling back to the natural ease of connection; as warmth spreads through your body, your sensual sexuality resurfaces into consciousness. Scratching a back stimulates nerve endings; the release of tension and toxins can set you purring. Luxuriate as fingers gently stroke your head and face, even as you nestle into the intoxicating mold on the soft, lower belly lap of your lover; your own fingers gently tracing the inside of the upper thighs.

Spasmed shudders, purrs, moans, coos...or sharp, intense, probing looks which vary between pleading and commanding...hugging 'til feelings erase the border between your bodies, and waves of subtle energy recycle in a flow between you. Deliberately prolong, almost suspend the motion between you; so that every throb, pulse and millimeter of groin to groin expression is a calling card of excruciating pleasure for you both. Drive and pound, almost viciously tearing at each other; consummation so intense you can barely differentiate each others touch. Almost numb in an avalanche of sensation, you're jerked in and out of your senses; as you conduit mental images between your nerve cells.

Peaceful, dreamy, cuddling, slow, absorbing, licking, tasting, intermeshing...or wild, abandoned, intense, overwhelming, explosive suck-fucking...Positions and pleasure of need; desires transforming needs; nuances re-stoking desires. Positions and pacing: When you get into the nitty-gritty of erotic enjoyment, that's what determines the qualitative pleasure of your variety.

You can go through every sexual position adaptable between two human bodies. You can lie entwined and motionless; soaking in each others embrace, yet it still may not seem different, special, or satisfying. You can play lovingly with each others nipples; stroking and licking them in slow provocativeness. Or you can squeeze, mold, and pull harshly in dominating command on breasts made victims. Still, it can be just another ho hum maneuver. You can rub, lick, suck your way through a cornucopia of penis / vagina, clitoris / testicles. Yet you may be only experiencing directly physical sensations, without any of that heart wiring psychosexual electricity.

Positions and pacing must be melded into a responsive recycling of the way in which you are both effected by the moment. To have timing, you must be beyond time (division of space by contemplation) and into the experience of whatever your awareness is processing—of course, that means each other. That will allow for the mutual synchro-meshing—of, at the least, the very best you've ever known—your mutual states of mind. In that dipolar fusion you create an energy flow which can only be tapped by the combined potential of male and female energies. It's like magic; it's that state of mind which makes everything always different, and every difference satisfying. All the rest become enhancers.

So that: unexpected urges; wham-bang fucks; adrenal rush indulgences in close proximity to public scrutiny; mischievous outings in dangerous, unprotected places; naked frolics on ocean beaches; getting head, driving down the highway; group orgies in suburban drag; romps with underage sexual veterans, etc...Or: simple between-the-sheets necking; drifting off into sleep, still inside each other; standing in masculine bravado, with her legs snaking around his neck; slow dance-like fucking; down in the dirt spontaneity; while cooking in the kitchen; gymnastically contrived; in command / being commanded, etc...So that every movement, stillness, or quivering spasm "twilighted" in between is, at the least, reminiscent of a very erotically attuned state of sexually enthralled satisfaction you'd experienced before.

To ejaculate, or not to ejaculate—that is a variation. Whether 'tis more satisfying for a man to release the psychosexual electrical energy concurrently building from his groin, or to retain and further escalate this energy. Ultimately, the decision rests with the male; however, in transcendent lovemaking, satisfaction is a joint psychic decision, where the female's energies must consciously work with the male in his intention to retain sperm. Either way, his decision is bound to dramatically effect him and his lover. Sometimes the two of you will want to retain and ride rhapsodically out of your minds on that energy. Other times you will find it just as beneficial to flood each other with emissions and melt into the womb of togetherness. Energy and relaxation have a lot to do with what is appropriate. If tired and / or tense, lack of focus and concentration can dull you, requiring a short, sweet release. When energized, you may find it more relaxing and invigorating to open the throttle.

Besides nutrition, there are other ways to override and affect your sexual responses. There are psychoactive herbs such as mushrooms, marijuana, opium, and caffeine. There are even more powerful, chemical like drugging agents such as L.S.D., cocaine, heroin, tranquilizers, amphetamine types, etc. With the wonders of modern chemistry, drugs are now being produced to mimic and amplify the direct brain control of recently discovered neuro-transmitters. And, of course, there is always alcohol.

Certainly, by altering your stimulus to response ratio of perception these substances can vary the way in which you experience. Like any form of power (energy given conscious direction), your intention and skill of application will determine how beneficial or detrimental it is to you. You don't alter your consciousness for no reason. If your actions are without reason, then the substance becomes your master rather than your tool. And it's lousy to be the slave of a slave.

Intention—why are you taking it? If it is to avoid facing something you don't understand how to handle, it will only deepen your confusion and anxiety. If it is taken with the knowledge of what range of possible effects it can have on your awareness, and your reasons for exploring those possibilities is in keeping with your level of progressed development, then at times it can be beneficial. The absence of pain is not pleasure. There is all the difference in your soul between contracting away from something, or expanding towards something.

Skillful application—how to benefit from body / mind altering substances and not be harmed. It may be relevantly necessary for you to accentuate and accelerate the quality of your functional, capacities. Still, this will put strains on your metabolic systems. You should ascertain what is being drained from you and nutritionally replace it as quickly as possible.

If lovers are experienced and skillful enough, and want to experiment with mutual augmentation of their psycho-sexual systems, I'd suggest being mildly judicious with the more natural agents such as marijuana, caffeine, and, perhaps for the advanced few who are ready and so inclined, an occasional psychedelic mushroom. Of course there is alcohol, which if used sparingly when appropriate, will not harm and can enhance you. In order to be healthy, to the degree that you self-actualize your individual potential, you must consciously take over directing the health of your body. It is a question of balancing the center of your awareness around its ever readapting needs. **Everything in moderation—including moderation!** *You must occasionally deconstipate the spirit.* The frequency and intensity of such excursions is an individual matter. Not to do so when needed can be as detrimental as indulging when psychomotionally unprepared.

If, when imbibing alcohol, it relaxes and stimulates you enough to re-center, your choice is appropriate. However, if it makes you headachy, tired, and unable to focus, or connect with your energies, it is not so appropriate...at least for lovemaking. There are times, for those so inclined, when a couple puffs of marijuana makes them clear, relaxed and extra-ordinarily focussed. While at other times, it is exhausting, draining, and disorienting. An occasional cup from a caffeine source may be exhilarating. But if your adrenals are down, it will just make you edgy, racy and unable to focus symbiotically through your feelings.

What you're doing with any consciousness-altering substance is decreasing focus on certain normal patterns of response and / or superseding normal focus. When lovers are consciously synched into each other's biochemistry and neurology, used intelligently, marijuana or light alcohol can deepen the connection, making them aware of other energy dimensions which they can access.

I could go on and on. The list of variables is endless; their possible combination, infinite. Variety is one of the four true aphrodisiacs.

Variety—everything's so exciting, I can hardly wait to play with it some more!

4. Belief

> *You can take as much as you want,*
> *As long as you give a little more than you take.*
> *And I want it all!*
>
> *Faith—acting on your belief.*
> *Confidence—being validated by your belief.*

It's not what you do, but rather the state of mind you're in when doing it that determines the quality of your experiences!

Is that a statement you can trust? Are you confident that it is so? Can you accept it as being true? Is it something you believe or disbelieve? Maybe you believe you don't have to believe in anything. Maybe your beliefs are very specific. Perhaps you believe that sex is only permissible under specific conditions...it's only justifiable in terms of procreation...that it is just a natural function...that you should get it whenever you can...whatever.

Your belief is your outlook. It is based on what you've inwardly come to feel and think about what you've experienced. It structures the way you approach circumstances and to what degree you allow yourself to interact with the potentials operable to your awareness. Optimally your beliefs should be open-ended and flexible; so that you can constantly update, upgrade, rearrange, and adapt them to the continuously changing sensibilities of any situation.

What do you believe LOVE is? How should it be approached by lovers? What are you making love to achieve? Then how conscious must you be of the process and your participation in it? Here is the ocean of Life. It is defined, shaped, characterized, sectioned, connected, and continuously animated into an almost unlimited profusion of forms and functions which manifest through it by currents of Love. Love, the meta-gravity which animates Nature. Love being sufficient unto itself, cannot be bound; yet it binds all things in a desire to be consciously immersed in it. *Love—God's desire to be!* Love, consciousness wanting to be aware of itself. Love, the movements (through manifestation) of wholeness enchanted by its own completeness.

Love permeates from everything imaginable by God, through every level conceivable to the human mind. Life's ocean of existence is shaped by it; seedlings alchemize into animated forms, pierce through the earth, drawn to the representational light of it; Love seduces instinct through biology; it polarizes feelings between pleasure and pain, approach and avoidance; it motivates our minds to try and contain it through structures. Love is the continuously repolarizing, reapportioning demarcating flow between Yin and Yang...between Nature and Spirit...between Receptive and Creative...between Female and Male. As we individualize and enter upon the self-actualized level of human awareness we call it *an affair of the heart.*

To the ocean of Life—continuously reshaped by Love— all consciousness must submit. The degree, combination and proportion by which you approach this state will determine how you interpret and characterize Love. To one degree or another, there are those individuals, paced well ahead of our collective inertia, who have come to represent the evolutionary path that humans must travel. If, for example, someone embodies Christed attributes (to some relative degree in relation to the needs of a particular psycho-socio state of development), they become a representation of the Way, the Truth and the Light. The Way to where; the Truth of what; the Light of whom? The answer to where we're going, what we'll find, and who will be revealed by this illumination is that which is motivating and drawing us through the living process—LOVE!

Ah yes, at the heart of things; it is humanity's birthright. But only a few have managed to catch sight of it. Fewer still have managed to center their consciousness there and operate from that perspective. Of course, that's all about to change. These are transitional times, you know. Obviously, our beliefs are similarly in transition. Just as when centered from the heart, you can see the reasons for all the shocks to which flesh and mind have been heir. They can be balanced and harmonized so that their attributes function optimally, without the grossly inadequate limitations of stupefying bureaucracy which has, for too long, incapacitated them.

Love, the attraction towards wholeness. At its base root is *Sex*; blending and re-blending individual differences to reproduce individual differences—*objectivity*. At its summit is God, the sublime procreator, assimilating the drives of individual existence into an homogenized apperception of Self—*subjectivity*. With humanity poised in between, trying to gestalt into a bio-psychic two-way flow-through valve.

To the primitive savage, love manifests as the ability to conform to the consistent rhythms of nature which motivate activity. As the savage evolves into the disciplines of tribal protocol—where identification as part of the group takes precedent—relatable rituals (which cohesively integrate each member to nature as well as to the other members of the tribe) form the motivating force which transmutes subservient containment into relatively secure contentment. When both the basics of survival and the rituals of group interaction have been mastered, the seemingly endless fascination with developing and directing one's individual capacities set in. Like the carrot before, but always just out of reach of, the horse which draws its burden while pursuing this reward...like a desert mirage to a thirsty man...like peace to a tortured mind...Love binds and draws all consciousness through whatever level of experience it is neurologically developed to encounter.

Love's one main personality trait is transcendence. In order to transcend whatever limitations through which you're currently working / playing you must lighten up. You must divest yourself of excessive structuring, so that you may be magnetized into a new stratum of greater encompassment. When you transcend, you go beyond your self-image. You strip that image down to its essence and let go of the structures you previously employed to give you access to the energies of a particular level of consciousness. By so doing, you gain access to a new level of consciousness. Then you try and stabilize that newer level of consciousness with suitable structures, 'til Love motivates you again.

Hatred (communication only with your own excuses) is a turning away from the urge to evolve. It is a perspective where the structures you've come to identify with as the energies of a particular rate of perception become mistakenly more important than the energy itself. You solidify, crystallize into form and function; which means you are stagnant in your intellect, putrefying within an avoidance-oriented pattern of feelings. You become heavy within yourself and with others. You do not move into new spaces easily. And too often you try to justify your position by dominating and commandeering the space and people around you to reflect your own perspective.

When you love, you transcend. When you transcend, you come into a more encompassing space; which in turn increases your psychomotional fields of activity and range of motion. You become something greater than your self-image. If you don't get derailed and fixated on this new self-image...if you keep loving, it will launch you still further.

Consciousness, through the male and the female circuitry, are drawn physically by nature to let go of their obvious structural differences long enough for the sexual act of intercourse to bring forth something beyond either of their individual capacities—a new life. To keep that life alive (the process matriculating itself), they are drawn to create structures that allow them to share feelings. These feelings, when lightened up and subscribed to, are pleasurably nurturing. A bond between the male and female is drawn to encompass more. From family to sociopolitical unit, structures are formed—however compromising—to facilitate states of consciousness which make it more worthwhile to be together than to be apart. Rituals, along with their mystically moralistic explanations, are set up to ensure orderly commerce by creating cultural toll systems to dole out the privileged activities that supposedly will allow participants to experience the benefits of love—courtship / marriage / family.

Eventually Love transcends, and if you want to keep pace with the wonderful satisfaction it provides, you must let go of these indoctrinated patterns and conditioned inhibitions and open up to more fulfilling levels of being. Bodies transcend their separateness in embrace. Feelings transcend polarized differences in affection. *Affectionate embracing engenders passion.* As for a while you can stew in your passions. Then the constant evolutionary—Love—once more entices you to transcend the limits of those structures.

Progressively you learn to direct your passions with a conscious sense of purpose—to enjoy yourself more.

Sexually, you become *romantic*. At first participating in the normal rituals of courtship. But increasingly you add your personal touch. Giving gifts (e.g., flowers, candy, jewelry) evoke certain responses; soft lights and music evoke other responses; entertaining or socializing provoke further responses. You become creative, artistic—Designer sex, anyone?

Designer sex, stylized for your mood and pleasure. Whether it be casual, intense, businesslike, flowery, athletic, sporty, brutal, religious...any and all of which can become associated mood-engendered environments, stylized for romance. Too often, everybody buys into their own propaganda and starts believing they're the part they've been playing. Romance at will; all the longed for externals seemingly become accessible. For those who are ready, Love takes you by the groin, whispering you into yet another state of transcendence.

Wispy inferential currents cascading over and into the mindless (thoughtless, timeless, holier than...) moment. Yes, yes...as you void your self-image and all the cumbersome structures of consciousness that go along with it. You're beginning to recognize that your body, feelings and thoughts are but a means of leveraging your awareness in order to channel energy. Energy, intellect blowing energy. All the cares, woes and sorrows of your structural fixations shown to be insipid. Another veil rent asunder. Energy: Oh, how you want to gorge and intoxicate yourself on the mentally transcending source of your human fountainhead.

Energy that can open you up to more conscious immersion in your spirit, simultaneously and concurrently opens you up to more sexual energy. *The more spiritual you become the more erotic you become!* Those accumulating sexual energies must be redirected. To what continued means? It depends on what your experiences bring you to believe.

Who is my *Father*?
 —That sublime level of intelligence who sires my consciousness.

Who is my *Mother*?
 —The apparent Nature of actuality which nurtures my sensibility.

If you want to polarize the game (of Life) through the lexicon of religiosity:

God — *Father*	*Mirroring Void* — *Supernal Mother*	
Christ — *Son*	*Rapture* — *Daughter*	
Spirit — *Consciousness*	*Nature* — *Manifestation*	

Christed Rapture—what a blissful, ecstatic, fucking joy!
 What an incredible turn-on. If such (or whatever) is your *belief system* and you manage to validate it, then you could potentially, with confidence, move mountains, re-shape the patterns of existence, turn into a sublime sexual recycling dynamo, etc.
 What would you do if such was the belief system that animated, activated, and motivated your awareness? Well, you could go a more or less traditional route. You know: The Diving Marriage—soul wed to spirit. As the believer turns away from more refined personal fulfillment to serve humanity. That is: No more nooky 'til we all safely meet on the other side, where you won't care anyway.
 Of course, that is only one way of distributing the

energy to which such a belief system would make you accessible. I mean, if you're going to be of service to humanity (God's pet creation) you ought to take stock of what humanity is most in need. In the past it may have even been a little suffering, sacrifice, self-denial; you know, a good kick in the psychic ass. Obviously, it doesn't need to be pulverized anymore than it has already been. There are a lot of things in which humanity needs to be instructed. And one of the greatest needs humanity presently has is to learn to handle its sexuality!

Making sex into a sacrament (like that Son and Daughter); what a thing to believe. Maybe you believe Rock and Roll is a kind of music. Or is it a state of mind (the music just being one of its aspects)? Did someone say Rock and Roll was originally hip slang for sexually getting it fucking on? Gee, what kind of life-style changes would such a belief system engender?

But don't get hung up there. Love never brings you down. It draws you to streamline, transform, and transcend into more encompassing fulfillment. No matter what you believe, or do—from a human perspective—*the function of the game is to evolve the human nervous system.* Sexuality is an undeniable part of that. And it's certainly time for sex to be approached as a *class act.*

When we think of being in love, we think of pleasure and openness—not pain and denial. Of course, you don't have to believe that. But do be sensitive, intelligent, careful, receptive, vital and joyful about where you put your mind (your beliefs).

Sex is not the highest aspect of consciousness. Sex has its limitations. But these can only be seen, put into perspective, and transcended when sex has been...and therefore, can be...taken to its limits. In order to safely do this, and get back with the goods for conscious perusal, you must first have access to more encompassing levels beyond sex.

What does it mean to live and sexually function without fear, doubt, confusion, shame, guilt, anxiety, jealousy and possessiveness? What are the social implications for such a belief system. That is the subject of the next chapter.

However, you should be able to now see how intelligence, health, variety and your beliefs can extend from little pleasures to quantum leaps of evolutionary potential in your sex life.

All, just for the sheer, joyous, fun-filled pleasure of it— a little recreational ecstasy, anyone!

Polarizing To Pleasure

I *want to give to those in-dividuals who are ready for greater actualization, what they need to help them accomplish it.*

I want to give to those who need to pace themselves more in relation to the mass collective rhythms, what will help them to feel more comfortable within themselves.

So that everyone can get the hell out of their own, and each other's way!

Most of the suffering on this planet—personal or collective—is unnecessary, and can be ended easily and quickly. All the tools that are necessary to rectify our age-old ills already exist. It is merely a question of intelligent deployment. Understanding must replace morality. Yet people who have gained their position of power (however personally dissatisfying or unfulfilling) through emotional manipulation, are reluctant to open up.

I'm not just talking about the obvious power-elite who control vast sums of wealth and all that goes with it.

Everyone, to at least some degree, has personal power. Mostly, power has been used to secure position, by being able to manipulate the deployment and utilization of other people and things. *The end doesn't necessarily justify the means*. Every end is also a new beginning. If the means used is inadequate and inappropriate, then the new beginning will be prenatally polluted and will have to rectify the imbalanced end.

Rather, it is the *means* which forms the frame of reference for any *end* (beginning...). Power being the supposed end has been for too long mistakenly used to justify war as its means. War: aggressively trying to overwhelm and subjugate others to your will by any means, including their annihilation in this existence. Thereby as a means, war has come to form the frame of reference for the end and beginning of the majority of our sociocultural cycles.

The war, in which most people's psyches are consumed (between what you feel and what you think) sets the stage for all other hostile aggressions. To gain power, people will sacrifice and distort certain aspects of their being to the supposed greater glory of other aspects. Which in turn has become the frame of reference for approaching God. From such a frame of reference, God, as the human limit of conceivable endings, has been depicted as sanctioning almost any means.

We war on our bodies supposedly to glorify our spirit. We war on our feelings to exonerate our intellectual conjectures. We war on the environment in an effort to convince ourselves that it is only a question of mind over matter. We've subsequently and consequently been warring on each other: Man against man; man against woman; woman against man; woman against woman. 'Til life has become an embittered resignation; this perpetual four-way crucifixion; a valiant but tawdry struggle between "damned if you do and damned if you don't." We even make war to end war.

Subliminally projected through a mass of patterned avoidance compromises, people make themselves sick to gain power over others. Against all reason, they often set themselves up to be hurt, then cling to their fixations, trying to manipulate by making themselves and others feel guilty and ashamed. So that now, with the high-speed, technologically souped up configuration of all these factors, we find parent and child continuously vying for emotional dominance. The only god that most people have been sacrificing and laying tribute to is the dark, false god of their own self-justifying ignorance!

So many holy relics leftover from our maddening headlong rush from primitive insecurity to intellectual competency. So many time-honored means of relating to the same expedient compromises we didn't know how not to make. Such an incredible burden to tote through the ages. We've confused where we've gotten to with how we got there. Yet by not fully understanding the process, we've held onto...dignified...glorified...justified...and religiousized our insecure compensations. Really, there are no sacred cows. Unfortunately, there is too much sacred bullshit!

Humanity has lived with fear, doubt, confusion, anxiety, guilt, and shame for so long—without seeing a way out of it—that people have tried to convince themselves that such unhealthful aberrations of their consciousness are inevitably normal. As it is time for us to live in a whole new strata of reality, so it is time for us to begin dreaming dreams where such demeaning and detrimental inhibitions are no longer activated. When people get what they really want, it makes them happy. But when they get what they think they want, and it still doesn't make them happy—then it wasn't what they really wanted after all.

What do people want? After feeling centered, peaceful, vital and controlled within themselves, they want to be able to open and extend their sense of self through interaction with others. To try and do so by aggressive warlike emotional dominance, is instead to become further locked into your own limitations. War is a shutting down, an attempt to reinforce the limits of structures obviously already inadequate. At times it has appeared as rightfully necessary. But that only reflects the inadequacy of the prevailing consciousness to understand the fears that have left them too paralyzed with personal insecurity to encompass more than their preconceived ideas.

Make love, not war! Love creates an approach to that which transcends the limitations of your present self-image. It requires sensitivity, receptivity, attunement, blending, merging, synergistically conscious combining of recycling energies which nourish your awareness to a level more encompassing than you could ever equal alone.

You say: "I love this or I love that...I love him, her, some of you, all of you...I love God...I love Life...I love the way it feels...He / she / it love me...I make love...I'm in love...I'm loving." What is being implied by all these inferences to love?

Whether it is: bestially animalistic, wildly abandoned, unabashedly carnal, sensual pleasure...courtly, stately, proper, dutiful, morally constipated, customized, compromised social obligation...artistic, esoteric, sophisticated, mind-altering, seductive, rhapsodic, consciously contrived sojourn into bliss waves of pleasure...and / or worshipful, inspired, divinely transcending, humanitarian, nobly sacrificing, cosmic evolutionizing of spiritual fulfillment...However you want to designate it, any human who is involved with LOVE is being consciously attuned to a particular rate of perception.

Obviously, what has come to functionally exist serves a particular need in the evolution of life on this planet. All evolution is a spiritual encompassment to more inclusive rates and ranges of perception. To accommodate these growths, biological forms must correspondingly evolve into appropriate manifestations in keeping with the quality of consciousness they must expressively channel. On the human level, sociocultural systems consolidate, integrate and designate conscious perspectives into workable formats of interpersonal relatedness. These are meant to protect the gains already made, and make them nourishing and accessible to the individual members of the collective whole. So nourished, individuals should be able to fulfill their own uniqueness; thereby offering a greater level for expansion of the collective social system.

You breathe in; you breathe out. But when the breath becomes inordinate to any degree, the neurological process and corresponding metabolic functions will be somewhat affected. Sometimes this is done with specific knowledge to achieve certain desired conditions (e.g., yoga, athletic training, psychological release). But too often, it is an unconscious process corresponding to subliminally suppressed aberrations in the psyche.

What is required at this stage of human evolution? We are only at the beginnings of Space Age Technology. Quantum leaps in accessible power are making us unavoidably aware of our potentials for new levels of greatness or complete annihilation. Stone Age emotions forged us through aggressive warring into the position we've attained today. However, this is no longer the path to continuous human fulfillment!

Yet how do we change and transmute emotional patterns ingrained at the most basic levels of neurological development...patterns with millions of years reinforcement through selective survival-breeding into the genetic makeup of our species? They say you shouldn't change horses in midstream. But the horse we're riding (the structural orientation of our egos) only knows how to function in midstream. As in the thick of it, we continue galloping through the onrushing crash-currents of emotional thoughts, up to our intellectual waist in potentially overpowering feelings. For millions of years we've galloped in midstream between the shores of Ignorance (lack of awareness; annihilation) and Knowledge (functionally controlled understanding; peace and plentitude). Juggling...always juggling our hopes and fears, pleasures and pains, approaches and avoidances. While looking ass backwards at the dark mystery of our own unresolved compromises, we kept moving onward. We became fit to survive. We persevered and conquered. To do so, we destroyed whatever threatened our determination and conscripted our bio-psychic energies—especially sexuality—in justification of our perspective.

The streams of competitive, combatant emotions have continued carrying us along; even while we were obsessively preoccupied with navigating them. Myriads of tributaries characterized by racial features, oriented by topography and climate, augmented by sociocultural refinement have kept flowing with the inherited legacy of their particular aspect of humanity. With the start of modern science and the technological revolution, these tributaries of nationalistic pride poured together into the melting pot rivers of mass media, mass transportation, and mass marketing. And now, as those in the forefront of these onrushing currents have already begun to see, the surging rivers of our idealism are emptying into an oceanic vision of global humanity. Which is already rising like a divine launching pad to galactic exploration.

Territories of space, be they physical or mental, denote a range of potential responses and the qualities of energy that can be experienced by a participating consciousness. A tropical rain forest connotes certain distinct probabilities of experience. Disciplined intellects immersed in devotional worship to a transcendent image will interact with the space around them in specific ways. Each level of orientation, each perspective includes not only a range of responses for possible energies encountered, but also those social modes of conduct most conducive to optimizing the potentials in any given experience.

War, aggressive avoidance of pain (inner insecurity) and its passive counterpart of pseudo peace (temporary cessation of hostilities) connotes a range of responses that have characterized our species since it first distinguished itself. Of course, we've accumulated a great deal of inestimable knowledge as we've battled through aeons. What seems appropriate for our current stage of transition, is to be able to transmute our awareness to functionally operate from a more encompassing rate of perception than the one that has structured our modes of conduct up 'til now. And that is exactly what has already begun happening.

However, as the level of orientation changes, so the forms of structuring our expressions must be appropriately transmuted. People need to relate according to their integrative level of development. People try to be—and are most certainly ready to be—living freer, more independent life-styles. Unfortunately, the only criteria they've had to adhere to or move away from are the archaic standards patterned into their formative years.

Now we want to talk about peace, love, and understanding as a modus vivendi for structuring our social interactions. Just about anybody can talk a good fuck. That doesn't mean they're ready to participate in one. Those who try to live their ideals, without understanding the energies and rates of perception involved, have and will continue to experience frustration and disappointment. We want to utilize modern opportunities to rebalance intimacy and closeness in light of emerging self-actualized patterns. This must be accomplished in such a way that the still existing tendencies toward hostile aggression are not set into motion. Which means the approach must take over and reorient all existing structures of social exchange from a perspective inclusive enough to simultaneously integrate all of them.

At the same time, such an approach must allow for maximum utilization of whatever is optimizing to our awareness. Accompanying bureaucracies, from petty innuendo bullying to grand mal dogmatic convulsions, must be disassociated from the neurological rates of perception they've for far too long moronically slandered. Instead of moving away from pain, we must orient towards pleasure. Peace is the pleasure of Love. Love is the pleasure of understanding. Understanding is the pleasure of harmonizing consciousness with experience.

Now let's get functional. How do we bring this about? The scope of this book is to deal with sexuality. Human sexuality is structured through interpersonal exchanges. What kinds of relations will satisfy the above criteria? Now that we are ready, how do we polarize towards pleasure?

In these transitional times there are three distinct levels of relationship possible. They interpenetrate one another. Yet none of them, as yet, possess adequate structuring to allow for their optimal functioning.

First, there are those people who are not ready for re-

lationships: Of course they will and should try to have relations, but they are not organized or integrated enough in their psyche to as yet be able to open up and honestly extend the full measure of themselves to another. They aren't yet ready to allow for a mutual synthesis, which would bring them into greater realizations and newly expanded energy states.

Secondly, there are those persons who are ready for relationships: Be it for two years or fifty years, this is the best way for them to be able to experience the fulfillment of their own potential. As for a given amount of time, under sympathetic circumstances, with an equally oriented partner, the relationship will become the vehicle through which the next phase of their spiritual maturity can unfold.

Thirdly, there are those individuals who are more than ready for a relationship: Their nervous systems have been exposed to, and integrated so much, that while they're certainly capable of having a relationship, they don't require exclusivity in order to process sexual intimacy. They can enter into and relate at will with all the intimacy and depth of feeling that it takes most people years (if ever) to remotely establish. Their nervous systems have to some degree self-actualized beyond the inhibitory limitation of their sociocultural indoctrination. It is possible, if not relatively easy, for such an individual to genuinely care for, share with, love and form personally fulfilling relationships with more than one person at a time.

Again, I'm not evaluating qualities as right or wrong, good or bad. Considerations are effectively harmonizing to the degree that you functionally understand and can thereby creatively control the energies involved. Health is where you consciously balance and control energies which can optimize your potential in any given experience. Privilege breeds responsibility. Responsibilities are made functional by their corresponding privileges. Regardless which of the above three distinctions the level of your relating moves through, there is in each of these perspectives, relative to your capacity, the opportunity for fulfillment and growth.

The problem with all three levels of relating is the lack of suitable social structures. Whether so-called conventional or unconventional, most relations today are derivative variations on the basic marriage theme. Marriage was never set up to be particularly satisfying, fulfilling or enjoyable. From tribal times 'til today, marriage has been a way of conscripting a work force, and keeping them in line to reproduce. This is not to imply that marriage can't be an adequate social structure by which some people can satisfactorily fulfill themselves. However, it is not the only way. And for it to become an effective modern vehicle for interrelatedness, it is desperately in need of some updating.

Now let's examine these three classifications of sociosexual relatedness as they could most optimally apply in today's transitional times:

1. Relating / Not Ready for Relationship

You can't relate any better with another than you're capable of relating within yourself. What is the basis of your self-imaging (ego)? From what perspective do you attempt to balance the inner workings of your mind; are you centered? Can you relate freely to the totality of perceptions available to you?

For some, the answer to these considerations is perplexity and watered down affirmatives. Their nervous systems are still too grossly patterned by emotional inhibitions, inadvertently conditioned into them during their formative years. Their indoctrination may have been uncultured, uncouth, superstitious, reinforced by a slobbered smattering of gut-grabbing emotionalism and brutish physical intimidation. Or they may have been raised in the best of economic and educational circumstance, by kindly well-intentioned people hoping to launch them into excellence.

What are the possibilities for satisfaction and personal fulfillment for people whose consciousness have been so conscripted? It depends to what degree their sense of self has been dominated by the moral dogma of others. If psychologically browbeaten into reasonless emotional subservience, then they will pretty much follow the party line of their upbringing. This will, of course, limit their range of responses, making them even more intimidated. But that is also their protective safety net against having to assume responsibility for their choices. Or even if exposed to the artistic sophistication of the more privileged side of life, they may still be caught in patterns of bohemian defiance and outlaw rebelliousness.

Whatever the reaction to their inner frustrations, what they are seeking is balanced integrative awareness within the wholeness of their psyche. Yet this inner seeking (usually subliminally devious and stoically denied at this level of inhibition) must go on within the scope of their social circumstances. Until the recent advances in this century, society mostly paced its social exchanges with the same repressive, restrictive sensual denial that it kept trying to convince its populace it should believe in. If people were uptight, confused, frustrated and the like, there was plenty to keep them occupied and believing that such was the proper nature of civilized spiritual citizens. So that after not knowing how to relate, nor how to satisfactorily exchange sexual energies, many people resolved themselves to the marriage situation. The frustrated sense of under par self-resignation only seemed to confirm the religiousized diminishing expectations they'd been programmed to accept.

Unresolved sexual tensions keep on building. To try resolving yourself to never being satisfied can be truly heartrending. Most people do so by forcefully making themselves believe they are relatively happy. *But you can't fake happiness; you're either satisfied or dissatisfied.* Even with all the socially coveted accoutrements to embellish one's status, great depressive wells of frustration can build around longings for interpersonal closeness which have never been truly satisfied.

Then what? People, so constrained, begin to lash out at those who are closest to them. They hurt what they love most. Why? To keep pace with the energies accessible through Love, requires periodically transcending the confines of your mental structuring. The structuring is undeniably useful as a necessary frame of reference for societal exchanges. But if you become lost in the identification with your concepts, you feel cut off from the flow of the living process. As the motivator for psychomotional attraction, when consciously attenuated to, Love is the continuously evolving artist of your composite awareness (soul). Now regardless of the apparent (coincidental) packaging within which circumstances seem costumed, if you can't open up to experience Love, you feel trapped. Trapped in what? In your psychomotional avoidances and alibied fixations. That is painful; and that pain is what is being avoided. But if you put yourself in a position where you're supposed to be able to experience Love...where all the supposedly advertised and sanctioned proprieties have been supplied, and you still can't open up to your own loving potential, then the pain intensifies. It is an inner composite of pains you were never able to handle in the first place. But at least you had an excuse. Or at least you thought you could rationalize your frustration away until this other person showed up. Being with them, doing all the supposedly right things, yet still not having Love can be almost unbearable. You'd lash out at your pain, except you don't know how to resolve it. So you lash out at what should be the fulfillment of your moment. You hurt your loved one because they fail to give you what you desperately desire. You drive them away from you to regain the excuse for why you can't have Love.

This kind of sociosexual confusion has become tenaciously recycled through the Hollywoodesque machinery of mass media. Hollywood has never really known what to do with Love. Rather, with brilliant artistry, it sells back to the public psyche an endlessly entertaining array of its own frustrated dilemma.

Sexual connotation in Hollywood so far has remained a heady mix between moralistically embarrassed hedonism and pseudo-cosmopolitan puritanism. Love stories are pursuit / wheel and deal / capture affairs of courtship. Slay dragons, defeat the bad guys, overcome negative circumstances to win your heart's desire. But finally, however the boy and girl get each other, the story ends. Once the lovers are together, the stories peters out and into the genre of situational comedies. Of course, tragedy must not be neglected; there is a huge market for expounding on people coping with love lost.

When lovers are sexually hot in Hollywood depiction, they are either bad asses and / or something negative is going to happen to them. Either their ability to experience sexual carnality and lusty passion is characterized as making them hard, mean, sophisticated and running emotional roughshod over others; or, by some inescapable moralistic retribution, sexually loving enthusiasts will be beaten, maimed, butchered, killed and / or socially chastised and branded by the likes of emotionally constipated bigots, deranged psychopaths, sci-fi / horror monsters, natural catastrophes, and life-altering circumstantial accidents.

How often have you seen a depiction of intelligent, freethinking, open-minded, attractive people living healthy, well-adjusted, creative, enjoyable lives in which their sexuality is comfortably resolved, so that their passions can be experienced within a life-style that functionally allows for growth, inclusive expansion with others, and greater intimacy amidst a mature atmosphere of accepted responsibility? Come to think of it, how often do you see it happening in real life?

Actors and actresses, in stories, work with the props— situational circumstances and psychological personality structures—which so far have been accessible. Lacking emotional clarity, society presently appears to be a commercial advertisement, trying to sell itself validation for its own progress. Hollywood mass-markets the symbols of what we've led ourselves to believe that life is all about. Madison Avenue astutely associates products with these symbols, and markets them so you can believe in the representations of what appears to be (yet never really can be) your existence.

The public watches media to see what they're supposed to be. In turn they go out and purchase the commodities which will allow them to feel acceptable. The media assesses the public and creates stories to depict where the public seems to be at. The blind leading the blind...who's leading who? We call it capitalism when there's enough leeway for personal inventiveness to individually restyle the kinds of commodities bartered. Supply and demand seesawing over and upon what? The continued open-ended recycling flow of the marketplace—humanity trying to intercommunicate.

And, are we ever an inventive species! We're constantly discovering ways to make life sleeker, more dynamic, more attractive, more fun, more...more...and some more after that. Fine, it's obvious that everybody—relative to their integrative level of perspective—wants to get even more turned-on to their potential. They want to be thrilled, enthralled, enlightened, satisfied, fulfilled, transcended— they want to be sexy! So we use our inventiveness to keep intensifying the pattern. Sex is the lubricant, the ball bearing, the pivotal balancing point in our frenetic, frantic juggling of supply and demand. As it has been since our most primitive misunderstandings, sexual satisfaction has been denied so that we'd have something to sell. Supply and demand has been 'til now—regardless of socially structured ideologies at any point in history—the formative nature of the marketplace machinery. Sex has been used to grease that machinery. Sexual frustration creates needs and desires. Commodities are created to fill those needs. But they never can, so commodities generate more needs and desires to be filled. We've used sexuality to sell the public everything, but satisfying sex!

Being highly turned-on sexually can be delicious, if you're psychologically set up to take advantage of it. If not, it creates tension. Being intense is enthusiasm incarnate; you're aimed, purposeful, moving into interactive immersion. But tension is a blocked flow of energy; disproportionate pressures build, weaken, undermine 'til things collapse and explode. Life is a flow; it's always in flux. Anything that interferes with that process creates a tension which is dangerous.

If you don't exactly understand what's causing the

tension, then you can't correct and eliminate the problem. You will either succumb to the negatively disorienting effects of its ever mounting pressure. Or you must find some means by which you can continually discharge its build. And this is exactly the frustration of sexual tension that so many people have to try and cope with every day.

Sexual tension, emotional fixation and other forms of psychomotional compromise doesn't mean that a person can't be sensitive and highly intelligent. Through the aeons, we've patterned plenty of religiously marriage-oriented structures to allow people to release their sexual tensions enough to let them function resplendently in the marketplace. But now, with the individualistic iconoclast opportunities afforded by Space Age technological innovations, many are no longer content to rely on these old-patterned escape valves. They've begun to break free of convention. They want to swing out and create their own more fulfilled activities for releasing their sexual tension.

Swinging life-styles for swinging people. In more technologically advanced places of abundant resources (e.g., California) there has been enough economic cushioning to enable people to shed old feeling-patterns and experiment. For most, this experimenting is basically an assertive denial of patterns of social conduct in which they were raised—in the course of which, they often seem to throw the baby out with the bath water (so to speak). Like a spiritual experience which is supposedly only accessible through participation in the religious structures built around it, most moderns only know how to approach intimacy, open affection, and deep caring through the structural commitments of contractual marriage. They mistakenly associate the few tidbits of interpersonal sharing, doled out to them through the family unit, with the restrictive limits of sexually repressive morality. So that in order to unshackle themselves from the obvious inadequacies of inept social structures, too often they give up the sweeter joys of deeply shared feelings. What good is freedom without increased intimacy?

What do you put in the place occupied by ordained soul-stifling commitments? Reactively, the answer has been a denial of sexual restrictions, and an assertion of all the seductive taboos:

Rock and Roll—open up your psyche to possibilities of connecting to pleasure; then go with the flow which is created. Rock and roll / connect and flow. Movements, looks, gestures, beats, tempos, rhythms, visuals...everything stylized to proclaim a pattern of living not shackled by a placid acceptance of calcified moralistic subservience and self-denial. If necessity is the Mother (nurturing motivator) of Invention, then what was the need which called forth such a social stratum of exchange?

Same old, ancient, archetypally primordial...eternally new, self-regenerating need to transcend limitations and encompass greater vistas of self-fulfillment—*Love to love you, baby.* Wow, a whole new restyling of the marketplace opening up. Fortunes to be made along with opportunities upon which to be capitalized. Music is an automatic doorway into the feeling level of consciousness. It creates a vibratory flux which can directly activate various mood swings. While it can't alter the basic patterns set in the feeling body, its resonance frequencies can coax a receptive mind into different emotional orientations. In our century, this mood-altering propensity has been and continues to be intensified by electronic amplification and spatial striation.

Soft, low, slow, steady, melodic instrumental music certainly can elicit different feelings than sharp, blaring, staccato, up-tempo backbeats of electronically enveloping

sound. Certain feelings make a mind more or less receptive to certain associative thought processes. Try watching a horror picture with the sound turned off; the images
will barely have an impact, When words—particularly lyr-
ical, cryptic poetry—are connected in synchronization to
the music, their message is driven far deeper into the
psyche than they would be if simply spoken.

Well, the consuming public has all kinds of tastes to
be catered to by the marketplace. And music runs the
whole gamut of civilized emotions. From ancient biblical
psalms, through lyrically mythological odes, medieval
choirs, waltzes, symphonies, jazz, country-western, cutesy
pop—the whole musical spectrum is available according
to the inclinations of individual taste. But what has been,
and still continues to set the "push point" pacing of music
in the future-orienting aspects of the marketplace? Rock
and roll / connect and flow: Amplify the beat—stimulate
the neurological frequencies—to where the entropy of
Stone Age emotions can be loosened enough to play with
some of the possibilities being created through Space Age
Technology. Correspondingly, the main message transmit-
ted so far has been break free and do your own thing.

That's right, babies: don't let them tie you down; don't
let them break your spirit; admit your desires and take
them for a spin. Where and how do you do it? What's the
big restraint that people have been trying to break through?
Don't you want personal satisfaction, more pleasure, fulfillment...don't you want to connect and flow into being
more sexy!? At whatever level of integrative social development, it is an unavoidable fact that people do want (will
pay a lot for) fulfillment. But the denial of restrictions is
not the navigational route to freedom. Refusing to participate in social structures which don't allow for pleasure

doesn't automatically mean that you will find the means of truly enjoying yourself.

So many people, who neither understand nor have free access to their psyches, are seeking to connect in a mutually satisfying way with others. They are willing to go through the external motions and emotional gymnastics of intimately sexual encountering. But no matter how much they look and act the part, they haven't yet integrated enough of their psychomotional circuitry to allow this to happen. Often, they get hurt and more confused by the ineptitude of their efforts. Then they may regress to justifying their pain, by subservience to the restrictions of their upbringing, from which they never really had detached. Some hang on in a confused emotional limbo. Hurt and curt, they cling to their more advanced idealistic conjectures, neither allowing themselves the limited emotional fulfillment of what they're denying, nor striking out for new vistas. While some, intent on getting what they think their self-assertion should entail, encounter their own avoidances through every kind of sexual experience in which they can get involved.

These are the people not yet ready for relationships. Then what are they ready for; what kind of social structures will enable them to grow more into self-fulfillment?

They've been playing variations of *hide-and-seek*: "Anybody around my base is it! Ready or not, here I come!" Hiding in secretly denied clandestine recesses of their mind—obscured by painfully compromised avoidances; overly structured through outmoded social proprieties; disjointed within themselves—they reach for connection with what they can never really be separated from. They seek in fame, wealth, power, status, affluence, exclusivity, community, conformity and status quo...they seek for recognition of themselves through others. The blessing and / or curse of being human (depending on your perspective) is that you need others.

In this game of pursuing the chase, anybody, who fits in with the basic criteria by which you've come to evaluate yourself, is a possible adjunct to this self-finding...self-deliverance...self-completion by validated recognition through the other. Whether you're ready with all the supposedly correct, outwardly mobile accoutrements; or even if you're uncouth, unkempt and haven't got the faintest clue of how to gain absolution from media standardizing pontificators...ready or not, life moves you on. In the process of which you touch others and are touched by others, you relate to whatever degree you're capable, motivated by your inclinations in any moment of considered circumstance.

Relating to something, someone, or some particular aspect of yourself...Relating is the process of continually recognizing yourself as existing. Relationships are an aspect of relating, being connected with another, under the structural limits of a specific range and quality of energy exchanges. Electrons, protons, and neutrons relate to form atoms; the bioelectric of plants and animals combine to form the relationships that are Nature; Nature and Consciousness relate in the formulation of Spirit. Male and Female relate in the form of...?

Human relationships depend on the level of development and quality of integration of participating consciousness. The level of development will orient the relaters to the particularities of their sociocultural circumstance. The quality of personality integration (i.e., between self-image and self-actualization) will determine whether the relating will reach the level of relationship, or perhaps even go beyond it. Some people may be too interested in relating to one or more particular aspects of their range of abilities to be interested in focusing on the totality of their own being—much less trying to extend it to another. Perhaps their vocation, hobby, study, travel, or immersion in Nature has so far proven to be more rewarding than trying to relate specifically. Perhaps the optimizing of some skill, athletic prowess, social grace, artistic insight, or paranormal ability has usurped their attention span. Perhaps subsistence workaday drudgery, hostile environments, poor health, limited mobility, material poverty preoccupies too much of their time and energy.

Relationships may be structured by circumstance, but they're never limited to any particular stratum of development. Primitive, culturally deprived, educationally indoctrinated, socially wealthy, brilliant exceptions... whatever, all are capable or incapable, relative to their integrative perspective, of having a relationship.

Human relationships, for a variety of reasons, take place with sexual bonding as the nucleus. On the most basic biological level, this is obvious as seductively genetic engineering endows our nature with the means to afford the continued reproductive survival of our species. But even though we are still a functional part of Nature, most humans today lives far removed from the dominant rhythms of their natural environment. We've taken our reproductive biology, and corresponding neuro-pleasure circuitry and manipulated them to the politico-religious jurisprudence of civilized expediency. So that gratifying sexual relating has rarely been socially accessible in a satisfying way. Because anything other than some form of maritally-structured relationship, if indulged in, was characterized as a sneaky, demeaning defilement of the highest qualities of human attainment.

Now, not everybody has the time, means, inclination

or even the need to experience the particular kinds of conscious evoking energies structured within a relationship. But everyone, to some degree (from lobotomized psychopaths through post-Einsteinian geniuses) has a need to relate to others. The problem is what to do with one's sexuality, when so far the only alternatives have been to succumb to a formal variation of relationship, defiantly rebel against it (which keeps you just as psychomotionally locked in), or deny and restrain your sexuality.

Whatever the particulars, people who aren't ready for relationships first need the means to actualize that for which they are ready. For them, relating—however, and to whatever degree—allows them to move more fully into an integrated recognition of the operative wholeness of all aspects of themselves. By their interaction with others, some people gain a chance to be objective, and thereby examine aspects of their own awareness which they haven't as yet understood how to directly perceive within themselves.

After the basics of hygiene, disease control, birth control, and economic subsistence, every person should have the option to be as sexual as need and circumstance allow. Obviously, not everybody is ready or so inclined to expend the time and energy necessary to adequately learn how to enjoy sex. However, the availability of choice would take pressure from them. Without the need to have to be in a structured relationship in order to experience communion of sexual intimacy, they could relax and enjoy much more of what they're experiencing.

Remember, its not what you do as much as the state of mind you're in that determines the quality of any experience. Rather than using relationship (up 'til now inadequately structured through the tenets of marriage) as a measuring rod for personal fulfillment, start geigering into the qualities of pleasure (not absence of pain) you feel. The first relationship you must fulfill before you can successfully extend yourself through others, is an ongoing integrated centering of your own consciousness within the wholeness of your being. Such centering must always take on the idiosyncratic characteristics peculiar to your own process of individual self-actualization. In order to break free of the emotional swamp of conditioned inhibitions, you must experiment. Inadvertently, most people do experiment with their indoctrination. But when they fail to liberate their understanding from the morally sanctioned proprieties conditioned into them as idealized value judgments, they either fall back into the bonded restraints of their upbringing, or exist in a pseudo, so-called individualized stance of defiant rebelliousness.

Now, if you cease having to defend what you feel your point of view should have to be...if there's nothing to have to rebel against or live up to— then you do what feels comfortably pleasurable to you. It becomes a question of how the feedback gained through consciously interacting in any circumstance can help to increase your awareness— your relationship to yourself. Instead of seeking a relationship, you are continuously relating, growing, exchanging, and fulfilling. You've taken the pressure off your self-image. You stop relating because you feel you have to, or you're afraid not to. You only relate when you want to, in the way that feels most comfortable. There is a great beauty in being with someone because you genuinely want to be. But you must consciously recognize the sense of this and set out to experimentally act through the perspective orientation. If you only read it intellectually, it will have no power for you.

Each person—relative to their integrative level of development—will, at least, start learning to relate to themselves through their consciously experimental interaction with others. Once this quality of relating to self has been assimilated, then they will be...

2. Ready For Relationships

There are many people, at various levels of social orientation, who are ready for a relationship. They have established a firm enough sense of their own uniqueness. In order for them to continue unfolding the potentials of their personal growth, they must extend and intermesh their consciousness with others.

Relationships take a definite number of forms and forces into consideration. They are structured and thereby must be purposeful. The purpose in any given relationship should be to synthesize the harmonious flow of available energies to allow for the expanded optimizing of the consciousness inter-involved. Circumstances do vary: the forces and forms at work in a primitive survival orientation certainly require far different handling than does a highly evolved, multidimensional society of extremely advanced technological know-how. The synthesizing of purposes between a well-adjusted young couple, following the ritual marriage rights of a fairly rurally isolated religious community, must certainly take on different characteristics than would a cosmopolitan hookup between a commando-business executive and a jet-swinging artistic personality.

In other words, what is the foundation for a successful relationship? What can you, as a participant, hope to achieve? What is the best way to commerce the energies inherent in the structures you create? What gives you and whoever else the right, authority, and power to step beyond the ricochetted random causation of continuous reaction and create an oasis of human fulfillment? What is the purpose of your activities?

For individual reasons, and the lack of reason, too often our purposes are obscured. It may be a reluctance to take responsibility for the consequences of your actions; or it may stem from a personal insecurity for which you try compensate by gaining a greater manipulative advantage. Instead of stating our needs, perspectives and intentions, we deviously contrive little rewards and punishments to cue each other in to how we want to believe the other should respond. Obviously, such an approach has rarely allowed most people to satisfy their real potential. But up until quite recently, couples weren't really looking for much; and even if they were, the means of effecting fulfillment really wasn't there.

The model for most relationships from Stone Age times up until the present has been some ritualized, rationalized, embellished variation on marriage. Marriage is a social contract in which a potentially reproductive man and woman are bonded together under the control of, and for the supposed good of, the collective community. The "good of the community" centers around its ability to perpetuate and enrich its existence. To do that there must be organization—control of the population. Unwanted, uncared for, unsupervised children in non-constructive, unchecked situations can bring about societal decline and possible downfall. Problems of disease, crime, and hunger can fester into a psychic cancer rotting away at the vitality of a society.

In the sexual act, which we've been engineered to find so pleasurable, so connecting, and so transcending, there is also the privilege / responsibility of reproduction. If this were not so, sexual intercourse would have little more relevance than having your back scratched. The good of any community seemingly has been best served by the most functionally productive deployment of the laboring power of its work force, as well as the continuous betterment of the lives of its individual members. Marriage was reactively conceived as the most obvious way to try and achieve this.

Marriage is a designated social responsibility, basically centered around reproducing, raising and integrating children to take their place in the societal schema. Because this function is the cornerstone of society itself, it unavoidably and automatically tributaries into the major concerns for turning the machinery of the marketplace. Politics (dictatorial or participatory democracy) structures and policies it; education transmits it; religion sanctions and glorifies its power through marriage (not from it); business packages and merchandises it as economics. And though there are those, whose nervous systems attenuate beyond the recycling mundaneness of it, by subscribing to expanded disciplines of science, philosophy and art, the foundational support of their efforts (personality structure) is still dependent upon marriage. Marriage has been the measuring rod for relationships between the sexes.

How do you keep them in line—for the supposed good of the community—which is supposedly for their own ultimate well-being? Whether they've learned how to take enjoyable advantage of it or not, the basis of uniting man and woman is their sexual attractiveness. Everything else is social bric-a-brac to structure, control and recycle the potentials produced by their union. Now when life is cheap—because the savagery of ignorance still overshadows understanding—you go for what you know, in any way you have to. Survival by Stone Age expediency of might makes right: If you want to survive, you'd better fall in line! Rewards and punishments are doled out in an advantage strategy of power brokering. Opportunities for sexual pleasure and all that goes with it, are distributed through a legislated merit system: If you want your survival to be enjoyable you'd better play ball.

Biological survival necessities, reactively catered to, produce pain-punishment / pleasure-reward feeling responses, which commandeer the intellect into structuring emotionally patterned rituals of social barter. Such has been the guiding force in the dynamics of the marital relationship. Marriage wasn't set up for satisfaction and fulfillment of the individuals so involved. Rather it was set up to commandeer and conscript a work force. With the exceptions of highly elite, rare, esoteric, spiritually oriented sexual disciplines and / or the cultivated bohemian life-style sensibilities of artistic types, eclectically indulging from the avant garde of cultural offerings, most of the populace learned to begrudgingly make do with their dissatisfactions. Laws were enacted to keep this process recycling. They were sexually restrictive laws which— under the religiousized guise of moral superiority—doled out severe punishment to anybody who breached their social contract.

It's not a question of right or wrong. Up until the twentieth century—in consideration of the gross inadequacies of our understanding—such methods for manipulating the public seemed most appropriate. Marriage, monogamy, conventionalism, and child rearing are how most people have been psychomotionally trained to approach the dynamics of a sexual relationship. Collectively, this was oriented around the greater good of the community. Individually, this was disseminated under the religiousized mechanics of spiritual salvation. Personal dissatisfaction, frustration, suffering and sacrifice were canonized as saintly. Material success and status were advertised as sexy.

But neither secular nor religious orientation had much good to say about personal sexual fulfillment.

Men and women cannot break this spell because it is formulated around and sustained by those sexually-oriented differences by which they are constituted (i.e., physiological structuring, metabolic flow, hormonal stimulation and neurochemical reactive rate). But the creative, individual propensities of our awareness can leap beyond the whole rigmarole of conditioned psychosocial patterning. As from this transcendent perspective an individual can refocus through their male or female orientation to create the means for a relationship that is truly satisfying.

It is becoming inescapably obvious that relationships may and should encompass far more than reproduction and child rearing. And whereas the social rituals connected with the perpetuation of our species can be a most beautifully fulfilling reason around which to structure a relationship, it doesn't have to be a consideration at all. We've sweated and toiled through the aeons to reach a place where we could really enjoy ourselves. Certainly, the relationships we've formed to sustain us through these growth struggles, which were based on compromised skullduggery and sanitized rationalization, are not what will allow us to finally capitalize on the successful fruits of our efforts.

Relationships take a definite number of forms and forces into consideration: they must be formed upon a foundation which is consciously structured to transmit the forces involved. The forces involved, by their nature, inherently pattern the kind of structure most optimal for their transmission. Marriage, as a social conscription of the reproductive process, is no longer an adequate enough foundation on which to base the structures of our socio-cultural exchanges. The forces we are now capable of intelligently dealing with can no longer find their expression through conventional marriage. It is not that marriage is wrong, or will suddenly disappear. Rather it needs to be revitalized as one of the means of human fulfillment; lovingly patterned within a more encompassing perspective. Space Age Technology requires Space Age Emotions!

Relationships were founded upon the family unit, because perpetuation of the species was an inescapable necessity, and binding children into the social order was an unavoidable responsibility. Religion loosely filled in for the emotional deficiencies in the way we expediently fudged things together. Whatever rearrangement of the particulars involved, marriage worked as a model because it structured the flow for one of our prime necessities; thereby doling out one of our main means to personal pleasure and satisfaction. In so doing, it created a series of ascending frameworks which were far superior to any petty-minded aspect of selfish desire man and woman could conjure. You married and related in the prescribed way for the good of your children, the good of your community, the good of your society, the continued survival of your species, the supposed morality pleasing to God, and as a means to achieve spiritual salvation. By all means let's give credit where credit is due; those are some incredibly viable reasons.

Relationships must be based upon something more encompassing and more important than the petty concerns of one individual's feelings. Feelings change; even true friendship, patriotic zeal, and religious fervor will not go the distance, if they're only predicated on how they make you feel. Computerization, mass media, and instant planetary accessibility is now changing all that. As more individuals begin aligning with the supra graphic input of our modern times, the faster their feeling patterns are shifting. Up 'til the advent of modern communication, emotional fervor—no matter how stifling, misguided or frustrating—could be sustained for a lifetime. But now that people can see all their perspectives dramatized in almost every conceivable manner...Now that they can step out of the confines of their community to access information from anywhere in the world...Now that they can record their own image and replay it for their own analytical consideration...Now that everybody's perspective is inter-penetrating into homogenization before the public's psyche...Now that they see how social organizations which govern them can be governed by them...Now that caste-prejudiced discriminations of programmed ignorance are leveling into equal opportunity for all to pursue happiness regardless of sex, race, religion...Now that sexuality has been intelligently dressed in the vesture of free choice...Now that all of this is being coupled with the ever accelerating, barely begun avalanching of the most sophis-ticated technology ever imagined...Now that all of our planet is becoming accessible, and almost limitless ter-ritories of space are opening up for exploration...Now that we stand poised on understanding and creatively control-ling the workings of our own minds, with paranormal abilities about to evolve into a new level of human stan-dardization...Now the narrow, blinded emotional conjec-tures of our primitive past can't even keep sex interesting; much less provide the basis for modern relationships.

The basis for everything we do in our lifetime is to fulfill our purpose for being here, by evolving our con-sciousness, by interacting as fully as possible through every appropriate level of our consciousness, in any given cir-cumstance—the *Human Prime Directive*. In consideration of that, where does a relationship become a constructive functional part?

It's gratifying, rewarding, healing, expanding and enlightening to be desired, enjoyed and appreciated! As your coming together (relative to what each person's nervous system is ready to intelligently integrate) progressively becomes a more conscious effort to help each "other" experience the expanding fulfillment of yourself, your relationship will start to become a positive tool for living. Whether for six months or a hundred years, a relationship may be the best means for some individuals to further their spiritual development. If we're going to achieve this as one of our more resplendently viable social vehicles, then the means of our exchanges must be clearly understood and flexibly formulated.

I will digress momentarily to discuss children. This book is obviously not the place for specific concerns and needs that I would like to address in relation to child rearing and education. However, in terms of inner development, you can do no more for your children than you can do for yourself. Children can handle almost anything except lies and avoidances! What they need is appropriate structures of love, caring, and honesty. Too often, parents use children as an excuse for what they're really afraid to accomplish for themselves. They claim they are making a sacrifice for their children, then try to validate their own avoidances by making their children indebted through guilt and shame. With guidance, children can handle anything. They can handle their parents being off taking care of business matters, as long as the time they do spend with them is quality time in which the bonds of love and honesty are continually renewed. What children, or anybody else for that matter, cannot handle is what they're not allowed to become aware of. To force a child to submit to moral structures of behavior, which the administering parent neither really follows nor even understands, is to sow perversion into the emotional integrity of a child's soul.

I'm now talking about relationships, whether or not they are, to some degree, involved as a child rearing family unit. Children are not a legitimate excuse for the dampening of sexual energies between parents. Unfortunately, too often, they've been held up as an excuse, so the parents won't have to encounter their own sense of confusion in terms of how satisfyingly they enjoy their sexual potential. One of the ways a child grows and discovers its expanding potential is by testing the limits set upon it. As much as they need to try, they also need the parent not to succumb or take their childish confusion too seriously. When a child, even inadvertently, can manipulate the parent's emotional field (e.g., the parent's almost blind, reactively dogmatic retaliation by punitive means, when the child defies a previously established mode of conduct), then the child becomes afraid. How can they depend on the parent to help them face their simple confusions, if the parent so easily succumbs to them already?

Children are children! They are not ready or capable of handling the same levels and complexities that the adult mind can perceive. They can be physically and emotionally addicted far more easily. Under positive nurturing supervision, children easily find and only too happily will subscribe to the natural cutoff point. Their infantile sexuality basically will only extend into sensuous massage-like stroking, affectionate cuddling, comfort of reinforced proximity; and emotionally into the initial phase of personality magnetism by reward through seductive attention-getting mannerisms for ingratiating others. There are exceptional, precocious, paranormal developments that may alter this. But by and large, even if a child was mistreated and manipulated to submit to prepubescent genital contact, they could only encounter out of the experience—even if marched through every position in the Kama Sutra—what their neurological development was capable of contacting.

Given an opportunity to watch a parental-like couple kiss and sexually caress, children will only be able to enjoy the energies exchanged up to a limited point. They will eventually seek to either move away from the action, or watch in inspired awe from a safe, uninvolved distance. The sexual energies stimulate them to a rate they are not ready to comfortably handle. Because they are not yet equipped to physically or mentally handle adult sexual energies, they really cannot be turned on—beyond their limited range—to what is actually taking place. So that what can be obviously so enthralling or rapturous for the participating adults may have very little meaning and only momentary interest for the observing child. The problem for the child arises when the adults in question do not know how to bridge their separateness and achieve satisfaction. As in a subliminally sneaky overflow of their discontent, their dammed-up unrefined sexual energies too often may seek compensation by taking on their children as psychological lovers.

Whether there are children or not, each person must learn to take their own space (i.e., centering of their awareness). Then they must learn how to take their space as a couple. If they do so, and there are children, there will be no problems. The parents will go off to do that wonderful loving thing that people get to progressively participate more in as they move into the privileges and responsibilities of adulthood. So that even if the children are allowed to view the sexual action, the privacy of the adults remains inviolable.

Alright, there is a fundamental fact which operates

through the human neurology that must be considered. When operating through the composite psychosexual orientation as man and woman, there is a limitation which must be structurally dealt with: Only two people can share the same space at the same time! That is, you cannot look more than one person in the eye at any given moment. Now the question must arise: When in need or desire, who gets first choice as to this level of attention? Who is it going to be? Them...others...or me? We're talking about the three conjugally patented ball-breakers—*insecurity, jealousy and possessiveness*.

Society is, in most aspects, the more vastly encompassing external projection of the inner psychic structuring of its component citizenry. Between the male and the female aspects of consciousness, *the collective and the individual*, continually reprocess each other. As sexual manipulation of pleasure has been used to collectively manipulate individuals, similarly has each individual drawn power from the public perspective to justify their sexual bartering, so that insecurity, jealousy, and possessiveness have mistakenly become the bartering medium for negotiating sexual exchanges.

Out of misunderstanding, most people confuse corralling the movements of others with justifying their own security. As I've said, such inner rationalizations become a shadowy substitute for communication—emotional one-upmanship. If you want to hide from the pain brought on by your own insecurity, you look for mental justification. Then you try and validate your position by gaining patterned manipulative control over other persons and circumstances. This becomes your *mask of security* by which you gloss over the suppressed denial of your insecurity.

Perhaps you're insecure about your ability to sexually experience pleasure and rapturous communion with another. Not understanding what is actually involved, you rationalize what sexual satisfaction means and how it should effect you. You rationalize a self-image. Then you seek validation by finding another person(s) whose way of not relating seems to you fit in with your expectations (including hostility, suffering, and nonfulfillment). This other person, along with the corresponding circumstances, is what you try to possess (control, manipulate). They represent external, societal justification for your mask of security. Thereby, over anything or anyone who threatens your validation, you become jealous of and act accordingly against what seems threatening. Ironically, nothing could be more threatening to such defensiveness than freely indulging in the ultimate pleasures of satisfying sex. You can't really handle pleasure 'til you let go of what you're trying to possess—an excuse for your insecurity. When you cease jealously resenting anything that might threaten your self-image, and reintegrate the misunderstandings you have about your own nature, the mask of security vanishes, leaving the true security of peace and inner certainty. Then you're ready for ecstatic lovemaking.

Because sex has been used as a form of manipulative barter, it is seldom allowed to truly express its potentials. Everybody—in some form, to some degree—wants sex. Every proper participant in the social order wants you to want sex. That is not to say they want you to be satisfied, pleasured and fulfilled. To want that for you, they'd have to first want it for themselves. They want you to be an obligated, attached, dues-paying member of their (and thereby your) mutual conspiracy: "You don't blow my cover, I won't blow yours." They want you to have sex, but then resent you if you don't feel shackled to them by the act.

Sexuality is an important part of a relationship but it

is only a part. It cannot take on its truer evolutionary potential 'til it is put into perspective as the part it plays within the wholeness of a relationship. The consideration is, how best can two people structure the dynamics of their exchange to allow for the optimizing of their own inner growth, the enjoyment of their outer circumstances, and the gestalting of a consciousness energy vehicle which enables them to transcend their self-image and participate in the vaster complex of energies of which they've always been a part.

When aberrations of insecurity, jealousy, and possessiveness are removed, they must be replaced by the only real security—consciousness freely centered in the experience of one's own being! People must deal with each other from the strength of their security, and the range of choices it provides. Participants in a relationship must both have access to levels of consciousness which transcend, and from which they can willfully direct the qualities and range of potentials inherent in the sexual-ego matrix of their personality. The closer you get to your *center*, the easier, more simple, calmer you become, while gaining more control over the energies which surround and interpenetrate you.

What you do out of ignorance may cause pain. But we can heal pain, learn from our mistakes and go on to greater fulfillment. But not to try...to be too afraid (inwardly constricted) to allow yourself to experience and learn— this is what will precipitate the mistakes you make and bring about pain in a relationship. You get hurt by holding back and not communicating. If you geiger through your feelings, you won't have to limit your feelings to emotionally fixated patterns. Go no further with your feelings than communication allows for understanding between you. Experience yourselves both intermeshing within a rate of perception more inclusive than the limits of your sexual identity. Then you're ready to make your relationship functionally romantic.

You keep regenerating your self-awareness through your relationship. You perpetuate your relationship through your renewed self-regeneration. Whether or not it is designed to last for six months or through sixty lifetimes, depends on the complexities and experiential energies which the combining of your consciousness are set up to channel. You are going to do what you do, anyway! You might as well enjoy the journey (state of mind). You bring it all into aspect and interact. When it ends, there is no pain of loss, if there has been open, honest communication. There is always, either way, the necessity of reorientation. People are not hurt by what they lose, only by their own avoidance compromises which they now must face up to once the other is no longer there to sustain their self-image. Conscious acceptance of continual change— voyaging in the heart of Love—not only makes change painless, but reveals it as a wondrously perpetual unfoldment to greater vistas of fulfillment.

A relationship is not a perennial excuse to become complacent. Rather, it is an opportunity to move lightly and freely, experiencing the more healing aspects of yourself as the giver. You, of course, must learn to be a *skillful giver*. You cannot love, if you can't discriminate. And each moment is uniquely individual, through which your consciousness may discover another movement of its own range and pitch. Usually, people are best at doing for others what they would enjoy having done for themselves. Men and women would be happier giving to and treating each other the way in which they believe they want to be treated. This is the essence of completing and balancing the four-way, inner-outer crossover between the sexes I mentioned in Chapter One, "Battle of the Sexes."

Because the male is usually seen as the external aggressor, and the female as the externally passive, receptive one, the man goes around thinking he wants the woman to be seductive and needy; while the woman thinks she's waiting for the man to be aggressive and assertive. In consideration of a sexual bipolar hookup, an inverted psychomotional reversal takes place. Inwardly, it is the female who is the assertive, creative one; and the male is more wanting to be pursued and seductive. What a person does to turn you on, is usually what they would like done to them (if they are ready to admit pleasure into their nervous system). As men allow themselves to express the qualities in their lovemaking that they thought they were sexually seeking in the woman, and as women do the same, relative to their own inner psychosexual temperament...As the four aspects of inner-outer sexuality are openly merged, relationships will become a lot more sexually satisfying.

Now marriage has its place as a structural means for relationships between the sexes. But it is only one of many dynamic processes for a relationship which is now due to surface. In light of the function it fulfills, centered around child rearing, it can be greatly expanded as one viable alternative for the Space Age. There are, however, whole new ranges of motion possible and highly beneficial between the sexes. As they begin to merge into the public consciousness, some old social structures will cease to be relevant, some will be brought into sharper focus to be even more meaningful, and some will completely transmute into more appropriate forms.

Next we want to consider the ways and means for those individuals who are...

3. More Than Ready For A Relationship

Through one means or another—lopsided and disjointed as they too often may be—some individuals have integrated their cultural conditioning beyond where their upbringing oriented them. These are the temporarily dispossessed, spiritually orphaned, new minds transiting their way into a futuristic standardization of human potential. As yet, they have little in the way of appropriate social structures to enable them to optimally participate in the energies to which their development has provided them.

There have been, throughout civilized history, the few isolated, exceptional forerunners of the evolutionary level of consciousness that is now beginning to overtake so many en masse. Their uniqueness—particularly with regard to their contribution to the marketplace—set the tone of their life-styles. They were exceptions, so allowances were made; though only begrudgingly. First, they had to suffer their way out of the common banality of their upbringing. They achieved rank by virtue of their special talents. Rank had its privileges. So within the accepted range of societal customs, they were privileged to indulge in some of the more pleasurable pastimes, without always having to submit to the morally policed order.

Business, art, inventiveness, healing, sports, politics, military, religiosity, entertainment...high achievement through any mode of social application—even antisocial, black market, underground, outlaw activities—could bring to the achiever wealth, fame, status, position, power and all that goes with it. What goes with it? *Mobility* to move more in the direction and at the pace of your own inclinations; *accessibility* to a greater variety of materials and services; and *opportunity* to further expand yourself by broadening the range of your interactions with people, places and things.

What is the first thing people would be inclined to do with their privileges? They'd usually try to obtain what they'd felt had been originally denied them by the limitations of their earlier circumstances. They'd go to claim their prize, their reward, the object of their desire which they'd psychologically enshrined, to goad them on to greater achievement. After some relatively appropriate degree of indulgence, they usually found themselves somewhat disappointed. They'd changed so much, in the course of their struggles, that what might have satisfied them originally, no longer meant the same.

Just when you get to where you can have what you thought you wanted, you no longer want it that way. Well, then what's left to want? The answer is usually more...more power and more self-justifying validation. That game is called: Pursuing a Chase...it's played by trading rainbows for wishes. So you have more food, drink, better environments and you can dictate actions to more people. But that was already accepted in the marketplace. What wasn't accepted in the marketplace was sexual gratification. That's it! Now you can afford to buy off the slings and arrows of outrageous moral restrictions; to indulge yourself in high-toned titillation.

Most relationships have been centered around some variation of adjusting towards or reacting away from the tenets of marriage. Marriage restricted and curtailed sexual activity within a fairly specific range of bio-emotional encounters. Of course, many people tried to sneak around those restrictions. Sneaking is disorienting and demeaning to the quality of conscious exchange being sought through sexuality. When coupled with the dire threat of severe punishment, it is not sex that is being enjoyed.

Rather, it is pip-squeak trickles of pleasure encased in nervous releases of tension and anxiety, in servile defiance of authority.

But what about these exceptional persons, who by measure of their talents have achieved either the liberal, protective permissiveness of the reigning authority, or have, themselves, attained a directive seat of power. Besides not openly displaying their lack of adherence to the moralistic structures used to herd and corral the more common folks, how can they best fulfill the opportunities of their social emancipation?

The first reaction is to indulge in all aspects of their sexuality which seemingly had been denied them. For those working from the level of discontented gut emotions, with only a hazy sense of intuition, but with little in the way of education, culture, affluence or social position— they become rebels.

Rebels don't know where they're going. They just react against where they refuse to feel they're supposed to be. They're too busy trying to break away from that restrictiveness to be particularly aware of the repercussions of their actions. In order to do this, they usually construct a personality veneer of toughness and emotional indifference. They have sex with whomever they can, usually with an affected, blase indifference to all but the intensity of their passion. They can be, within the sexual exchange, exciting, intense, driven, challenging, offensively tender, brutally passive, stimulating, and extremely needful. Such an approach is usually characterized by a short interim of staying power. Unless circumstances bring them to harness their efforts around more thoughtfully constructed means of discovering and integrating their uniqueness, they will burn themselves out. Then they may become a lackluster caricature of their former actions of the social defiance by which they'd identified their right to be different. Or they may so totally associate their sexuality with their defiance that they prolong their own sense of personal excitement by progressively escalating from rebelliousness to criminality. Mostly, they will simply fall back into the patterns they sought to defy. In turn, they often will become the repentant sinners, vehemently (if not ruthlessly) seeking to repudiate others in the same patterns they had formerly denounced.

On a far more sophisticated level, we have the Bohemianesque cultural infidels. These are sociosexual heretics who believe more in the quality of their own perspective than they do in the established dogma of the ruling morality. Rather than submit to a workaday routine, they barter the services of some aspect of their talent for commodities. With artistic sensibilities they can get far more mileage out of form and function. They create environments and social interrelationships that most people work to be able to afford trinket representations of. Art imitates, or rather, attempts to capture through some medium of expression, an intrinsic quality of the living process. To do so, one must be sensitive and unfettered by the inhibiting restraints of social conformity. Freedom to indulge in the arts of living and loving...but at what price? Art is an imposing, disciplinary spiritual master. It requires extraordinary vitality and effort to transform one's consciousness into the subtle complexities of transcending, simplistic receptivity. There being only so much time and energy available to an individual, something will usually be neglected. It cannot be the extraordinary sensitivity which makes the artist's life possible in the first place. However offbeat it may appear to the more normally conscripted, there must be some semblance of working order through which an individual's creativity can be channelled. What then is sacrificed to allow for enrichment of artistic sensibilities? Usually it is the order of the inner feelings where chaos reigns with counteractive intensity. No matter how avant garde, experimental, or even accepting the artistic soul strives to be, much like their scientific counterpart, the psychologist, they still remain mostly on the outside, looking in. After all, artists have never really resolved their indoctrinated patterns of feeling. Rather, through their art they transcend the realm in which such emotional subservience has relevance. However, there still remains a quiet desperation of not being forced back into that level of relating where all their guilt and shame lies waiting to restrict them.

So the Bohemian lives and loves, hoping for a marketplace bingo that will enable them to support their life-style. In their lovemaking they hold nothing back—except themselves. There can be passion, romance, frenzy, spontaneity, eroticism, depth charges of emotional dalliance; there will be tempo, rhythm, beat, shading, texture, form, and gradation...there will be a kaleidoscopic collaging of morsels from every known life-style and philosophy throughout the ages...ingenious delicacies of social style will be reciprocally dined upon in flash nuances between the souls of participating lovers...and the sex will at times surprise them with the white heat fervency of orphans denying their tears on Christmas Eve. All of this will become their suffering; as they become cauterized by their inability to retain access to it. Their passions imprisoned in hip cynicism; their ideals smoldering on pyres of never-to-be-fulfilled love. For art is their salvation, their refuge from the middle class. But not even the greatest art can ever equal the living process itself. The unsorted feelings it saves you from, the hypocritical inadequacies of conformity it lifts you beyond, are the very doorways which must be entered and understood to gain the fulfillment only Life can bestow; and they cannot cope with both that and the inevitable demands of survival. Far-outness can cost a lot of money to sustain—indefinitely. But unless they make it, as their youthful vitality gives out, they may have to finally face the social patterns they sought to transcend. Still, what a glorious try.

Then there are all those darlings of the middle class. From blue-collar workers through highly credentialized professionals...from prejudiced fanaticism through arch-liberal insipidness...from superstition to psychism...from puritanism to hedonism...from demand to supply...from marketplace to consumer. They uphold the integrity of the phenomena of civilization; valiantly struggling to maintain a balance between earning their daily bread and trespassing against each other.

Still, some will want to more than just religiousize their frustrations. Some want to obtain the joys of sex. They accept marriage as the basis of proper conduct. They just don't want to be so proper. They want to get down into their baser instincts, get dirty, and have a swinging good time.

Here we see sex as the ultimate commodity. It's consciously kept separate from love, then overlaid onto a relationship. It's a tool of barter; a notch on one's ego; a measuring rod for attractiveness; a reward for achievement; a healthful exercise; a merit badge for sophistication; a knowing of the score; a semblance of adulthood; a means of release; a form of escape; a break in loneliness; a means of retaliation; an establishment of intimacy; and a taste of ecstasy. It's looking the part and acting the part. The part is one's right to accumulate enough money to afford sensual gratification. For every incoming generation it becomes the newest product of an old marketplace. Sex is always kept subservient by its ability to be packaged and merchandised for profit. As now, with so many quantum breakthroughs in technology, sex has reached competitive market value for orienting one's life-style. Brilliantly stereotyped with modern metropolitan urbanity by *Playboy*, sexuality as a life-style has come to rival religion and politics for a hefty, accelerating share of the marketplace.

Like any major commodity, sex in the rough, obviously needs some refinement to make it a worthwhile product. Now that's not necessarily true. But from the bourgeois perspective, such is the main functioning criteria of sexuality. Because the middle class has so hypnotically projected its inner values into the form and function of its commodities, it can barely experience itself except through utilization of its products. This associative identification of the quality of sex also takes on the success-oriented formulations of the pecking order in the marketplace. In other words, quality is something you must be able to afford. So for sex to be rewarding, it must be rearranged through a seemingly endless variation of associative materials. We enhance it with fashion, power, status, cars, music, dress, drugs, alcohol, food, environments, lighting, nature, technology, movies, textures, culture, education, and anything else that's accessible. The trouble with baubles, bangles and beads is that they are limited in the stimulation they can provide. So we distract ourselves from our own emotional response patterns with thrills, chills and spills. Sex on the run; sex in the sun; underwater; in hot tubs; on the sly; against commitments; near public discovery; and all the other offbeat variations that can be so unusual or risk-taking as to make us pay more attention. 'Til finally with puritanism deconstipating from our libidos, the taboos start coming down. Swinging, swapping, groping, grouping through the lubricity of any friendly inviting orifice. Of course sex can be made into an unnatural act; but to do so there can't be any human bodies involved.

The problem here is not enough heart; because you put the cart before the horse. First you should learn to explore your sexual neural circuitry. When you have free access, even if it's twenty times in a row with the same person under the same conditions...even if you've known this person for years and only made love to them, it should always be differently fulfilling. Then you can embellish it with anything that suits you. But to become primarily dependent on material form and circumstance, can obstruct and lead you away from the very essence of the experience you were seeking. Oh yes, you certainly will catch a smattering of it here and there when you can stimulate and / or distract yourself enough to relinquish your self-image. Then your consciousness will flow into the pleasure zone. But hit or miss insecurity makes it hard to escalate the feelings and sensations with any degree of reliability. Instead, continuous variation must be resorted to—if you can afford it—just to allow you to experience the same simplistic energies.

Finally we get to the modern aristocracy of the financially privileged elite. They've attained success in the marketplace so far beyond subsistence that easy access to material goods and service is guaranteed. However, that never has, nor ever will be a direct guarantee of the capacity for self-enjoyment. Suicides, cancer, neurosis, psychosis, and all the other manifestations of an imbalanced psyche have never been particularly respectful of the wealthy. Neither does money guarantee wit, charm, charisma, taste, brilliance, or any of the other cultivated talents which make existence more than a drudging struggle for survival. However, money can provide far greater access to explore your inclinations. The opportunity to buy the productive efforts of rebels, artists and the middle class can enable one to live nonchalantly at what for most people would be a jazzy, juiced, luxurious pace.

Sexually, the wealthy are often self-congratulatory and insistent; while being less prone to taking chances. They already have access to what most everybody else is struggling to attain. Therefore, they already know that, in terms of personal satisfaction, the populace is chasing a phantasm. They may question whether or not sexual satisfaction even exists. Of course, there is pleasure, amplified by the little niceties they can afford. If lucid enough, it will become apparent that the real thrills were in the struggle, the climb, the combat, the contesting of wills for personal advantage over others—power often seems to those in such a position to be the ultimate aphrodisiac.

This is the turn-on of conquest and control; with sexual tribute being laid on the lap of might makes deserving. What a variety it affords. Then, to increase the sexual titillation, those in positions of power learn to prolong the sport of manipulation. It can be done vicariously through manipulating the socioeconomic circumstances of others. Or it can be done directly through close personal involvement. How stimulating: you can challenge the integrity of the human spirit and force it to battle; you can create hopelessness and despair, then revel in the other's agony, as you move in to crush all resistance; you can seduce with extravagance, flaming delirious desire in others; you can motivate with nobility, experiencing the adoration and gratitude as you guide with generous benevolence. Often—in the unadmitted flickering of their sexual gusto—those who can afford to manipulate power, congratulate themselves. Not so much for their ability to enjoy sex; they may never get that far. Rather, they are pleased to be beyond that supposed illusion, while in a position to savor the teaming emotions of those struggling to reach what they already control.

Of course, that may be very comforting if the apparent material conditions of the world are the only criteria upon which you base the quality of your life. Yet there is— even more importantly—the way you feel inside. If you want to believe that what you've attained and the way in which you happened to achieve it was the right and best way, then inwardly you become very defensive. You use the power at your disposal to continually reinforce the correctness of your belief system. You insist things go the way you want to believe they should. That takes strength of will and power; for you not only want to maintain control, but to do it in such a way as to ward off anything that might demean the quality of your life-style. Which in turn may leave you feeling less inclined to take chances; except within the confines of the criteria you've so vehemently established. All of which can make for an aristocratic sexual trade-off: You get the best of everything, except you can't enjoy it to its fullest. Because in order to connect, you have to relinquish control, re-sensitize, and merge into the conscious energy fields of the other.

Rebels, Bohemians, the bourgeois, the aristocracy—it sounds like a panoramic caste system for historical change. In the sixties—with one generation having invented it, the next generation putting it into access, and a third generation having grown up on it- modern media came of age. In the first intoxicated gush of enthusiasm, the caste system seemed to disappear. A new gestalted level of consciousness appeared to intone a point of relatability that functionally transcended all cultural class boundaries. Everybody who was competitively aware of modern achievement wanted to be "hip." The boats of realizable futuristic possibilities were sailing, and they didn't want to be left, stuck on the shore of yesterday's limitations. Humanity gave the impression of being ready to come of age. The voyage towards greater actualization was underway. But in naivety, and for the most part in innocence, these New Age sojourners overlooked the necessity of weighing anchor and casting off from their emotionally fixated moorings.

In relation to how they didn't want to feel restricted, they shouted out rearranged variations on how they thought the past should have been handled. In defiance, they rebelled against their inner uncertainty. With artistic sensibility—amplified by drugs, consciousness techniques, and media—they created visionary situations of how they'd like to relate. Denouncing middle class morality and its technologically productive achievements, which had made this spiritually pubescent sharing of minds possible, they rampaged through successive cultural encounters. How charming that with social values pleading temporary insanity, the aristocratically well-heeled could afford to nitty-gritty with the middle class. Barriers weren't completely broken, but they were catalogued and targeted for future healing.

And for an intense shadowless moment, the marketplace was disoriented. Its advancement into Space Age Technology had created access to the first glimmerings of a rate of perception that transcended its structures. But there was no real psychic foundation for this state of awareness. The old patterns were stretched and varied by the sacrificial expenditure of youthful enthusiasm; yet never broken. As the vitality began to subside, childish visionaries plumbed the esoterics of the past, looking for confirmation. They found it; but it was almost inseparably attached to the bureaucratic structures of antiquated mind sets. Then the marketplace caught up; made allowances and exceptions; it followed the new demand for idealism with the appropriate supply tactics. Hipness, awareness, were the newest of marketable commodities. And what do you know, it still seemed to boil down to a financial caste system.

Space Age Technology—we now possess the means to functionally rectify the physical deficiencies and economic improprieties that have plagued humanity since it first distinguished its evolutionary existence. Yet we are so deadlocked and hypnotized into the pecking order of the power structures we'd compromised to initiate, that we keep reverting to primitive-survival-of-the-fittest patterns even though they're no longer relevant. The real cost of labor-saving, robotic, computerized Space Age Technology can no more be accounted for by monetary units, than can the now arriving Space Age level of consciousness be structured through the patchworked updating of primitively based emotional reactive patterns. The true cost of humanity finally realizing and operating from the level of its own potential, is the functionally applied evolution of its consciousness.

Now in these transitional times there is a need for experimenting futurists to become more deft in the integrative handling of their physical and mental energies. And sexual satisfaction is one of the prime areas of consideration. For those who are awakening with a readiness to handle all of this, there is coming into focus the unique opportunity to creatively develop the structures that will go beyond marriage. New modes of sexual etiquette more suitable to our times can provide the means of realizing the personal satisfaction that has all too often eluded most lovers.

What's involved with sexual satisfaction—at whatever level you're ready for—is the ability to access it within yourself and harmoniously recycle it through others; along with creating the most nurturing of sociocultural structures to support your activities. Throughout this book I have related extensively as to what, at the least, goes into beginning to satisfyingly turn-on, tune into, and sexually inter-extend your nervous system. However, the finer the instrumentation, the greater its capacity is to function at ever increasing levels of exquisite sensitivity, the more exacting become the circumstantial conditions in which they will serviceably function. And by far, some of the most sensitive equipment on our planet lies beneath the surface of our skins. They psycho-physio inhibiting factors which have masked the majority of our potentials are finally starting to disperse. What sort of perspectives will enable us to fulfill our potential? How can those who are more than ready for a relationship most effectively channel their personal exchanges in order to optimize the evolution of their spiritual potential?

Good sex is not where you should be aiming for. At the very least, it's from where your relationship should take off. It's not that we've been wrong in our sociocultural structures; we've just been inadequate in our choices. Too often, we've invariably encased the essence of our insights in frighteningly cumbersome bureaucratic procedures. For tidbit moments of sexual pleasure we trapped ourselves into lifetimes of reactively hostile, indentured conformity. We blamed it on love instead of misunderstanding. You can't have love without freedom; anymore than you can have love without truth. And honestly: Don't you just want to be free to come and go as you please, and live your life in the way you find most satisfying and fulfilling!

We want, at the least, to extract the best from every form of exchange, while doing away with all the bureau-

cratic red tape that usually goes along with it. We want
the power and passion to go after what we desire without
having to slander the foundation which nourished our
growth—if rebels had a cause which gave purpose and
meaning, their movements would be an expansion towards
pleasure; not just a contraction away from pain. We want
the sensitivity and discipline to access and integrate the
vast dimensions of consciousness through which the
human mind can experience its own spirit—if artists could
operate from their insights, their means of expression
would be a functional orientation for human fulfillment;
not just a dramatically pathetic yelp for a validation beyond their personal futility. We want self-acceptance and
participatory service in the human potential of which we
all are a part—if the middle class consciously used its
collective power to optimize each of its individual citizens;
it wouldn't have to waste so much of its power trying to
convince them to be grateful for what they lack and have
to endure. We want the privilege of being more aware and
having greater access to power, while simultaneously and
synergistically accepting the responsibility (ability to respond) to understand and direct the territories of space
over which we've been given dominion—if the aristocracy
understood their balance as co-creators between what
they're creating and how they're being created; they'd feel
secure enough not to waste their precious opportunities
by keeping others down in order to assure themselves the
right to be up.

We want to eclecticize the best of all approaches, and
gestalt them into a means for loving freely. Remember: It
is not so much what you do, but the state of mind you're
in that determines the quality of your experience. You may
come and go as you please sexually; make love to whomever you please; indulge in every kind of erotic coupling

possible—none of which may really provide the satisfaction you were seeking. You may commit yourself in every way possible to the exclusive sharing of life and love with a partner—yet the tender warmth of deeply shared intimacy may still elude you.

Closeness, intimacy, tenderness, nurturing support...Passion, lustiness, sensuality, eroticism...Freedom, exploration, experimentation, multiple partners, group sex...Trust, reliability, honor, integrity...How can we have access to all these aspects without bludgeoning each other with jealousy, possessiveness, and the other hostile, disqualifying mechanisms of emotional retaliation? We need a new etiquette for relating. Let's illustrate what is involved and how it works:

You're one of those self-actualizing individuals who never quite fit in with the supposed scheme of things...though you did try. For the first thirty years of your life you attempted to adapt your needs, desires and perceptions through the conventional gamut of sociosexual alternatives. You had madly impassioned affairs; group sex; bouts with celibacy; sentimental romantic courtship; bar-hopping; live-in monogamous relationships; sport fucking; and you even gave marriage, with all the trimmings of commitment, your best shot. There was something enjoyable in every approach you took. Yet the ability to relax and lovingly share the depth of your feelings with another on a consistent basis somehow was always compromised.

You want more than ever to experience more expanded realms of fulfillment through your sexual nature. It's become apparent that sexual satisfaction is not a separate aspect of your life, but a dependently integral quality in the composite of your being. You don't agree with the way in which other people try to structure their relationships, but you no longer need to fight their approaches. They're just not right for you. It never made sense to you as a child anyway. But now that you've actually tried on their orientation, you know that all rationalizations for accepting personal dissatisfaction are etched in self-deceit and cowardice. When you consider the already established alternatives, you know they hold nothing that can truly satisfy you. Obviously, you have no threatening delusions left to lose. Your solutions have not yet come into existence. It is up to you to discover them. You will have the great joy of inventing psychosexual modes of communication which will allow you to process your awareness with others in the most mutually optimizing way.

It is your consciousness to explore, and your life with which to experiment. How you choose to exercise your options is up to you; but you must always retain the option to choose. Your ability to give, receive and share pleasure is personal. Pleasure must remain beyond the pressures of social bartering for compensation; no compromises with your freedom to do as you see best. Never again will you allow yourself to be placed in a position where you can't make love. Whether it be for a brief encounter or an ongoing lifetime relationship, never again, if you and another person want to touch and share lovingly with each other, will you deny yourself the freedom to partake.

But equally as important as your right to establish relationships with whomever you want, to the degree that feels comfortable, for the duration of time that communication is dynamically active...just as necessary is your ability to share with great joy, tenderness and intimacy the depths of your feelings. In the past you might have bought into the intimated promise of the closeness you were seeking, if you played ball the way the other person was convinced they should to secure their relationship. Who is everybody kidding—but themselves! If they really knew how to open up to all those warm, wonderfully nourishing aspects of themselves, they wouldn't waste time trying to housebreak you into modes of conduct that had never done the job for them, in the first place. Now you want what you want in the way that is most satisfying. All social proprieties must ever more take a structural back seat to what works for you.

Whether or not it's exclusively with one other person, or multiple relations with numerous people at the same time...it is in actuality always yourself becoming aware of the vaster aspect of your higher Self through the living process. Each relationship is exclusive to the moments when you are consciously focused on the other person. All other considerations are merely taking place in your mind. No matter how vitally significant any interaction is, its validity only extends through the moments of experience. As such, everything that has seemingly taken place in your life up 'til this moment has no real existence anymore. The significance of what past sojourns through experience has made out of you, can only have meaning by its effect on the overall dynamics of your perspective.

In other words, even if you're neurologically integrated enough to successively and simultaneously handle relationships with more than one person, you're still only having one relationship at a time. At any given moment, the person you are having a relationship with is the only person to whom you are actually relating. Whatever might have preceded that moment—even if it was the same person with whom you are still relating—it doesn't exist. Nor does what you might project that future moments might turn out to be. However you've been effected by your past, will certainly influence the quality of what you can share in the now of any given moment. If you've been making love with others and that doesn't demean or take away from what, at the least, has been the quality of exchange the person you're currently with has previously been able share with you...If it has enriched the quality of what you can share in the present moment with whomever you're with, then the person you're with has no real grounds on which to reproach your actions. But if you cannot move honestly and lovingly from one person into another...If you drag in affects from the past that diminish the quality of the present, then in frustration of not getting and / or fear of losing what they need and want to share with you, there can be a hell of a price to pay: "It's not so much what you do when you're away from me. Rather, its what you do when you're with me that counts!"

At the same time, it is necessary to understand that whether consciously activated or not—there is no relationship you've ever established in your life to which you are not still connected. Unless you have actually experienced that level of consciousness where those connections exist, it sounds like a complicated mishmash of mysticism. Normally, the only connections most people are capable of recognizing with each other, are the ones which are somehow affecting their senses. The reason I'm mentioning this here—though this book is not the place for a working explanation of the process—is that those people who do open themselves up to the freedom of relating, when and with whom they want, in some way come in contact with this supra normal level of connectedness.

That is, your connection to everything and anyone with whom you've ever made notable contact still exists. You might say that each object or level of integrative consciousness has its own composite vibrational rate; which is its energy signature. In a manner of speaking, your awareness, at any time, to any energy signature, connects in your consciousness a sympatico through which you could experience that energy. Through conceptual imaging of symbols we mentally categorize our senses. That mental dividing of the territory of space we're capable of perceiving at any given moment we call time. So that normally what exists for us, only has relevance in the sequenced part of the space of which we're currently aware. From our normal level of consciousness this is true; and that rate of perception has been the basis from which we've established the ground rules for interacting with the apparent manifestations of material reality. However, from more spatially experiential levels of perception, you start to perceive that any access is and always does remain constant. Crudely analogized: It's like being tuned to one television channel, where the contents of whatever you're viewing occupy your consciousness for the moment. If you switch to other channels, the channel you were watching, in the greater composite of video as a whole, still persists. If you amplified your access through more monitors, you could partake simultaneously of several of the available video connections. But such an example is too linear and sequential to convey a rate of perception, beyond time (as we know it) that is experientially holographic.

When two lovers tantracize each other into an ecstatically more encompassing energy state, they, at least momentarily, are operating from such a level of consciousness. They are experiencing supra normally, the energy pathways that are connecting them. And quite often they experience connection to much more, although as in dreaming, their inability to reference their experiences may leave them unable to transmit what they were experiencing when they refocus into their more normal rates of perception.

Making love with more than one person is like jump-
ing reality tracks, from one connective cord to another.
Sexuality, in its higher octaves, is one highly evolved,
spiritual tool for allowing your consciousness to experience these extended hookups. Yet access to this rate of
inter-exchange, for the most part, up 'til now, has been
hopelessly mired in rituals of heavily inhibited, emotional
protocol. Think for a moment: You're making love to someone because you've established a relationship. You approach them as lover, marital partner, whatever. Because
certain emotional procedures, that you've both been
trained to feel must be validated, have been fulfilled, you
can exchange to some limited degree with each other
through your sexuality. Later, you go out and find yourself attracted to another person. According to the situation and their acceptance of what you can offer, you will
again connect to some degree through your sexuality. It
may be no more than a look, sigh and wishful thought. It
may be the almost casually accidental touching of each
other. It may be a hot fuck in some place of clandestine
convenience. However, what you are capable of sexually experiencing with each other, is determined by the set
of cultural role models into which you fit. Marriage partner; lover; prostitute; pickup; casual fuck; chance encounter; illicit indulgence, spiced by betrayal; good friends;
the currently accepted in-thing; daring and risky; healing;
merciful; retaliatory; convenient; experimental—each
designation carries its own protocol for how to, and how
much of your hookup can be accessed sexually.

What this has always amounted to, is letting outer
circumstances dictate how and to what degree you experience sex. But you've come to understand that the subjective orientation of how you perceive things is more
valid for the decisions you make than for the objective

world at large. You can more than adequately deal with the social patterns that exist. They're okay, but inadequate to your needs. Besides, you know that these patterns are just a reflection of how people perceive themselves. As you reorient the dynamics of your inner consciousness, then—and only then—are you in a position to change the world. And at the least, you'd like to change that part which you move through enough to hook up full access to sexually transmitting through the cords which connect you to others.

New skin to contain new wine: How are you going to relate with others in order to make this sexual satisfaction and personal fulfillment possible? You are going to consciously establish an individual relation—to whatever degree is desirable and appropriate—with each individual with whom you sexually share. Your validation and authority must come from within (as throughout this book, I've given you enough means to determine whether you understand or are faking it). No matter how passionately, affectionately, lovingly and intimately you share, it can never be enough upon which to base your relationship. You cannot always be lovers, but you can be friends. If your sexual attractiveness has temporarily run its course, it only exists as one aspect within the greater dynamic hookup of which you're both a part.

That which works in keeping you centered through each moment is what will work in extended form between you and another. One of the great constants of Life is continuous change. It is the energy of Life—of which you are a functional part—with which you are seeking to harmonize. Relations, operating as systems for processing available energies within a comprehensive whole, must partake of the characteristic nature of that wholeness to be optimal / successful. Conscious readjustment to continuous change is part of the primary foundation on which you will base your relating.

For you to relate as completely as possible with another, all you need to do is have the desire, become receptively attracted, and keep it honest. That's not morality in holy drag. Your decisions are based on understanding; your movements are advanced through pleasure; your responses are valued and validated by accepting no less than the best you've ever known in the quality of your connections. No guilt, no shame—no sexual barter. But what about the other person who finds you so attractive, but doesn't know how to relate with you because you don't fit into any of their established psycho-cultural categories?

From their perspective: "Who are you? What are you to me, if I can relate like this with you?" Priest, psychiatrist, lover, marriage partner, soul mate; these are the categories most people have been oriented to correspond with another person when a certain lucid depth of intimacy and / or extreme sexual pleasure becomes relatable. For the most part, probably no one before has ever really gotten so close to their inner workings. Either they were categorically kept at a distance by the definition of their role model, or in the course of sexual encountering, both participants tripped each other into the obvious familiarity of Stone Age patterns of reactive avoidance. Well, you must keep it respectful; and you need to make it clear: "I'll only come in, if invited; I'll only stay, if wanted. I will always respect the sanctity of your individual privacy. And I will accept no less than the same respect for me."

Fine, now they know they won't be invaded by force. But you've put the ball in their court. Because, if they invite you in, you can walk past all their barriers to commune with them at levels they've been afraid to approach within themselves. You're a fucking catalyst. Either they explore new aspects of themselves, or lock up even more deeply into their avoidances. You're centered, peaceful, vital, and alert. What they see in you must also be accessible in them, or they couldn't see it in you. But you no longer buy into the emotional distractions; you don't avoid encountering the misunderstandings that keep most people off center. They can't even seduce you into compromising yourself. There's no bit of sexual-emotional distraction that can remotely compare with the feedback of being centered. For it's when you are able to center your consciousness, that you can experience the greatest sexual pleasure.

Of course, not yet having had such experience, this might not be quite conceivable for the other person. They go for what they know. But they can't find the cutoff point with you. Because of the sexual mastery you've gained over your own nervous system, you can open up and control the sexual pleasure flow of the cords connecting you. They keep getting more and more turned-on. They find themselves disoriented in barely believable, exceedingly pleasurable territory.

"Hey, you're not tired; you're giving pleasure; you're tender, gentle and sensitive. It's getting easier to feel comfortable with you. You're so responsive, alert, receptive. Does that mean...is this it...?" Have they finally discovered that special someone? The answer is yes, they have. But its not who they think it is. They're really discovering their own uniqueness. You've been centered and open enough to enable them to reach more deeply into the experience of their own potential. You understand; you've already been through it. They don't understand and insist on giving their power to you.

That's another distraction into which you're too balanced to fall. They're trying to find some way to intrigue you, to bundle you up like a commodity they can emotionally purchase to fulfill a need. You know they're only coming on that way out of confusion. If they knew a better way, they'd go for it. Like you, they must learn to validate themselves by understanding, connecting through and taking control of their own center of awareness. No one but their own self, can make them secure enough to be able to open up at will and access their nervous system to any degree, and in any combination within their self, and with others.

How far are they ready to go in obtaining their inherent rights as freethinking, open minded, spiritual individuals? That choice, most of all, is up to them. They've been dancing on the energy that you know how to access. Now that they know it's possible; are they willing to understand, heal and expand themselves? Are they ready to assume responsibility for their own success and satisfaction?

They are fortunate, through you they've been presented with the opportunity to learn from someone who can help them, because you're already there. But what gives you the right to assume such a position? You have understanding and knowledge; you're a concerned, sensitive, experienced person who really cares (If you weren't, you could never have reached this position in the first place). The respect they give to you, you hold in trust for them. They are giving to you what they actually need to give to themselves.

So you can take it, huh? Okay, they're going to find out. Out of force of habit, they can't stop looking for those emotional levers that will give them manipulative control over you. Of course, you already found those a long time ago. You ripped them out and reprogrammed your nervous system minus such levers. You make it clear that you won't barter, sexually. Sex is absolutely wonderful, but they can have a share of your love and understanding without it. They want to place you on a pedestal, to excuse themselves from assuming responsibility for their own actions. You assure them that you're not God—you just love and bring your consciousness as close as you can to God. You're a fellow human being; like them, you're another soul of awareness voyaging through the circumstances of this existence. You've just worked hard, learned a lot and have some wonderfully functional insights to share with whomever that might interest.

You let them know from the get go—clearly, straightforwardly, with no "ifs", "ands", or "buts" about it—that you do not want to be in an exclusive one-on-one relationship with anyone. You have already tried out possessiveness, envy, jealousy, guilt, shame and other such obstructions and could find no beneficial use for them under any conditions. You make sure they understand that you feel free, do see other people when you want, and exchange sexually as it pleases you. And, of course, they have the same options. No, you're not trying to prove anything and you're not afraid of commitments. You reserve the right to reconsider and change your mind any time it seems appropriate. You love your own company, and sometimes like to be alone in the quietude of your own heart.

They are attracted and intrigued and can agree—at least verbally—with anything you say. However, their only real criteria is to justify the way their feelings were structured—they want what they want. Neither can they stop looking for that emotional control lever in you; nor can they believe they are so obviously following repetitive patterns that you can easily discern the rationalizations behind their movements. Now it is true that the man or woman aspect in you is vulnerable. However, you're not vulnerable. You only open up the playground of your sexual ego when it suits you. The psychosexual potential of man and woman can be a wonderfully pleasurable, fun-filled level at which to playfully exchange. But you are far from limited to that perspective.

Any balanced person wants to love, exchange, communicate. You know, if they hit you with anything negative, it's because they're at least temporarily lost within themselves, cut off from the heart of their awareness. If you took them seriously in that state, you'd only be adding to their confusion. To begin with, they're already taking themselves too seriously. Instead, you don't activate your consciousness through your feelings. You move into a different mode of operation. Depending on what's called for, you become the friend, the healer, the teacher. And if they don't respect that position when it's offered to them, you must take it away from them until they do. You let them realize (figuratively speaking, regardless of gender)—*These balls are blessed and cannot be broken!*

Maybe you don't have the authority to call them out as a man or woman. But as a self-actualized individual of centered spiritual adulthood, you must certainly have that right; which if you choose to exercise, it becomes a responsibility / privilege. You want—and you know that every individual, in their heart, wants—to perpetuate through their relationships, an extended honeymoon; a continuous rediscovering of each other. This is possible only between equals (centered, and genuinely self-accepting). Each person, by first pleasing themselves, makes the other a part of their pleasure; minus the competitive struggles for psychological power dominance. You understand how to bring forth the healing potentials that sexually exist in male-female relations, and you've started to do so.

Meanwhile, you are perplexing them by actually fol-

lowing through as stated. Every time you see them emotionally fixating, while trying to tell you it's love, you pull
back. You always leave your friendship and concern open
to them; unless they violate your space by volatile trespass against you. You tell and show them that the place
they find so pleasurable sharing with you will only be
made accessible when they keep it worth your while. You
can work with, help, teach, or communicate with anybody.
However, whom you share your time with as a psychosexual identity is particular. The least you ever accept is
the best you've ever known. You've already earned the right
of self-acceptance; you genuinely enjoy your own company. Anybody with whom you spend time on a personal
level is going to be at least as enjoyable as you already find
yourself to be inside. You've never met a person you
couldn't understand: You forget nothing; forgive everything;
and understand anything in between.

They get pissed and tell you that you're a self-centered,
selfish egotist. You congenially admit that you are centered
within yourself. You instructively point out that when you
can make sense out of a nebulous emotion, you gain control over it. Selfishness is demeaning and self-defeating;
that to be self-interested in enjoying your life shows an
intelligent use of reason...And about the egotistical part,
you say: *"I bet you tell that to all the mirrors!"*

Ah...oops, we slip from anger to anguish, as they cry
that you're breaking their heart. You explain that no one
can really break another's heart. The worst they can do
is con you into doing it to yourself. After all, only a person so involved with the actual pain of what they haven't
yet understood or integrated within themselves, can fill
in the emotional space of what another is psychologically
intoning. Besides, you assure them, you're a heart mend-
er...not a heart breaker!

So what is there left to complain about?: The two big-gies—sex and money.

In another ploy to try and press those illusive phan-tom buttons of emotional subservience, sex is referenced: "You're just using me sexually. I'm more than some sex object to satisfy your whims. I can't really enjoy sex ex-cept in a meaningful relationship." To which you play-fully pull their mouth from their crotch and remind them that it has not been a one-way exchange. That your sex-uality is, at least, as valuable as theirs. You can relish being a sex object, as long as you're enjoyed and appreciated, when it suits your purposes. You've always honestly accorded them the same rights and options you've as-sumed for yourself. Never have you lied or misled them. Anyway, how can they experience successive bliss waves of some of the finest sexual pleasure they've ever known; pleasure they weren't even sure existed before; and com-plain. If anything, it's their own sexual whims—and a heaven of a lot more—they've been satisfying.

From sexual outrage to sexual dependency: "But I need you. I'll do anything for you. I just want us to be togeth-er. Why do you have to be with other people? I haven't been with anyone else; I don't need or want to be with anyone else. Everybody else says you're really being un-fair with me; that I should teach you a lesson and leave you."

And you respond with warm understanding: "So people are trying to convince you that you're wrong for enjoying yourself. What are they offering you that's even as good...much less any better? They're telling you that hap-piness isn't any good unless you do it their way. And their way doesn't make them happy. Try to understand. If you can manage to live your life the way you want, and be sex-ually satisfied, so can they. They don't want to believe that.

Marketplace protocol has taught you that you can have special privileges when you achieve financially measurable success and / or bankable notoriety. Now, of course, it's nice to be able to afford the extra trimmings; but, obviously, they don't guarantee satisfaction."

You continue: "The reasons they don't want to open up to qualities of perception that could make their lives more satisfying, are the same reasons you're fighting me now. There's all that deep-seated pain that made you turn away from your true feelings in childish ignorance. Anybody who wants to feel whole and centered within themselves, must sooner or later come to grips with all their compromises! Ultimately, to get to the heart of the matter, there is no other way! Mistakenly, out of ignorance, they feel it's easier and more profitable to justify their unhappiness, then it is to pursue happiness. They've got endless excuses. As you start to feel better about yourself, you become a threat. You threaten their identity. They know who they are—they're the ones who are suffering. But if you—with whom they can't help but identify—can change, so can they. You're becoming a threat to their excuses for not dealing with their fears. Besides, even if everyone is telling you how wonderful you are, but you don't feel it inside, then what good are their acknowledgments for you? But even if the whole world is against you, yet you feel clear and peaceful inside, then life is good to you."

They admit what you're saying seems to make sense. But they alibi in protest that they don't want to fight the world. You laugh: "Sweetheart, I'm not fighting with anybody. I'm too busy having this wonderful love affair with life! Anybody who enters into my life becomes a part of my love affair."

Ah, the mental sword thrust for emotional confirmation. As if everything else was just to get you to emotionally capitulate. As if you're finally going to consign yourself to their terms, they ask: "Then you do love me?"

You respond: "Yes, in my own way. As much as I can connect through that space with you. Then again, there are many people I love. I find the more fully I share love, the more people I find with whom I can and want to share it."

How contemptuous they'd like to be. You've belittled their uniqueness: "You're saying that making love with me is no different than it is with anybody else."

You smile. You can already see the change in them. They're running the gamut of habitual protest. But their eyes are gaining light. Against their fears, they're starting to reach for themselves. For the first time in a while, you sense a real current of sexual energy stimulating their circuits. You take a moment to tenderly hug them, and lightly stroke sensual remembrance over their erogenous zones. You continue: "If you're really paying attention, every time you make love with somebody, it's different. And each person can bring out a uniquely different quality of response from you. Nobody can touch me the way you can. But that's just as true about the uniqueness of others. The key to attractiveness is allowing yourself to open up and be attracted. That's why you find me so attractive. I'm secure and integrated enough to see an extended aspect of myself in you. When I'm with you, I give you my real attention. With me you feel wanted and connected, because you are. Understandably, you want more of the same. You're just approaching it ass backwards. When I'm with you, it's because I want to be. I see the opportunity to beneficially exchange some pleasurable energy. You think you're seducing me, but nothing could be farther from the truth. And the more you persist, the more boring it becomes."

With indignant defensiveness they go wide-eyed: "Are you saying that you find making love with me boring?"

Now you get them to admit what they really feel: "No, lovemaking is always wonderful. But that's not what we've been doing lately. It's a negative cycle which can discharge potential lovers into sexual insipidness. Admit it. Hasn't it become progressively less satisfying to you lately?"

Okay, they admit it. But then they tell you that's because you're not close enough...not committed enough.

You continue to tutor them: "Think of what you're saying. You're trying to make me believe that if I do things the way you want me to, then you'll reward me with greater sexual appreciation. Now, you know that's not true. Look, when we were first together, if we wanted to pursue the attraction we felt, then we both had to really pay attention to each other. We didn't take each other for granted. That's what made it so interesting. But you haven't, as yet, learned how to operate from your center. Instead of using your mind, you let it dictate to you. You remember what you think you experienced. You've started to intellectually rearrange what you think with regards to how you think you would or wouldn't like it to be. And you're going about it in the way you were indoctrinated to do; with whatever cultural variations that are appropriate to rationalize these days. You've stopped paying attention to what's really going on between us. Instead of making love, you're just fucking around inside your head. The more you do that; the more cutoff you feel; the more desperate you become to hold onto what you remember as having given you so much pleasure. And that's very boring—isn't it."

A true note of humility seeping into the other person's

eyes; they're learning. They're admitting they don't know. But their edging it with too much self-negation: "Then why do you bother being with me?"

Humility is fine, but you're not going to let them play bullshit false modesty games: "Because you're a warm, intelligent, caring human. And when you allow yourself to open up, you're one sexy, fun person to play with. That's why I enjoy seeing you become more secure and in control within yourself. The better you feel about yourself, the more of a turn-on you are to me. It's one of the ways I cater to my own self-interest. You can only share with some-one, what it is you have to share. I enjoy when someone feels good about their space. Then we can mix and match into whole new qualities of being. I'm most comfortable with people who don't resent me for liking myself. Which means, they have to first like their own space."

In challenge, they ask you: "And then what? More...I suppose."

You like it; they're starting to think and probe. "Exactly, more...! But that doesn't mean extended amounts of the same thing. More, alchemizes you; it gestalts your aware-ness into something quite different. But you're trying to play it safe by figuring it out first. Beyond reasonable deliberation, that's dangerous to the health of your spir-it. You can't figure out what it's like to be wet, before you've immersed yourself in the experience. If you fudge in too many expectations, you'll block out the sensitivity you need to really experience."

Finally they get down in the pit and drag forth their last excuse: "That's why I need you. You're special. But I just can't do it myself. I don't know why, but I just can't seem to handle things on my own."

Well great. Now that they've finally admitted what's

really bothering them, you can give them some help. "Okay, so obviously there's some things you need to learn. If you don't know, then you can find out. You can only deal with what you look at; you can't deal with what you refuse to look at. When you expose those vampiric shadows of soul-sucking ignorance to the light of your understanding, they disintegrate."

. . .

"First you've got to stop hypnotizing yourself."

"What do you mean?'

'You've been buying your own propaganda. You've been casting spells on yourself."

"How?"

"Look at what you said about yourself. You could have said that you may not have it all together yet, but you're learning...it's getting easier to understand and take control...that you're becoming sensitive enough to be drawn to people who can relate with you at more inclusive levels...that soon you'll have real control and be able to handle anything you choose. You could have seen yourself in so many positively expanding ways."

"Oh, I'm starting to see what you mean. I was limiting myself."

"That's exactly it. You cast a spell, so to speak. You project that you're limited; that you lack some ability. Then you walk into your projection, and start believing your own propaganda. Then you turn around and wonder how and why you got stuck there in the first place."

"But it seemed so real."

"Well of course. You masturbated a lot of emotional associations to lend a kind of negative credence to your illusion."

"Then I truly am responsible for my own life."

"Yes, the part of which you're conscious enough to take creative dominion over."

"Then there's also that which I'm a part of that's creating me...through me..."

"Greetings from the Heart of things: welcome to the world! Now you know upon what to anchor your choices."

. . .

You become still inside, letting them savor the connection. It is one thing to become aware. It is yet another to learn to operate consciously from such a level. You wait for the next, most obvious question. They feel neither here nor there. Yet they know themselves to be uniquely alive. After all, what good is an insight that can't be made functional for the betterment of one's everyday activities? What does such a perspective do to your relationship?

Calmly they approach you. They notice with whom they're relating. They ask without anticipating the answer: "Why is it that my love isn't enough to keep you satisfied?"

Okay. Now there is honor and respect...an intelligent and reliable structure through which open-minded, free-thinking, heart-centered individuals can honestly transmit love. Now you can talk about the world you live in, and how it relates to the world in which we're all living:

. . .

"If we ended our relationship today, would it negate the quality of all that's come before?"

"No, I'll never be sorry for what we've shared."

"Just, not sorry?"

"No matter what, I'll always be grateful for what we've exchanged."

"Then you, too, can enjoy loving freely in whatever the present brings; however much it suits your purposes."

"What suits your purposes?"

"Good food, good friends, nice environments, fun times aren't what I'm looking for. They're the least I'll accept. They're the least any intelligent individual should accept. Once you've taken care of those as basics, what else is there to do but see how much you can evolve and functionally activate your potential. Once you've brought your personal awareness into balance, what else is there to do but see how much you can expand that with others in the world. That's human."

"How do you go about it?"

"You work from the highest, most encompassing quality of consciousness you can access, understand, and control at any given time. You predicate your interactions from understanding."

"Explain yourself, my dear friend; please."

"What enables me to stay clear, centered, vital, peaceful and connected takes precedence in my life. Without it, nothing feels right. Without it, neither I nor anybody else can really keep it together in the world. In the light of it, anything can be brought into focus. You truly become the master of yourself, when your self is consciously mastered by your heart!"

"Then what?"

"Everything is still there...life goes on. It's just that the way you perceive, and thereby interact with it, is irrevocably changed. Instead of looking up, searching for glimmers of an answer, you experience yourself as the answer, and start observing where and how best to focus yourself. You not only see the condition of the world as it exists, but even more clearly, you see how it really is. You become a healer. A healer doesn't wrestle against the dark. That is only how it appears to be, to a person whose imbalances have patterned them into some sort of affliction. A healer sees in wholeness, and merely helps others to remove the obstacles which delude them into thinking they're cut off. Once blockages are removed...once you become aware of the nature of your wholeness, in relation to other's wholeness, within a still vaster wholeness...once you are optimally connected, the form and function of your body, mind, and life follow suit."

"Then your mind becomes a joyous servant of its master, the heart. Then your thoughts are structured, and structure through the nature of your experience. Now you're ready for whatever Life has in store for you...whatever the moment calls you into being."

"Which is?"

"Well, consider for a moment. The closer intimacy, clarity, and dynamic sexual pleasure we've been sharing— have they been like this before?"

"No, nowhere near this."

"Yet we're not relating under the guise of any of the ways you've been led to believe must structure an intersexual exchange."

"True. I see. None of those approaches allow for this quality of sharing. Yet we're beyond what I thought was possible for two people to share. And it feels so simple and natural."

"That's because you're ready for it. People are moving from degrees and combinations of the neuro-spiritual orientation. Only when you've accepted where your own orientation is in the scheme of things, can you comfortably work with the acceptance of each other's needs. Humanity is on the way to making the world safe for diversity."

"I see. Despite all my avoidance and protest, I still go through what I'm going to go through anyway."

"Exactly. So you might as well open up and enjoy it. That's the best way to show you're grateful. Enjoy it, and you get more. Don't enjoy it, and you start to lose what you have."

"Of course. When I enjoy you, I get more of you. But I've been so preoccupied with how I thought things ought to be, that I've been pushing you away. But you already knew that."

"Yes..."

"Yet you chose to be with me anyway. My God, what a beautiful, loving friend you are."

"Thanks. It's nice to be appreciated. Anyway, I bet you tell that to all the mirrors."

"You know something? The reason I get uptight isn't because you see other people. It's because I've always doubted—limited, that is—my ability to move about and exchange the way I really wanted."

"Okay. Then let's spell it out. If communing as a lover is one of your modes of operation, then there are also some economy-based logistics involved."

"I can already see it. If I were independently wealthy, I'd do as I please."

"That's part of it. If you want to combine any part of your finances, that's an aspect of voluntary partnering. But lovers must always have the options to come and go."

"Yes. So there's no lopsided, forced dependency, subtle coercion or resentful retaliation. What's the other part?"

"To be honest with yourself about what you're really ready for. Be aware that it changes as you change. There is no right or wrong; good or bad. There's either understanding and creatively controlling the energies accessible to you, or misunderstanding, being controlled, and suffering the consequences."

"Not everybody's that conscious."

"Then they'll move through their relations in the way most suitable to their needs. It's misleading to rely on comparing yourself to others. To know what you want in a love relationship, you have to gauge it by your own potential."

"Yes, I understand now. I'm so glad you're a part of my life...that we're friends. I won't try to restrict you anymore. That would only be avoiding myself. And I do want to make love with you as much as it feels good to us both. Just tell me one more thing. The one thing I should have asked you, but never did. How is it that you want to re-late?"

"I'm here to help out with the transition in conscious-ness which is now taking place on our planet. I'm not here to be an excuse for fighting. I'm here to help create struc-tures that will allow all existing systems to come into optimal focus. It is not my intention to tell people what to do with their lives. That should be, and basically is, up to them. I do want to share with any who are interested in better ways to optimize those faculties which should be under their control. I'm here to teach men and wom-en how they can optimize personally and between one another, their physiology, consciousness, sexuality and communication. Though I enjoy giving (and receiving) suggestions, what any individual makes out of it, is their own business. The most effective teaching is to function-ally embody your being through your actions—I teach what I practice. The levels of consciousness, and their subsequent beneficial effect that most people are trying to obtain through relationships, are already accessible to me. I view—in keeping with the Space Age openings of our times—whole new ranges of motion to be socially plausible for human beings. I'm in the process of helping develop them into accessible reality. I make friends and share as honestly and intimately as is mutually desirable / appropriate with whomever I can. I reserve the right to make my own decisions; come and go as I please; change my mind anytime new information necessitates reevaluation; make love when it suits me; develop and fulfill my every potential; and suchly, to love and serve GOD with every aspect of my being! In Light of That—in my close personal relationships as a lover—I'm up for anything that pleases me."

"What have you got in mind...?"

Afterword

Belief...

    People can, and too often do, believe just about any-
thing.

Trust...

    Even if you know what to base trust on, it still takes
time for your trust to be validated.

My job is to empower you...!

    In consideration of the erotic art, my intention is
to show you: what it is, how it's constructed, the
particulars of its interactive range of motion, and
how you can access it for yourself.

                 The first book in this se-
ries—ACHIEVING SEXUAL ECSTASY—is an overview of
human achieving sexuality. It's purpose is to provide you
with clear insights that will enable you to understand your
erotic nature. It is not merely a book of intellectual categorizing and wishful thinking. This book is philosophically crafted to move your awareness into more profound
and satisfying rates of perception. Read it; and when appropriate, read it again.

    By challenging the contents of this book, you will be
challenging your own beliefs. See if the insights provid-

ed hold true in the situations that you've been in; that other people you know have been in; and even in the depictions of love you've read about, or seen enacted in movies and television. In so doing, you will come to make sense out of your emotions, thereby gaining control over them. The more you truly understand your sexuality, the more secure you'll feel about experimenting with aspects of your erotic nature.

The second book in this series—EROTIC ALCHEMY—will deal more specifically with various methods for unfolding your erotic potential. These techniques will deal with amplifying the physical health of your mind and body; sexually increasing your capacity for experiencing pleasure; ways of safely using sexual energy to expand your consciousness; along with ways of taking constructive advantage of the opportunities afforded by socio-sexual interaction.